Emily Dickinson, Daughter of Prophecy

EMILY DICKINSON
Daughter of Prophecy

Beth Maclay Doriani

UNIVERSITY OF MASSACHUSETTS PRESS
AMHERST

LC 95-11037
ISBN 0-87023-999-6
Designed by Susan Bishop
Set in Adobe Caslon by Keystone Typesetting, Inc.
Printed and bound by Thomson-Shore, Inc.
This book is published with the support and cooperation of the University of
Massachusetts Boston.

Library of Congress Cataloging-in-Publication Data
Doriani, Beth Maclay, 1961–
Emily Dickinson : daughter of prophecy / Beth Maclay Doriani.
    p.   cm.
Includes bibliographical references and index.
ISBN 0-87023-999-6 (alk. paper)
  1. Dickinson, Emily, 1830–1886—Religion.   2. Women and literature—New
England—History—19th century.   3. Christian poetry, American—History and
criticism.   4. Sermons, American—History and criticism.   5. Women—New
England—Religious life.   6. Prophecies in literature.   7. Authority in
literature.   I. Title.
PS1541.Z5D64   1995
811'.4—dc20   95-11037

British Library Cataloguing in Publication data are available.

Acknowledgment is made for permission to reprint material under copyright:
    From *The Poems of Emily Dickinson*, edited by Thomas H. Johnson, Cam-
bridge, Mass.: The Belknap Press of Harvard University Press, copyright 1951,
1955, 1983 by the President and Fellows of Harvard College. Reprinted by
permission of the publishers and the Trustees of Amherst College.
    From *The Complete Poems of Emily Dickinson*, edited by Thomas H. Johnson.
Copyright 1929, 1935 by Martha Dickinson Bianchi; copyright © renewed 1957,
1963 by Mary L. Hampson. By permission of Little, Brown and Company.
    From *The Letters of Emily Dickinson*, edited by Thomas H. Johnson, Cam-
bridge, Mass.: The Belknap Press of Harvard University Press, Copyright
© 1958, 1986 by the President and Fellows of Harvard College. Reprinted by
permission of the publishers.

For Christopher

Contents

Preface

THIS STUDY began to take shape as I increasingly realized that American women need not and, indeed, do not totally reject their religious heritage, despite the tensions they experience with it, when it comes to literary practice. A common feminist attitude today is to disparage most Protestant religious traditions as patriarchal and to view them as phenomena that religiously and historically astute women can only reject, radically revise, or, at best, live with in anger and resentment. But my own personal and literary experiences have led me to an alternative belief. Despite the patriarchal biases of American Protestant Christianity as it has been historically expressed, that religious tradition and the Bible itself offer vehicles through which female writers, thinkers, and potential speakers can be affirmed and even empowered in their practice. That empowerment may be motivated by biblical theology—a theology of creation, fall, redemption, and restoration that emphasizes the creational value of all people and their voices, regardless of their gender, race, or class. Certainly, American evangelicalism affirms the priesthood of all believers, as Emily Dickinson well knew. In increasing numbers, evangelical women today are discovering the liberating possibilities of the Scriptures, even as they remain within their evangelical circles.

The models and devices found in the scriptural rhetoric have especially appealed to female Christian writers and speakers as a principal vehicle of power and authority. Recognizing the power of words to define reality, women historically have incorporated the rhetorical patterns of sacred texts into their art. If an audience accepts particular texts or voices as authoritative, a female (or male, for that matter) speaker may well adopt the rhetorical techniques and voices found in those texts to legitimize her own words. We can detect this practice in evangelical preaching, when ministers adopt the voices and tone they perceive in the biblical writings. Female religious writers also do this, as we find in the works of two prominent Americans, Anne Bradstreet and Harriet Beecher Stowe. As I have argued elsewhere, Bradstreet looks specifically to the Psalms for poetic techniques and adopts the psalmist's voices in her Andover Manuscript poems; she emerges with what she suggests is sanctified poetry, verse that is authoritative and

immortal because it is acceptable to God. In another body of literature, she patterns her work on the wisdom literature of the Bible and
calls the resulting "Meditations" first "Divine" and, second, "Morall."
Likewise, Stowe draws on nineteenth-century sermon techniques in
Uncle Tom's Cabin, speaking a political-religious message that is so
persuasive in part because she employs sermonic strategies. Given
the practices of these two noteworthy female writers who share with
Dickinson the broadly Calvinist tradition of the Puritans, I began to
explore the idea that Dickinson, too, looked to that New England
tradition for an authoritative voice even as she revised much of the
dogma of nineteenth-century evangelism.

Emily Dickinson, Daughter of Prophecy is the result of that exploration. Dickinson, aware that the biblical, classical, and romantic traditions identify the figure of the poet with the prophet, could find usable
and adaptable models of a prophetic voice—an authoritative, wise
religious voice—in the Bible. She could also find accessible models of
that voice in the customary homiletics of her time, which she knew
extended the scriptural prophetic mode into her own era and locale. In
adopting and making innovations upon those Judeo-Christian prophetic models, Dickinson allied herself with a tradition of American
female writers who sought to express a religious vision within a context of male claims on religious authority.

Indeed, a sensitivity to a female writer's womanhood and to her
understanding of her religious surroundings will prove to be key, I
believe, in developing theories through which we can best read America's nineteenth-century female poets. More and more of these poets'
works are being rediscovered and recovered, yet we still do not have
adequate ways of reading their verse. These poems, some of which are
anthologized in Rufus Griswold's *The Sacred Poets of England and
America* (1849), a text that Dickinson herself owned, and in his *The
Female Poets of America* (1848), as well as in Caroline May's *The American Female Poets* (1848), demand new ways of reading that take seriously the poets' experiences both as women and as inheritors of
religious traditions. Although Dickinson may be more daring than
some of her poetic sisters, her strategies and themes may illuminate
those poets' religious verse. If she is understood as a daughter of
prophecy, her poetry may even inspire female religious speakers of our
time, showing them rhetorical possibilities as well as speaking wisdom
across the ages.

Acknowledgments

I EXPRESS my appreciation to Charlene Avallone for helping me to think through and articulate my ideas. Her encouragement and incisive comments on earlier versions of this manuscript I could not have done without. My thanks also go to Thomas Werge, Erskine Peters, and James Dougherty for their comments on the manuscript.

Individuals at my present institution deserve much of my gratitude as well. First, a research grant from Northwestern College (Iowa) enabled me to complete the final version of the manuscript, as did the special-emphasis contract on research that the college was able to offer me. To Robert Zwier and James Bultman, I am grateful for Northwestern's show of support and commitment to scholarship. I am also indebted to my colleagues Joel Westerholm and Lee Cerling for reading and commenting on portions of the manuscript. Thanks also go to Richard Reitsma, reference librarian, who always knows where to find research materials, and to Michael Cole, a Kent State University librarian who helped me to track down numerous books and sermon manuscripts in the early stages of my research. Several student research assistants helped on the manuscript in its various stages: Carla Carlson Hibma, Cory Mattson, Stephanie Grandia, Jill Haarsma, Kellie Gregg, and, most of all, the ever-faithful Scott Isebrand.

Versions of two chapters of this book were published in scholarly journals: Chapter 3, as "Emily Dickinson, Homiletics, and Prophetic Power," in *The Emily Dickinson Journal* 1, 2 (1992); and Chapter 6, as "Power through Prophecy: Emily Dickinson and the Scriptural Prophetic Tradition," in *Studies in Puritan American Spirituality* 4 (Winter 1994): 225–51. Both are used by permission. I am grateful for permission granted by the Harvard University Press to reprint Dickinson's poems from Thomas H. Johnson, *The Poems of Emily Dickinson* (Cambridge, Massachusetts, 1963), as well as portions of Dickinson's letters from Thomas H. Johnson and Theodora Ward, eds., *The Letters of Emily Dickinson* (Cambridge, Massachusetts, 1965). Paul Wright at the University of Masschusetts Press deserves my thanks for his helpful comments and his persistence in seeing this book through. I am also grateful for the work of Pam Wilkinson and the staff in the Amherst office of the University of Massachusetts Press.

Acknowledgments

Finally, I express appreciation to my family for their moral support. In particular, Betty Boucher Maclay and William Maclay have shown consistent interest and confidence in my work on the project. Over the years, they have valuably modeled perseverance and discipline in tackling long and hard projects. Bonnie Maclay Schaefer has stood beside me in ways that only a twin sister could. Kara and Andrew, my children, deserve my gratitude for their flexibility in adapting to my schedule. Most of all, I am deeply indebted to my husband, Christopher, whose steady encouragement sustained me over the long haul. His unfailing moral support and practical help with our family made this project possible.

Emily Dickinson, Daughter of Prophecy

Introduction

> *And it shall come to pass afterward, that I will pour out my*
> *spirit upon all flesh, and your sons and your daughters shall*
> *prophesy, your old men shall dream dreams, your young men*
> *shall see visions.*   (Joel 2:28; reiterated in Acts 2:17)

FROM THE TIME that Anne Bradstreet defied each carping tongue and picked up her pen to write poetry, women in America have been struggling to assert their poetic voices. Lacking authority within American culture—authority that is crucial to the ability to speak, as Sandra Gilbert and Susan Gubar have admirably shown—American women poets have explored various poses and strategies for sustenance and empowerment. In this study I examine one of the principal strategies through which Emily Dickinson sought to gain authority for her poetry: her method of drawing on the Christian prophetic tradition to achieve power and authority as a women prophet.

Surrounded by the prophetic voices of contemporary male and female orators, preachers, and self-proclaimed seers such as Ralph Waldo Emerson, as well as the didactic religious voices of contemporary female poets, Dickinson responded with a wisdom literature of her own making, revising the conventions of faith and expressing her vision through her poetry. In revising Christian dogma, Dickinson often drew on the very rhetorical resources whose doctrines she sought to undermine. Thus, Christian prophetic tradition, which Dickinson and her contemporaries saw extending from the Old and New Testament eras into modern America through a line of authoritative, wise religious speakers, provided her with stances, rhetorical structures, and a style for her poetry. She adopted these not only from the writings of the scriptural prophets and wisdom speakers but also from, as she would have understood it, a contemporary expression of that prophetic heritage: the traditional sermon. Adopting features of Judeo-Christian prophecy, Dickinson found a way to speak as an authoritative daughter of prophecy in the tradition of Joel 2:28: "Your sons and daughters shall prophesy."

The biblical prophetic tradition to which Dickinson was exposed offers a way to understand her poetry that both feminist scholarship and conventional religious criticism have missed. Focusing on the patriarchal elements of nineteenth-century Christianity, feminist scholars have, for the most part, dismissed the potentially positive contribution of Christianity to Dickinson's art. Although they have correctly challenged critics who have ignored the importance of Dickinson's womanhood to her art, almost all feminist critics have assumed that Dickinson was distanced from the repressive nineteenth-century American culture around her, including her religious heritage.[1] Similarly, religious critics of Dickinson's poetry have generally seen Christianity as a negative influence on her work, either limiting her in some way or, more often, stimulating her to protest against her theological heritage. Often the religious critics have failed to consider how Dickinson's gender might have shaped her art.[2]

To be sure, Dickinson did question her New England culture's understanding of deity, but at the same time, she found within the Christian tradition ways to empower her protests. By assuming the voice and stance of the prophet as she drew on biblical and homiletical rhetorical techniques, Dickinson as a woman poet spoke to her culture with a sense of authority and justification, despite that culture's patriarchal slant. Her religious tradition and her innovations upon it were precisely what enabled her to write her distinctive, unforgettable poetry.

In the introduction to *Feminist Critics Read Emily Dickinson*, Suzanne Juhasz sums up a feminist stance: "All [such critics] show Dickinson, of necessity, responding to the repressions that surround and threaten to control her, change her into something other than she is or might be."[3] Thanks to the work of Juhasz and other scholars sensitive to cultural and literary contexts, we are now in a good position to explore those elements that liberated Dickinson from the "repressions that surround[ed] her"—specifically, her religious tradition, or, more precisely, her participation in current innovations of that religious past. Instead of regarding Christianity as just another patriarchal structure, Dickinson scholars would do well to test the ways in which she drew on her religious surroundings to achieve liberation within her own cultural context, patriarchal as that culture was. Focusing on the elements within her religious heritage that give her a voice, a purpose, and authority as a female poet can illuminate her poetry in ways that feminist and religious scholarship may miss.

Conventional critics have generally acknowledged that Dickinson made extensive use of concepts and terminology adapted from New

England Congregationalism. While her broad indebtedness to that tradition has received wide critical attention over the years, more precise definitions of the relationship of that past to her poetry demonstrate specific formal and conceptual connections that illuminate the positive contributions of her heritage to her art. Dickinson's interactions with her religious tradition go well beyond the commonly acknowledged imitation of nineteenth-century hymnody. Critics have noted the concrete language, aphorisms, and antinomies of Dickinson's poetry, but all of these are best explored within the tradition of scriptural prophecy and wisdom and within the New England tradition of homiletics, both of which share an emphasis on those same literary devices. The two traditions offered Dickinson and other poets not only forms of artifice for their verse but also models of religious poets and speakers that could help shape their religious voices. Taking into account the ancient identification of poet with prophet or seer (which Dickinson knew from her classical training) and the pervasive romantic emphasis on the poet as prophet (found, for example, in Ralph Waldo Emerson), we can more clearly understand the appeal that assumption of the stance of poet-prophet would have had for Dickinson. Not surprisingly, to help position herself she turned to the tradition she knew best, one that also identified prophecy with poetry and empowered speakers: the heritage of scriptural prophecy and its extension in homiletics.

The form of prophecy as song, modeled in the Scriptures by the female prophets Miriam and Deborah, seems to have especially appealed to Dickinson, as does wisdom literature, which is related to the prophetic writings through the genre of poetry and the shared emphasis on vision and which also includes song (for example, the Canticles). Dickinson's poems often have the form and rhythm of song, because she often adopted for her basic pattern the "common meter" of the hymns she learned as a girl. She even identified herself as a singer, in one letter declaring, "*My* business is to love. . . . *My* business is to *sing*." In a letter to her Norcross cousins on the death of their father in 1863, she wrote, "Let Emily sing for you because she cannot pray" (*L*, 2:412, 421). For Dickinson, poetry as song is a displacement for the more conventional religious use of words such as "prayer." Singing, not the scolding of the jeremiad, links her poetry most obviously with the prophetic tradition associated with women.

Another pointed connection to the Judeo-Christian prophetic and wisdom literatures lies in Dickinson's adoption of the proverb or epigram. Loosely defined, proverbs are short, insightful statements that usually reflect a nation's inherited wisdom. They can take a number of forms, as in, for example, the Upanishads and Russian literature. Certainly, proverbs came to Dickinson from a number of sources—Greek and Latin traditions, English poetry of the classical era (1596–1616), even Benjamin Franklin's and Ralph Waldo Emerson's epigrams. But Dickinson's epigrams reflect a distinctive form and character, most notably derived from Judeo-Christian wisdom literature. Like the scriptural proverbs—as I explore in greater detail in Chapter 5—many of her epigrams have the form of two lines that echo each other in rhythm and often in form:

> Lazy hands make a man poor,
> 　　but diligent hands bring wealth.　　　　　(Prov. 10:4)

> Wonder—is not precisely Knowing
> And not precisely Knowing not—　　　　　　　(#1331)

Like the sayings in Scripture, Dickinson's proverbs offer profound insight; they are not simply clever rhetorical exercises like those penned by Benjamin Franklin. In content and tone, Dickinson's sayings are more like Anne Bradstreet's in "Meditations Divine and Morall" than like "Poor Richard's"—not surprising, since the women shared a common religious heritage.

For generations, Dickinson readers have noticed the poet's preference for what William Shurr calls a "fourteener," a two-line statement divided into an eight-syllable line and a six-syllable line, to transmit her insight:

> A nearness to Tremendousness—
> An Agony procures—　　　　　　　　　　　　(#963)

> Best Gains—must have the Losses' Test—
> To constitute them—Gains—　　　　　　　　(#684)

In his study of Emily Dickinson's letters, Shurr has isolated hundreds of proverbs that take this form.[4] Although the poet sometimes chose, in her poetry, to lengthen the line to include more syllables, fourteener proverbs abound among Dickinson's poems as well as in her letters. Perhaps more than any other single device, these proverbs, in both their richness and their abundance, distinguish the poet as a prophetic speaker. Expressed within the rhythm of the hymn, they elevate Dickinson to a position of American Sappho.

Yet, as I show in this study, Dickinson's poetry of prophecy goes beyond her use of the proverb in drawing on the stance, style, structures, and themes of the preachers and biblical prophets. The Judeo-Christian prophetic tradition, broadly defined, provided Dickinson with a voice to speak about her own vision of spirituality and her experiences of human suffering. These concerns constitute her version of prophecy as she translates conventional Christianity into other terms, often those of the emotions or of her psychological experience. She redefines the center of spirituality as not renunciation and submission to a conventional Christ but rather a more general renunciation and submission to the realm of spirit. That renunciation often inspires pointed observations about human living and experience, as Dickinson appropriates the terms of conventional Christian theology—God, Jesus, faith, redemption—but revises their meanings according to her own vision.

My procedure throughout this study is to draw on literary and, to a lesser extent, historical contexts to illuminate Dickinson's art. In Chapters 1 and 2, I discuss nineteenth-century ideas about and contexts of prophecy, as well as the definitions of prophecy that Dickinson would have embraced. Along the way, I show how these ideas and definitions apply to Dickinson's poetry. In Chapter 3, I consider sermonic prophecy as one of the most accessible forms of the prophetic tradition in Dickinson's day. There I offer some close readings of Dickinson's poems, exploring the influences of homiletics on her art while noticing the innovations Dickinson made upon the rhetorical strategies she knew from sermons.

The next three chapters show Dickinson drawing on particular prophetic stances and strategies that she knew through her exposure to the scriptural prophets. First, I explore in Chapter 4 her understanding of poetic inspiration, as shown in a range of her poems; then, I look in Chapter 5 at the genres she appropriated (with her own revisions) from the biblical prophetic writings—traveler to eternity, indicator, consoler. Chapter 6 focuses on the particular rhetorical devices she adopted from the scriptural prophecies, strategies that, combined with the preacherly ones discussed in Chapter 3, helped Dickinson shape a memorable and distinctive poetic voice.

In Chapter 7, I turn my attention to the connections between Dickinson's poetry and the prophecy of other American women writers. I consider Dickinson as continuing a tradition of American female prophecy, as well as overcoming (as other women had to do) public resistance to women speaking in a culture that discouraged their prophecy. In Chapter 8, I look at a stance central to Dickinson's prophetic vision—renunciation—which she could discover in the works of both female prophets and the male preachers of her day. Dickinson, like Anne Hutchinson before her, was able to turn renunciation into an assertion of power. Chapter 9 attempts to outline some of the emphases of Dickinson's wisdom or prophecy as these emerge from her renunciation to a godhead she understood to be absolutely wondrous.

Although for the purpose of study I have separated the contributions of scriptural and homiletic traditions to Dickinson's art, they have to be considered in tandem to illuminate her poetry. The homiletic tradition extends the scriptural one into Dickinson's time and shares its primary prophetic features, yet it differs in specific ways, most notably in its rhetorical structures. Dickinson brought the two together, learning key ideas about prophecy from her own reading and from the oratory of her day and combining them with romantic ideas about poetry and prophecy—ideas that have their own roots in biblical tradition. She shaped and modified what all of these sources could offer her. With these backgrounds in mind, I focus in my study on Dickinson's poems. My intention is not to offer a biographical reading of her art but to uncover Dickinson's motivations and strategies as they are suggested through the poems themselves, in light of her complex identity as a nineteenth-century poet, woman, and inheritor of the Puritan tradition.

This identity remains central to my study as I show that Dickinson, in the antinomian spirit of Anne Hutchinson, claimed a sanctioned inner voice that might defy cultural norms. Further, Dickinson's Puritan heritage provided a rich fund of material that she manipulated in order to speak within a patriarchal culture. Shaping the styles, genres, and techniques she found in literary and oral sources, Dickinson challenged the terms of conventional religion and expressed her own wisdom. She wrote out of a sense of being "Baptized . . . of Grace" to speak truth (#508, "I'm ceded—I've stopped being Theirs—," lines 8–9). In the biblical tradition articulated by the prophet Joel, she thereby made herself a daughter of prophecy.

1. Prophecy, Poetry, and Dickinson's American Contexts

"R ATHER THAN LOVE, than money, than fame, give me truth," Henry David Thoreau admonishes his audience in a famous line of *Walden* (1854). "Say what you have to say, not what you ought."[1] Thoreau's earnest exhortations to speak and live the truth exemplify the surge of interest in prophecy as a truth-telling and visionary mode in Emily Dickinson's day. This interest came from both secular and Christian circles—not surprising, since prophecy, as a specific oratorical and literary mode, has strong Judeo-Christian roots. The New England religious context remains inseparable from understandings of prophecy and from the broader practice of oratory, since the religious sensibility colored even political rhetoric. The emotional intensity of prophetic voices such as Thoreau's ultimately derived from the models of the prophets of Israel.

The Great Awakenings, understood as revivals of Bible-based faith, helped to stimulate the American interest in prophecy, as preachers exhorted their audiences to return to faith in much the same spirit that Old Testament prophets had demonstrated centuries earlier. By the time of the Second Great Awakening in the early part of the nineteenth century, preachers as well as such figures as Thoreau, Ralph Waldo Emerson, Margaret Fuller, and Walt Whitman (all of whom either only loosely associated themselves with Christianity or rejected it entirely) demonstrated New England's preoccupation with prophecy, especially as the Civil War approached. As I will show in more detail, Dickinson herself experienced her most direct contact with prophecy not through secular speakers such as Emerson (who emphasized the importance of it for all of nineteenth-century America) but through ministers' books and sermons, with which she had a far more extensive experience than she did with secular prophets. Nineteenth-century Christian prophetic texts, both verbal and written, extended the Hebrew prophets' tradition into her own day.

To be sure, in her secular contexts Dickinson could not have escaped exposure to prophecy, especially as the Civil War approached. As Shira Wolosky and others have pointed out, the imminence of the

7

Civil War encouraged a rhetoric of apocalypse and millenialism, as ministers, politicians, and other orators prophetically warned Americans that the war was God's divine judgment for the sin of slavery, which had not been sufficiently opposed. The rhetoric of apocalypse infused the nation as a whole, Wolosky notes, so that America believed itself "to be witnessing the coming of the Lord and the Final Judgment." Seeing the war as part of a millennial pattern, orators spoke on the apocalyptic drama and on issues that they saw as universal and spiritual, rather than local and political only. The atmosphere of apocalypse was conducive to the emergence of a wide variety of prophetic speakers—clerical, political, and popular—including Emily Dickinson, who, as Thomas Ford and others have pointed out, had her most creative period during the time of the war: she wrote more than half of her entire corpus between 1861 and 1865, and she questioned the significance of suffering in an age that tended to romanticize death. Perhaps, as Wolosky argues, Dickinson's poetry should be seen as part of the range of responses to the Civil War offered by contemporary writers.[2] Her verse, emerging from an era that was questioning the purity of the nation, certainly challenges audiences to consider their spiritual groundings.

The war and the rhetoric surrounding it understandably sustained America's interest in prophecy, and probably also Dickinson's. Prophecy also formed the center of transcendental poetics. Emerson had proclaimed a gospel of poetry as spiritual medium, the poet's office consisting of articulating the "spiritual facts" of earthly existence, with the effect of emancipating humanity through the poet's "sublime vision." For Emerson, the poet was prophet, utterer of spiritual truth—an idea Dickinson knew from reading Emerson's essay "The Poet," which she owned.[3] Emerson had seen this convergence of speakers modeled in the Bible, as had other romantic writers. We will consider this idea in more detail, but here we can say that, overall, the idea of writer as prophet was immensely stimulating for Emerson, Dickinson, and other writers of their generation. Emerson, for one, believed all extant religious systems to be expressions of the same divine spirit and that the individual had direct access to that spirit. He carried the new literary approach to its conclusion in his call, at the end of the "Divinity School Address," for the "new Teacher" to complete the "fragmentary" "Hebrew and Greek Scriptures."[4] Whitman assumed a similar prophetic or demiurgical role as the speaker of *Leaves of Grass*, hoping that it would be the "New Bible."

Margaret Fuller saw the feminist implications of transcendentalist thought. Like Emerson, she viewed women as oracular and intuitive beings, possessors and speakers of wisdom, but she went farther than Emerson in the ways she explained women's particular gifts of prophecy. Her conclusions are not farfetched for her day and certainly are ones that Dickinson could have drawn.[5]

Pointing out "two aspects of women's nature, represented by the ancients as Muse and Minerva," Fuller describes in *Woman in the Nineteenth Century* (1845) the "Muse" as "the especial genius of woman," that genius being "electrical in tendency, intuitive in function, spiritual in tendency." "What I mean by the Muse," she pointedly defines, "is the unimpeded clearness of the intuitive powers which a perfectly truthful adherence to every admonition of the higher instincts would bring to a finely organized human being." What is its literary expression? "Prophecy or poetry," Fuller declares, going on to describe some ancient precedents for female prophecy. Women, with their special gifts of intuition and spiritual power, have always been specially suited to express weighty vision, she says; their vision would take the form of prophecy or poetry—or, presumably, prophetic poetry itself.[6]

Fuller expresses a view of women's spirituality held by other female speakers of her time—that is, that women are more suited to "religion" than men are—but she goes farther than many in specifically attributing spiritual authority through prophecy to women. Underlining the importance of prophetic "sight" as a component of intuition, Fuller holds "women . . . to be especially capable" of this "sight of the world of causes," an emphasis that would have appealed to Dickinson. (Even if Dickinson did not know Fuller's ideas directly, Fuller's interest in female prophecy indicates the conduciveness of the New England milieu to the topic.) In women is the soul completely developed, Fuller says, identifying feminine nature as "the lyrical, the inspiring, and inspired apprehensiveness of her being," such that woman's soul "flows," "breathes," and "sings." Fuller thus suggests that women are specifically suited not only to be inspired but, through that inspiration, to express new visions of spirituality, taking the form of prophecy or poetic song. Like Emerson—indeed, perhaps influencing Emerson—Fuller calls for "one incessant revelation": "let it take what form it will."[7] She herself offers an early female precedent for Dickinson's project of prophesying—one that makes Dickinson look conservative, for Fuller was all for jettisoning the entire Bible.

Yet, even nineteenth-century women more conservative than Fuller

9

expressed a specific interest in prophecy and its possibilities for women. Curiously similar to Fuller in her perspective, yet claiming herself to be no feminist, Lydia Maria Child in *History of the Condition of Women* (1835) includes a discussion of Hebrew women, considering whether women were thought to be naturally more prophetic than men and arriving at the belief "that women were in more immediate connection with Heaven," including among the biblical female prophets Miriam, Deborah, Mary, and even the witch of Endor.[8] Despite the fact that Child was conservatively religious in some ways, the book caused a stir when it first came out, and indeed, Child's attitudes toward women challenged her contemporaries' devaluation of women and their religious powers. She offers to Dickinson a nearly contemporary popular source for a focus on women prophets in the Bible.

Sarah Josepha Hale, best known for her almost half-century editorship of *Godey's Lady's Book* (1837–1877), in *Woman's Record* (1853) similarly reads the Bible as giving much religious power to women, a reading indicative of the possibilities for women that some nineteenth-century cultural leaders saw. Indeed, *Godey's* itself was so widely read that Dickinson knew it, and probably, being an astute reader, she saw the deeper meanings of Hale's writings. As Nina Baym points out, Hale is usually interpreted as having impeded egalitarian feminism through her espousal of the ideology of separate spheres for the sexes (and through her championing of a sentimental, consumerist aesthetic sensibility for women). But Hale, according to Baym, shows in *Woman's Record* her fullest expression of her theory of womanhood, one that challenges the interpretations of her that are based solely on surface readings of *Godey's*.[9] In fact, in *Woman's Record*, Hale defends the religious case for female superiority, describing woman as a repository of intuition, which makes her superior to man.

The argument sounds surprisingly like Fuller's—surprising because Fuller is usually seen as "radical," Hale as "conservative." But Hale, implicitly if not explicitly, agrees with Fuller's belief in the prophetic powers of women. Through her nine hundred pages of entries recounting the lives of some 1,650 women from all historical eras and nations, Hale offers an elaborate historical narrative that sees women as crucial to the march of Christian history. Hale's vision of the progress of world history conflates the progress of Christianity with that of women; the moral improvement of men and the rest of culture depends on women, whose nature is specifically suited to Christianity and religious power.

Reversing a Puritan argument by depicting women as closer to heaven than to earth, Hale encourages educated Christian women to speak out their religious convictions. Indeed, instead of only speaking softly among themselves, women are invited to prophesy, to address each other in public, and to exploit the power of the word. They have the right and obligation to speak, Hale maintains, because they are correct and because it is necessary for men to hear them. Dickinson would have found such an emphasis attractive, even as Hale advocated women's use of "stealth" when they spoke out, "as though it were wrong for them to be recognized doing anything which has a high aim."[10] Obviously, Dickinson and many other antebellum women chose poetry for their expression of religious vision, preferring the "stealthy" possibilities that this medium offered over the more direct and, in some ways, more public mode of oratory.

Women were not the only ones to urge prophecy on their audiences. Through their books and sermons, ministers, including those with whom Dickinson had direct contact, encouraged and modeled prophecy, advocating the direct proclamation of spirituality. Although they did not figure women as prophets per se (because they accepted the nineteenth-century strictures on women's religious roles), nonetheless their directives remained available to women such as Dickinson who could see the broad applications. One of the books in the Dickinson family library was George Faber's *A Dissertation on the Prophecies* (1808), in which Faber, presenting his argument in the form of a sermon, analyzed in depth each of forty-four biblical prophecies and exhorted his readers to "be mindful of our duty . . . to endeavor, each according to our opportunity and measure, to promote the conversion of the house of Judah" and so "fulfill the prophecies."[11] Although Dickinson would later reject much of orthodox Christianity and thus prophecy as Faber defined it—that is, as the task of "promoting the conversion of the house of Judah"—his work may have presented early encouragement to Dickinson to pursue her own prophetic "labor of love"—her poetry. But instead of seeking to extend Christ's "spiritual kingdom" in an orthodox fashion, she would redefine Faber's notion of prophetic duty to focus on the giving of wisdom and vision. Faber and others served to encourage her to prophesy, and she would find her own way, exploring the emotional states of spirituality and translating the orthodox into the unorthodox, the conventionally religious back into radical Christianity, the spiritual into the psychological.

Perhaps more important in shaping Dickinson's poetry of prophecy,

F. D. Huntington, whose collected sermons the Dickinson library also contained, preached that their era was an age for new prophecy: "We are in a day of a new order of worship. . . . The day of the prophet has come,—bold rebuker of kings and chieftains—sharp discerner between light and darkness, between truth and lies,—the unsparing censor of the corruptions of government, of the abuses of law, of the idolatries and worldliness of the people."[12] As in Dickinson's poetry, Huntington's emphasis is on "true" (that is, emotional) spirituality, that which "may go on in the individual heart, yours or mine, . . . when we pass from mere outward compliance with religious forms to a hearty adoption of their life."[13] In emphasizing such emotional spirituality, Huntington and Dickinson participated in the historical shift in their century toward a new kind of religiousness. Dickinson adopted the spiritual and emotional forms or structures of prophecy that Huntington called for, more than the content or dogma that can prove hollow when not rooted in heartfelt spirituality. She radically revised, even invented and contradicted, some of the dogmas of orthodox faith, but as a prophet-preacher, her emphasis on spirituality is the same as Huntington's.

Dickinson readers are well aware of the emotional quality of her poetry, but when we consider the spiritual vision that she expounds, we see that her interest in heartfelt religion sounds much like Huntington's. Still, she often revises Christian dogma. A poem such as #234 emerges naturally from Dickinson's contexts of prophecy, at the same time capturing her own version of a spirituality that is more than skin-deep:

> You're right—"the way *is* narrow"—
> And "difficult the Gate"—
> And "few there be"—Correct again—
> That "enter in—thereat"—
>
> *'Tis* Costly—So are *purples*!
> 'Tis just the price of *Breath*—
> With but the "Discount" of the *Grave*—
> Termed by the *Brokers*—"Death"!
>
> And after *that*—there's Heaven—
> The *Good* Man's—"*Dividend*"—
> And *Bad* Men—"go to Jail"—
> I guess—   (#234, unfinished poem)

The poem reads as one side of a conversation between the speaker and an unquestioning, Scripture-quoting Christian of Dickinson's era. The emotional intensity of the speaker is unmistakable; the exclamation points and underlining in the poem help to communicate the high pitch. Clearly, this is a situation in which crucial religious tenets are at stake. "You're right," the speaker ostensibly concedes, seeming to confirm the pat articulations of the simplistic Christian's beliefs. But the reader detects the irony and even humor behind the phrase. The speaker, in reiterating the platitudes of nineteenth-century Christianity, exposes the easiness of the formulations and suggests the shallowness of the beliefs. Reducing "death" and "heaven" to economic metaphors—"discount" and "dividend"—makes those states seem ordinary and routine, not cosmic, mysterious happenings of spiritual import. Certainly, this poem suggests that religion needs to avoid superficiality—a concept frequently propounded by both Hebrew and nineteenth-century American prophet-preachers. Easy religion, the kind that can be iterated in a list of simple tenets, is found lacking by the poet, who pokes fun through her speaker's ironic responses: "You're right," "Correct again," "And after *that*." We sense the poet's preference for a spirituality more complex, a religion that goes beyond logical propositions.

But the poet's spirituality may not be conventional, either. The "I guess" of the last line undercuts all certainty that the quoted tenets are correct. Thus the poet challenges not only religious shallowness but also the very dogmas of the faith; as we will see again, these two stances are characteristic of Dickinson's prophetic mode. Her poem thus continues the nineteenth-century interest in prophecy as a way to urge moral and spiritual depth, even as she goes beyond the usual practices in her rejection of accepted doctrine.

It should be noted that speaking the truth in defiance of cultural conventions had long been identified as key to the prophetic role as Dickinson's Protestant contemporaries saw it. Of course, one could go only so far in challenging societal practice, but nonetheless, oratory, the most public form of societal challenge, was seen as the genre most conducive to prophecy. We will see that oratory provides an important context for Dickinson's poetry.

Among Dickinson's contemporaries who associated oratory with prophecy were both ministers and professors. For example, as Boyleston Professor of Rhetoric and Oratory at Harvard from 1819 to 1851, Edward T. Channing lectured and shaped the assumptions of the generation preceding Dickinson's: writers—such as Emerson, Thoreau, Thomas Wentworth Higginson, James Russell Lowell, Oliver Wendell Holmes—and clergy alike, and through them, one could argue, New England culture in general. In his *Lectures Read to the Juniors in Harvard College* (1856), Channing describes "the exhortation, warning and instruction, which the prophets addressed to their countrymen as religious beings," as "a kind of public preaching which, in its design at least, resembles our sermons." By "design," Channing apparently means the aim of the form of oratory, which he describes as "moral influence" and the "affect[ing] of human conduct."[14]

Dickinson would have known this association of oratory or "public preaching" with "the prophets' addresses," for the importance of the passage reached far beyond the students who read Channing's lectures, since he shaped antebellum New England thinking on rhetoric and oratory. Dickinson's culture vested the public speaker, whether of the church (the preacher) or the public platform, with prophetic importance, as Channing did. The idea also appears in the thinking of Channing's student Ralph Waldo Emerson. As I argue was also true for Dickinson, Emerson claimed the prophetic role for the poet, in "The Poet," the "Divinity School Address," and other essays. Emerson linked the role of prophet and preacher, and thus the genres of prophecy and sermon.

From her reading of "The Poet" and, perhaps also, the "Divinity School Address," Dickinson would have known that for Emerson, the prophet and the preacher—and the poet—were "seers" and "sayers" of spiritual truth, wielding great cultural power. She knew of Emerson's acclaim as a lecturer, because he spoke in Amherst and in the vicinity at least six times in her lifetime, and she may have heard him speak, thereby directly experiencing his oral prophetic voice alongside those of her ministers.[15] Serving as modern-day prophets for Dickinson and her contemporaries, Emerson, the ministers, and the other orators in New England society established an oral tradition of prophecy that was inescapable. The antebellum culture's oratory was pervasive, teaching Dickinson the influence, value, and power of the spoken word.

In addition to the sermon, all around her Dickinson saw Americans giving speeches in all kinds of situations: political events, business occasions, celebrations, electioneering, legislative contexts, and forensic or courtroom situations. The institution of lecture halls provided an opportunity for many would-be prophets, such as Ralph Waldo

Emerson, who, with many writers, ministers, and other speakers, took advantage of the lyceum movement to gain opportunity to speak his understanding of truth. "The prestige of oratory overshadowed that of poetry," Lawrence Buell points out, "not to mention fiction and drama," to the extent that belles lettres were defined neoclassically, as a branch of rhetoric, "well into the Romantic period."[16] The effect of oratory on other genres can be seen as a collapse of twentieth-century generic distinctions, making Dickinson's adoption of oratorical, sermonic structures for her poetry more understandable.

Significant for the influence on Dickinson's art, her own Christian tradition had associated preaching with prophecy since the Reformation. John Calvin saw ministers as performing a prophetic role; he identified them as the "successors" of the apostles, who are the New Testament analogues of the Old Testament prophets, and called both prophets and ministers "the very mouth of God," apparently the most important role of prophet-preachers as the Reformers understood prophecy.[17] William Perkins, a seventeenth-century Puritan minister and rhetorician, assumed Calvin's identification of preaching with prophecy in calling one of his studies of preaching *The Arte of Prophecying, or A Treatise Concerning the Sacred and Onely True Manner and Method of Preaching* (1592; translated in 1607). This text shaped views of homiletics even into the nineteenth century. One hundred or so years after Perkins, Jonathan Edwards still assumed the extension of prophecy in preaching, urging preachers, in one of his ordination sermons, to imitate the "great prophet" John the Baptist, who was a "burning and shining light" in his ardor and clarity of teaching. According to Edwards, ministers were to share John's prophetic task of imparting divine truth, consoling those who mourn, and directing people in the ways of holiness.[18]

In Dickinson's time, the association between prophecy and preaching had become implicit among Edwardsian ministers. Edwards A. Park, a minister whom Dickinson heard speak, described the preacher as Calvin had described the prophet, as one whose words "come with power" because they are the words "of God." F. D. Huntington, whose volume of sermons Dickinson owned, described prophets in terms applicable to ministers: prophets were "teachers" who communicated of "religious wisdom" when they expressed "larger vision or insight"; their role was not restricted to prediction. Giving "wisdom" or "vision" was central, and, Park also pointed out, even their written sermons would retain power. Those texts would gain a literary immortality in their enduring influence on posterity, so authoritative did Park consider preachers' words as divine, prophetic messages.[19]

With this cultural emphasis on oral prophecy, it is not surprising that one of the distinguishing features of Dickinson's poetry is the spoken quality of the verse, as we saw in #234, "You're right—'the way *is* narrow'—." Yet scholars have not associated that quality with the popular or sermonic oratory of her day, perhaps because they have tended to read the poetry with the twentieth-century understanding of genre. Nevertheless, the spoken effect of an oral tradition of prophecy, replicated in Dickinson's verse, is distinctive. Brita Lindberg-Seyersted argues throughout her *Voice of the Poet* that "the prevailing impression conveyed to a reader" in Dickinson's verse is "of the spokenness of her poetic message'; Lindberg-Seyersted in fact attempts in her study "to establish the character of an immediate, 'spoken,' often confessional message, which is one of the essential marks of her poetry."[20] David Porter agrees, calling Dickinson's poetic discourse "flattened speech, a *talking* that was depoeticizing and an escape from pomposity." As he strikingly describes:

> Dickinson interrupted nineteenth-century poetic discourse with a vernacular so direct it seemed crude to her first public. She disarmingly called it in poem 373 "my simple speech" and "plain word." . . . Into her poems and particularly into those outrageous first lines came a natural breath and diction that created the illusion and the impact of real speech acts.[21]

In adopting natural speech for her poetry, Dickinson followed, as we will see, the practice of the preachers of the Puritan legacy, who were taught by the homiletical rhetoricians to reject an affected style or an eloquence not characteristic of ordinary speech. The sermon gave Dickinson access to a tradition that could provide her with strategies and a structure for her own wise voice, and preachers offered her models of contemporary prophets in her own locale.

Despite the widespread American interest in prophecy, Dickinson's culture did experience some ambivalence about it when New Englanders considered the expression of prophecy through art. Antebellum New England, if Buell is correct, was "characterized by a tension between the impulse to seize visionary authority and the awareness of the quixoticism of that desire—by a skepticism about art's authority that came both from without (the general public) and from within."[22]

That skepticism about art undoubtedly fueled the public's interest in oratory at the expense of poetry. Perhaps in reaction against such skepticism, Dickinson attempted to appropriate scriptural-sermonic authority for her poetry, as other poets did (most notably, the popular female poets of her day), even as the cultural force of that authority was being undermined in some circles by the Higher Biblical Criticism movement.

Dickinson could vary her prophetic-poetic voices (to include irony, doubt, consolation, even despair) yet remain in the prophetic and wisdom traditions through the rhetorical structures and genres she drew on. Indeed, the scriptural prophets themselves and, to a lesser degree, the preachers of her day expressed a range of voices. Dickinson was not limited to the oratorical jeremiad as an expression of prophecy, and neither were the biblical writers. The Bible, with its inclusion of poetry in the prophetic writings, offered a range of expression beyond the jeremiad—consolation, proverbs for daily living, descriptions of afterlife experiences. And in including poetry in the prophetic books, the Bible sanctioned verse as a medium of prophetic authority, an association that dovetails with Fuller's and Emerson's emphasis on the prophetic possibilities of poetry. Even if the "secular" art of Emerson, Bronson Alcott, and others might have lacked prophetic authority outside of the limited circles of the transcendentalists, Dickinson would have realized that poetry drawing on the models of the Christian tradition should have greater authority within a culture informed by evangelical Christianity, even if particular audiences in their shallowness dismissed her or her poetic prophecy. To her, as to colonial Puritans who acknowledged David as a poet favored by God, art had sanctity, even if that sanctity went unacknowledged by an ambivalent readership.

To regard poetry as prophecy is to recognize its sanctity according to ancient traditions surrounding poetry, ones that undoubtedly had more weight for Dickinson as a poet than for contemporary audiences. As she well knew, poetry has been associated with prophecy for centuries, both as written and as sung—an emphasis that the romantic poets of Dickinson's age renewed. In classical times, poets were identified with the divine, seen as the mouthpieces of the gods because they composed under divine inspiration. Giving their oracles in song, poets in ancient times were often regarded as seers or priests, when they guided people in the ways of life through their oracles. In the biblical tradition as well, prophecy is associated especially with sung poetry.

Dickinson, familiar with the Bible, certainly knew that the prophet Moses led the Israelites in song when they defeated the Egyptians at the Red Sea. Part of the song is repeated in the prophetic writings of Isaiah (in Isa. 12:2), one of Dickinson's favorite books of the Bible. The prophecy-song is also quoted verbatim in the collection of poems in the Bible, the Book of Psalms (Ps. 118:14). When the prophet Miriam led her choral dance at the same defeat of the Egyptians, she repeated part of Moses' victory hymn in her song (Exod. 15:20).

King David, understood as the writer of the Book of Psalms, also exemplifies the intersection between poetry, prophecy, and song. Calvin habitually referred to him as "the Prophet," influencing generations of Calvinists to consider the prophetic spirit of many of the Psalms. By generations of believers after Calvin (including conservative audiences of Dickinson's day), David was at the same time looked to as modeling a sanctified poetics, the exemplar for anyone aspiring to write verse acceptable to God. In his songlike psalms, prophecy, understood in its wider definition as wisdom literature, takes the form of poetry.

Beyond the Psalms, Dickinson and other writers of her day found an even more extensive literary source modeling the convergence of the poetic and the prophetic: the biblical prophetic writings themselves. By the time that Dickinson wrote her first poem, British romantic poets had already discovered that these writings—the books of Isaiah, Jeremiah, Ezekiel, and the twelve minor prophets—constitute an enormous body of biblical poetry. Afire with a sense of the "lofty function of poetry as a spiritual guide for mankind," as Murray Roston puts it in his study of poetry and prophecy, the British—and, later, the American—romantic poets saw themselves as specially equipped to reveal profound truths to their age. With the nineteenth-century interest in and discovery of the particular forms of Hebrew genres, including poetry, came the romantic writers' realization that scriptural prophecy often took the form of "poetry . . . filled with passion, fire, and moral vision"; here was a literature that could provide the "model for which they had been searching."[23]

Dickinson also found that source, participating in the romantic movement's impetus toward prophetic poetry. Her era increasingly saw the blurring of distinctions between sacred and secular writing, resulting in the exploitation of the Bible as a literary model to a greater extent than ever before. At the same time, secular writing was gaining spiritual legitimacy as a revealer of truth. It is not surprising that

Dickinson looked to and found in the Scriptures rhetorical possibilities for her own verse; in many ways, she was following the practice of other writers of her era, both in America and in Great Britain. Like these writers, Dickinson saw the opportunities that the "literary liberation" of the Bible made possible.[24] What distinguishes her prophetic poetry, of course, is her preservation of a female identity for her prophetic persona, even as that voice draws on and adjusts the style and devices usually preferred by male prophets.

The plundering of the Bible for literary models arguably began as early as the late eighteenth century, with the practice becoming increasingly popular by Dickinson's time. With his 1772 address *On the History, Eloquence, and Poetry of the Bible*, a clergyman, teacher, and poet, Timothy Dwight, initiated the American tradition of viewing the Bible as a piece of "fine writing" apart from "its purity and holiness."[25] Significant for both American religious history and literary history, Dwight attempted to examine the biblical rhetoric as distinct from its truth content. Following the model of Robert Lowth, who in 1753 was the first scholar to analyze systematically the Old Testament poetics, Dwight and Hugh Blair (who summarized Lowth's findings) intended to present the Bible as beyond comparison; but in their literary approach to the Bible—their isolation of the stylistic element and their comparison of sacred and secular rhetoric—they unwittingly encouraged the relativization of Scripture and the view that Scripture was culturally determined. As Buell points out, the effect was that they lent support to the idea that latter-day poets might be equally inspired as Scripture—a point that explains Dickinson's rhetorical decisions. Dickinson took Dwight's approach even further when she examined rhetorical form as a discrete element of the Bible but, unlike Dwight, rejected many aspects of biblical dogma. She and many other writers of her day attempted what Buell calls "literary scripturism": reworking biblical texts into their own writings, but without regard for the distinctive biblical vision that undergirds those texts. Like other romantic writers, Dickinson wrote according to her own vision of spirituality, thus undermining scriptural authority even as she turned to Scripture for a model of authoritative prophecy.[26]

In her reading of Keats, Wordsworth, Byron, and Emerson, Dickinson undoubtedly shared these writers' dislike of the restriction of the prophet to the role of *vates*, or foreteller of the future.[27] Indeed, even the ministers of her time, such as Albert Barnes, pointed out that the biblical prophets' main role was "to promulgate the will of God," not to forecast events.[28] The romantic writers saw the real identity of the prophet and poet centered in concern with the "eternal, the infinite elements of life."[29] As Roston explains, "The ethical, reforming element of Romantic poetry, the belief that the poet had a more sublime function to perform than merely to amuse or instruct in the limited Augustan sense . . . derive[s] directly from the biblical consecration of poetry to a diviner purpose."[30] Dickinson shared the biblical and romantic impulse to influence the moral improvement of humanity, perhaps most specifically in her use of the proverb, which, in its terse, parallelist form, derived from the biblical prophetic-poetic writings. Offering proverbs in the stance of wisdom giver, Dickinson showed that she, like Emerson, Shelley, and other romantic poets, as well as the biblical prophets, saw her purpose as being not simply to write didactic moralisms but to provide her audience with ideals of moral excellence and spirituality. As a religious visionary, she wrote to reveal the inner workings of the soul, her individuality becoming marked, like that of the biblical prophets and the romantic poets, as her religious impulse took firm hold.

Not only the romantic poets disseminated this biblical poetic; the popular rhetoric books of Dickinson's time also schooled her in a poetry of prophecy. Hugh Blair's *Lectures on Rhetoric and Belles Lettres* (1783), which devoted a lecture to the poetry of the Bible, remained vastly influential in Dickinson's day and could have been the source that taught her about this body of prophetic poetry. Her father's readings of Scripture to the family, her religious training, and her father's library further exposed her to the prophets' techniques and stances. And of course, she knew the biblical tradition of prophecy through her own reading and study of the Bible. As Jack L. Capps points out, among the books of the Bible that Dickinson most often cites are prophetic books: Revelation, the Psalms (which were understood to continue the themes and forms of the Old Testament prophets), and Isaiah, as well as the Gospels, which obviously include the sayings of Christ, himself a prophetic speaker.[31] Not only would she have associated prophecy and poetry, but she also would have been aware of the variety of Judeo-Christian prophets and the distinctive features of prophecy. Through all of her sources, Dickinson would have recognized that the central connection between the poet and the prophet in the romantic and biblical traditions remains the word spoken in a stance of authority. Both figures come to their audiences uttering truths revealed not by reason but by special insight. (Indeed, the romantic conception of the poet as prophet derives from the biblical notion of prophet as poet.)

From her religious training among New England Congregationalists, Dickinson certainly knew the important details of the Christian prophetic tradition—for instance, that it had a long history dating back to Moses, who was understood as the author of the Pentateuch and considered the first or "normative" prophet by Calvin and other Reformers. Conservative preachers of Dickinson's day reminded their audiences that the tradition of prophecy continued into the New Testament with John the Baptist and with the pouring out of the Holy Spirit at Pentecost in Acts 2. This was a crucial tenet for evangelicals, since it meant, at the very least, that all believers were equipped to do evangelism, whatever their gender, class, or race.

But even more specifically, astute readers of Scripture, such as Dickinson, understood that the "pouring out" of the Spirit on all of God's people carried with it the result that every Christian is potentially a prophet in a more profound sense, as described in Acts 2:17–18 (which reiterated Joel 2:28): "Your sons and your daughters shall prophesy." Students of the Bible knew that a specific group of prophets in the New Testament were those who used their gifts to issue spiritual guidance to the Church. Their work as preachers to the Church is described as exhortation (Acts 15:32), edification, and consolation (1 Cor. 14:3), all of which take prophecy beyond the narrow idea of future-telling. And the word "prophetic" in the biblical sense connects authority, sanction, and special, divine selection—experiences that nineteenth-century women like Dickinson rarely publicly enjoyed.

Yet Dickinson knew from her own reading of the Bible, as well as from sources expressing female interest in biblical prophecy—Fuller's, Child's, and Hale's writings among those—that the Scriptures sanctioned women as prophets. Women's claim of spiritual authority was certainly not a new pattern in Dickinson's day; the Bible witnesses to a tradition of female prophecy. Dickinson would not have missed the numerous references, in both the Old and the New Testaments, that affirm women as prophets, leveling gender distinctions and specifically citing women's prophetic potential. Female prophets specifically named in the Old Testament include Miriam, sister of Moses, who led a choral dance in celebration of Israel's deliverance from Egypt (Exod. 15:20); Deborah, "mother in Israel" (Judg. 5:7), who was consulted as an intertribal judge; Huldah, wife of the keeper of the royal wardrobe, who declared the divine will to Josiah after the discovery of the law book (2 Kings 22:14); and Noadiah, who joined other prophets in attempting to intimidate Nehemiah (Neh. 6:14). The New Testament writers mention as "prophetess" Anna, who praised God in the temple at the appearance of the infant Christ (Luke 2:36–38) and Philip's four daughters, who prophesied at Caesarea (Acts 21:9).

In the early church, as Paul's Corinthian correspondence indicates, the gift of prophecy was exercised by various Christians, irrespective of sex (cf. 1 Cor. 11:4–5). This was in accordance with Joel's prediction that both sons and daughters "shall prophesy," presumably in greater numbers than ever before. And with the beginning of fulfillment occurring on the day of Pentecost, the abundance of prophets apparently was the case, as both men and women assumed active roles in the early church. It is no surprise that many women are numbered among the martyrs who died for the cause of Christ at the hands of the Romans, since those women heard the gospel as a gender-inclusive message and stood alongside men to defend it with their deeds and words. In all of these cases, whether or not they claimed the special office of "prophet," women recognized their call to participate in prophecy by acting as speakers for God. The New Testament Church opened the doors to women's participation even wider than the Old Testament had, through such proclamations as Gal. 3:28: "There is neither Jew nor Greek, there is neither bond nor free, there is neither male nor female: for ye are all one in Christ Jesus."

Of the biblical models of women prophets that Dickinson would have known, many women functioned specifically as divinely chosen leaders and speakers. Miriam, perhaps the most widely remembered female prophet of the Scriptures, in Num. 12:1–2 pointed out her belief that God had spoken through her (and Aaron) just as God had done through Moses, a belief that is later confirmed in Mic. 6:4, which cites her as a leader of Israel. As in the case of the male biblical prophets, the Scriptures suggest that Miriam was divinely inspired through visions and dreams, the modes of transmission that God cites in Num. 12:6. As we will see in Chapter 4, Dickinson continued this tradition. Equally important, Dickinson practiced other patterns demonstrated by the women prophets of the Bible. Like the male biblical prophets (whose prophecies constitute the bulk of scriptural poetry), the biblical women prophets chose Hebraic poetry with its paired lines, but these women often spoke their messages through poetic song, their way of awakening in their audience a response to God.[32] In the women prophets' utterances, Dickinson could see that a woman's visionary verse could fulfill an important cultural function as audiences looked to the female prophets for spiritual guidance. In filling the role of prophet, these women served as spiritual leaders who authoritatively exhorted their audiences in regard to the divine will. Dickinson apparently attempted to appropriate the same role, as we can see over and over in the poems that reveal her sense of special selection. "Title divine—is mine!" her speaker claims in #1072. "Acute Degree—conferred on me— / Empress of Calvary!" As a presumably divinely sanctioned female speaker, she continued the pattern presented by the women prophets of the Bible.

Dickinson thus observed a range of prophetic styles in her time, ranging from the prophetic writings she read in the Bible to the preaching she heard. Her comments in letters regarding sermons show sharp discernment as she criticizes sermons that bore her and praises those that transport her, the latter including those of Edward S. Dwight and, later, Charles Wadsworth. Other contemporary models of prophecy or wisdom giving she could find in the verse of antebellum evangelical women. These versions of religious vision are necessarily sentimental, the poets constrained both by cultural expectations and by their own understanding of verse. Dickinson both continued their practice and went beyond it to make, paradoxically, innovations upon the tradition of women poets as truth tellers.

Dickinson's creativity in transforming female literary practice is striking when we consider the cultural barriers she and her contemporaries faced. As we will see even more clearly in Chapter 7, after the close of the New Testament canon, the female prophetic tradition met with obstacles from a patriarchal expression of Christianity that would keep women "in their place," submissive to their husbands and silent in matters of the Church. We will later explore those obstacles and the ways that Dickinson and other would-be female prophets dealt with them. But first, let us examine some of the defining features of Judeo-Christian prophecy and the ways that Dickinson adopted these to attain a particular poetic voice. We will discover a tradition that enabled her to express a religiousness that could be at odds with nineteenth-century practice while paradoxically associating her with what her culture would have seen as conventionally Christian. In her poetry, Dickinson attempted to reclaim the prophecy exemplified best by the Scriptures, the practice of speaking the truth even at the cost of being misunderstood and rejected.

2. "A Word that Breathes Distinctly"

WHEN EDITOR Mabel Loomis Todd sent a copy of the 1890 *Poems*—the first series of Dickinson's poems published—to one of Amherst's summer visitors, the Reverend E. Winchester Donald of New York's Episcopal Church of the Ascension, Donald responded with enthusiasm. To his mind, he was encountering "a mind & imagination that could tell . . . more of nature and the mysteries of life than the combined wisdom of the College." Dickinson was, for him (as for many of the poet's readers of the 1890s), a giver of wisdom. And she was more: Donald recognized Dickinson as working within an accessible prophetic tradition, making the same difficult choices as the scriptural prophets who went before her. He went on to ask:

> One other thing: was the inexorable cost of all this illumination her seclusion renunciation & ache? Would John Baptist [*sic*] be forerunner without the years in the desert, the locusts and all that? Is the nun's self-effacement, her veil and her virginity, the explanation of her unquestioned power? We cannot wear lace and pearls—go often to town & the play, be experts in salads beers and truffles, know what to do with our hands—and expect either to see heaven or to have anyone believe we have seen it.[1]

Clearly, Donald saw Dickinson's seclusion and renunciation as the source of her power. Like John the Baptist's, her countercultural decisions resulted in "illumination" and "unquestioned power," an ability to see divine relations and meanings. Misunderstood by many of her later readers as being eccentric or strange, Dickinson followed the path, as Donald recognized, of those who would speak wisdom to their culture at the cost of social nonconformity.

Although for the most part in this study I do not make hard distinctions between the scriptural genres of wisdom and prophecy—Dickinson's generation hardly did—it is important to point out here that this nonconformity to societal expectations sets the prophet apart from the wisdom giver, at least in the scriptural tradition. While the latter figure positions himself or herself within the community (Solomon is the most obvious example), the prophet in the Scriptures usually speaks from a place just outside the community, figuratively if not literally. Distance rather than social acceptance seems to be prerequisite for prophecy, as it was for John the Baptist and Jesus. It is also the response that the prophet often elicits from an unreceptive audience. Jeremiah, thrown into a cistern for his prophecy, and Jesus, despised and rejected by most of his contemporaries, exemplify the prophet's tenuous relationship to the community. Dickinson, along with her contemporaries Henry David Thoreau and Walt Whitman, continued this tradition of prophecy in nineteenth-century America, even more than did the evangelical preachers whose sermons she drew on for rhetorical techniques.

Yet Dickinson's poetry is a wisdom literature too, as Donald identified in the letter to Mabel Loomis Todd. We will explore in Chapter 6 the techniques that the poet adopted from both the wisdom sayers and the prophets of the Bible. In speaking wisdom, Dickinson continued a literary tradition shared with an earlier famous American female poet of Calvinist sensibilities, Anne Bradstreet. As Rosamond Rosenmeier has so ably demonstrated, Bradstreet selected and used the voices within the biblical tradition (as I argue also for Dickinson) to restate the workings of the divine presence, to portray a healing, revitalizing presence gendered female. Bradstreet spoke from the text in the female voice of Wisdom, relying on the wisdom tradition of the Bible, French Protestant poet Guillaume du Bartas, and Sir Philip Sidney. Dickinson went further than Bradstreet had in setting her wisdom ultimately against the sayings of her religious heritage, including the Bible itself. Moreover, she tended not to create a distinct female figure of Wisdom, as Bradstreet did (for example, in the person of Queen Elizabeth, whom Bradstreet portrayed as the sister and mother of Christ, or in the figure of Woman Wisdom from the Book of Proverbs), but she did continue Bradstreet's pattern of re-creating the self through a female voice that speaks the salvific words of divinity.[2]

That the wisdom literature of the Bible is important to women's spirituality and art should come as no surprise, since Wisdom in the Old Testament is so often hypostatized as female; and the wisdom genre is frequently poetry, a form that may have more appeal to women speakers than the more public expression of oratory. Like Bradstreet before her, Dickinson could find in Woman Wisdom a figure that not only represented her chosen genre but also embodied just power relations and spoke in voice both female and authoritative, one so powerful that it could address audiences across time. All of these aspects of the wisdom tradition were important to Dickinson and complement the salient features of the Bible's prophetic literatures.

As we discussed in Chapter 1, a key distinction of Judeo-Christian prophecy—that found in the Bible and the kind practiced by Dickinson's New England contemporaries—is that the role of the prophet is not restricted to foreteller of the future. Dickinson, like Keats, Byron, and Emerson, shared this broader biblical and romantic understanding of prophet as an inspired religious visionary. This understanding of the prophet's role helps explain how Dickinson's vision can be at times very orthodox, radically Christian, often ethical, yet, alternately, secular, abandoning Christian dogma and principles. Both stances are underwritten by the perception of the prophet as a visionary who speaks ideas that may, and often do, conflict with tradition. But the conflict is not for conflict's sake. The prophetic voices that Dickinson created—and there are many—attempt, overall, to influence the moral and spiritual fiber of humanity, as she found those voices modeled in the Bible.

Dickinson's version of spirituality is not creedal; hence the difficulty for—and disagreements between—scholars attempting to articulate the outlines of her religious vision or prophecy. Dogma remained one of the irritating aspects of the nineteenth-century spirituality she knew, and she avoided it in her poetry. Her poetic voices often contradict one another. We should not attempt to reconcile them, since Dickinson did not seem to care about consistency. After all, as Emerson points out in the "Divinity School Address," great speakers are usually inconsistent and thus often misunderstood, and this is the case with Dickinson. At the same time, however, we can detect a few patterns of thought that she seems to have returned to in her poetry. We will explore those patterns and the content of Dickinson's "wisdom" more directly in Chapter 9, but here we can say that her spirituality touched nearly all (if not all) aspects of her life—from nature and domesticity (she often attributed sacred qualities to these) to her experiences with people, expressing impatience with hypocrisy and shallow religiosity. Perhaps most notably, Dickinson seems to have prized suffering as a way to triumph, an idea we detect in many of the poems on pain or death. All in all, she seems to have been impatient with easy formulations of spirituality yet found true religiousness difficult to attain, even for herself. As we consider various poems and aspects of her prophecy, we will discover the multiple facets of Dickinson's prophetic message, one that involves wise living, experiences of wonder, and encounters with the divine.

The connections between the Christian prophetic tradition and Dickinson's poetry become more apparent when we consider some of the defining features of Judeo-Christian prophecy. Two bodies of such material we know Dickinson had access to are the Bible itself and the traditional sermons she heard as a young girl. I suggest four features that the scriptural and the nineteenth-century sermonic expressions of prophecy share, aspects that Dickinson would have noticed from her own experience with the Bible and as a churchgoer. These include: (1) the stance of the prophet as inspired visionary or guide; (2) the prophetic voice, which can include a range of expressions but is always emotionally charged and spiritually intense; (3) the style of Judeo-Christian prophecy, with its colloquial simplicity and vivid, concrete images; and (4) the rhetorical structures and strategies of the biblical prophets and the nineteenth-century traditional preachers. Here we briefly explore these features of prophecy as Dickinson would have encountered them in the biblical prophetic writings and the traditional sermons of her day; we will consider them in more depth when we look at pointed aspects of Dickinson's poetry.

Perhaps most important as a defining feature of Judeo-Christian prophecy—and one that would have appealed to Dickinson—is the prophet's stance as an inspired visionary who attempts to revitalize faith because of an experience with the divine. In the Judeo-Christian tradition, prophets are people who are divinely inspired to speak their vision. Not satisfied with the mere practice of religion, prophets— both those of the Bible and many preachers of Dickinson's day, who saw themselves extending the scriptural tradition—speak a message of spiritual vitality, challenging empty rituals and hollow religiosity. Unlike mystics, who also share a preoccupation with spiritual vision, prophets experience a compulsion to speak, even at the risk of sounding, as Isaiah often does, iconoclastic or even blasphemous. Unlike those who speak in tongues, prophets require no intermediary to interpret their vision. The intelligible, if sometimes baffling, word remains central for the prophet, a concept that influences the plain style of Judeo-Christian preaching. In this tradition, prophecy is the utterance of an authoritatively inspired "I" who has special vision and therefore a privileged position as religious speaker. Because of his or her special insight or inspiration and the prophetic commission to speak about that insight, the prophet stands as one set apart from the culture, a speaker who is specially qualified to serve as spiritual guide.

Dickinson rejects her culture's formulation of the doctrine of election and much of the dogma of nineteenth-century Christianity, but she does not reject the idea of being set apart as a visionary speaker. She has prophetic authority "by the right of the white election," her own version of the doctrine she iterates in #528, "Mine—by the Right of the White Election!" Her election is, in her mind, due to her ability to speak, not because of any assent to conventions of faith. "Eternity's disclosure," after all, is only to "a few" favorites (#306, "The Soul's Superior instants," lines 13–14). Thus, as she indicates in #303, her soul "selects her own Society—"; few people can be her soul mates. For Dickinson, the idea of the prophet as spiritual visionary is key, offering her the opportunity to redefine and revitalize conventions of faith. Dickinson's prophecy is akin to that of the sermon and the biblical prophets, the kind that Wendy Martin describes as evolving (from Puritanism) in the work of Bradstreet, Dickinson, and Adrienne Rich—prophecy "not in the sense of foretelling events or assuring a bright future for the saints . . . but in the preclassical [and biblical] sense of the utterance of truths that well up from the depths of awareness deeper and more complete than that afforded by reason."[3] As we have seen, American prophecy continued the biblical focus on articulating profound truths, de-emphasizing the prediction of the future.

A second feature of Judeo-Christian prophecy, related to that of the prophet as visionary, is the spiritual intensity of the voice. Focused on their task as articulators of divine truth, the biblical prophets, as well as the truly prophetic preachers of Dickinson's time, all addressed their audiences with earnestness, emotional fervor, and a sense of ultimacy. Speaking as individuals who know God and the ways of spiritual life, Judeo-Christian prophets express their personal involvement with their task, deeply committed to their purpose even when it results in personal sacrifice. They are confident in their God-given authority, and they are compelled to speak the truth. Their delivery is direct and natural, not stylized, and they earnestly emphasize the importance of personal holiness and purity of worship. Explaining doctrine and offering morals are secondary to affecting the imagination, will, and emotions of their listeners. Indicting, consoling, and pointing the way toward holiness, the Judeo-Christian prophets often give their prophecies in the form of absolute pronouncements, their emotional charge and sense of ultimacy expressed in short, declarative lines as the prophets focus on themes of wise living. And when the biblical prophets turn to report on their visionary trips to eternity, their spiritual intensity may be heightened as they focus single-mindedly on their vision, as seen in the later chapters of Isaiah and in the Book of Revelation.

This zealous, spiritually intense voice can be said to have distinguished the truly prophetic preachers of Dickinson's day from those preachers who misused their cultural position as speakers for God. The Calvinist tradition envisioned preachers as extenders of the prophetic tradition, but many, of course, missed the mark as articulators of divine truths. The biblical prophets model a spiritual compulsion that seems to authenticate a prophet as authoritative speaker for God.

In expressing her spiritual vision, Dickinson exhibits a similar spiritual intensity and compulsion. The breathlessness conveyed by her poetry's dashes, the exclamatory language, the colloquial style, the imperatives, and the questions all contribute to the spokenness of her poetry, a tone of immediacy and urgency. The addressee, like an audience rapt by prophecy or a congregation listening to a sermon, never becomes a speaker; the "I" is always at the center of interest as the poet focuses on her spiritual vision. In the tradition of the Hebrew prophets, Dickinson's concern with ultimate truth and pure religion is so great that she at times challenges conventional religion with its hollow practices of faith and morality. She even moves out of the Judeo-Christian tradition to offer her own definition of the terms of faith, challenging the dogma of the biblical prophets and contemporary preachers while retaining their emphasis on spiritual vitality (recall #234, "You're right—'the way *is* narrow'"). "God is a distant—stately Lover—," she proposes in #357, revising and challenging the evangelical emphasis on God's proximity and personal qualities through her oxymoron "distant . . . Lover." Speaking with emotional fervor and earnestness, she attempts to purify faith from simplistic, easy understandings of God. In a tone of prophetic certainty, she speaks directives on wise living that take the form of absolute pronouncements: "To lose one's faith—surpass / The loss of an Estate—," she admonishes in one poem (#377, line 1); "Trust in the Unexpected—," she urges in another (#555, line 1). Over and over in Dickinson's poetry we hear the intensity of the voice, a voice that her early readers aptly called "didactic" yet "strange" in their observation of the emotionally charged messages that frequently surprise.

A third defining feature of Judeo-Christian prophecy is the simple, colloquial, imagistic style of the biblical prophets and of the nineteenth-century preachers who continued that tradition. The Judeo-Christian prophets employ plain language, free from artificiality, and they use immediate, accessible examples and images, although these may convey complex, even opaque, ideas. Their images, often taken from daily life, are vivid, distinctly focused pictures that convey intensity of feeling through their concreteness. The colloquial, plain language and sharp images enhance the directness and earnestness of the prophetic voice.

Dickinson likewise relies on the colloquial style found in Judeo-Christian prophecy. As in the biblical prophecies and the traditional sermon, we see the syntax of speech in her poetry, or the illusion of such syntax—as if she were speaking instead of writing. She employs the sentence structure and parataxis characteristic of spoken English and retains the spoken word order (subject–verb–object). Dickinson followed the example of the orthodox preachers she heard, who strove for the plainness, simplicity, and colloquiality of daily speech. The contractions and signals such as "you know" and "you see" further heighten the effect of spoken English, in her adoption of the simple language of common people. "I'm Nobody! Who are you?" she writes in #288 (line 1), capturing the direct, colloquial quality of the biblical prophecies. Prophets do not speak through elegant, rhetorically elaborate speeches; neither does Dickinson. Despite the presence of her own rhetorical innovations, in Dickinson's poems we hear a voice speaking personally to us.

Part of Dickinson's rhetorical power, like that of other prophets, comes from the imagistic quality of her style. Like the Judeo-Christian prophets, Dickinson often chose her images from daily life and relied on vivid pictures to convey her thought and the emotional charge of her vision. In #241 ("I like a look of Agony"), for example, she focuses on "the Beads upon the Forehead / By homely Anguish strung," a concrete image drawn from her experience (lines 7–8). Through that simple picture she communicates both her impatience with hypocrisy and the truth that is impossible to avoid when an individual experiences intense pain. The sharp images and direct, simple language enable Dickinson to communicate her vision with force. As in the Scriptures and, often, in the traditional sermons, Dickinson's style and language are simple although her thought and rhetorical strategies, as well as their significance, can be very complex.

The biblical pattern of rhetoric affirmed the individual personality of the prophet, allowing for some differences in personal style, as we can see in comparing prophetic books of the Bible. But both the biblical prophetic writings and the conventional sermons of her time showed Dickinson particular rhetorical structures and devices, a final defining feature of Judeo-Christian prophecy. Nineteenth-century traditional preaching, while sharing with the biblical prophetic writings the other fundamental features of Judeo-Christian prophecy, took a form different from the prophecy of the Scriptures. Both sources of prophetic expression are important to Dickinson's art, neither one sufficient alone to explain the influence of the prophetic tradition on her art.

The biblical prophetic writings showed Dickinson particular kinds of paired lines that define these prophecies as poetry, a structure that obviously appealed to Dickinson. The scriptural prophets also modeled for her the techniques of biblical paradox and aphorism. While Dickinson, of course, saw these devices in other sources, she nonetheless incorporated both of them in striking ways alongside the other prophetic and wisdom techniques, a pattern too striking to be mere coincidence. From the sermonic rhetoric of her time, Dickinson drew on the basic pattern of the traditional sermon, as we will see illustrated in Chapter 3. In perhaps as many as half of her poems, she adopted the four-part structure of the sermon to give logical shape to her verse. The traditional sermons, her most immediate link to the prophetic tradition, showed the poet a contemporary model of spiritual vision that vividly appealed to the senses while engaging the intellect. The combination of a reliance on argument and evidence, on the one hand, and an emotional intensity that remains centered in colloquial simplicity, on the other, makes nineteenth-century New England preaching distinctive as a rhetorical form. Dickinson adopted these rhetorical structures and devices from the scriptural prophetic writings and from sermons to accomplish the same effects on an audience. The sermonic form provided her a structure through which she could capture the defining features of prophecy, including the paired lines of the scriptural prophecies, even when she left behind the sermons' dogma.

Of course, John Calvin, Jonathan Edwards, Albert Barnes, and others would not have regarded all preachers as fulfilling their commission to speak prophetically. While preachers could adopt the style and rhetorical structures of Judeo-Christian prophecy, it seems that the stance of religious visionary, along with the spiritual intensity of the biblical prophets, remained the features that distinguished a speaker as prophetic. Indeed, Edwards's phrase to describe the prophetic preacher, "a burning and shining light," captures both of those features.[4] As we will see, Dickinson's poetry is prophetic not only for its rhetorical links to the Christian prophetic tradition but also for its combination of the qualities of the prophetic stance and voice.

In a poem such as #1442, we hear Dickinson's own prophetic voice. This poem is one of her more orthodox ones in terms of the image employed and the theme she articulates, but the implications of the poem are characteristic of Dickinson's innovations upon tradition:

> To mend each tattered Faith
> There is a needle fair
> Though no appearance indicate—
> 'Tis threaded in the Air—
>
> And though it do not wear
> As if it never Tore
> 'Tis very comfortable indeed
> And spacious as before—

Dickinson adopted her central image of the garment from the Bible, which speaks frequently of spiritual garments: clothes of righteousness, holiness, or spiritual power (as in Isa. 61:10; Luke 24:49; Col. 3:12, to name only a few passages). The lengthiest scriptural passage that includes the image, one that Dickinson surely knew, describes the specific pieces of the "armor of God" (Eph. 6:10–17).

In #1442, the speaker's assertion that the "garment" of faith can be mended by a heavenly "needle" sounds traditional, even quaint. But what is striking here is the voice itself—authoritative, propositional, one that suggests an application of the message implicit in line 1, that is, "Have hope" (a pattern that, we will see, the sermons modeled). Indeed, despite the ethereal nature of the needle, it can sew faith so well that one can hardly tell that the faith garment has been torn, stanza 2 tells us; the needle yields a garment that is not constraining in its reparation. Equally striking is the insight suggested by the image of "tattered Faith"—that is, this prophet admits that faith can be strained to the point of tearing, so that it needs to be mended. Nowhere in the Bible do prophets or other writers describe spiritual clothes as being (or able to be) torn. Therefore, we see here Dickinson modifying a Judeo-Christian idea, probably in response to the emotional needs she witnessed in those around her and, undoubtedly, even to her own. That revision heightens the prophetic power of the poem. The voice in the poem is hopeful in pointing out that the garment can be mended, prophetic for its authoritative tone as well as for its message. In speaking so propositionally, Dickinson also reveals a voice compelled to speak, in the manner of, for example, Isaiah: "The Lord has anointed me to preach good tidings unto the meek . . . to comfort all that mourn . . . to bestow on them . . . the garment of praise for the spirit of heaviness" (Isa. 61:1–3). Dickinson's prophetic voice, this time comforting as well as teasing, confidently plays on the same image with the same sense of authority: "To mend each tattered faith / There is a needle fair."

Other poems capture Dickinson's humor, irony, sometimes even ambivalence or uncertainty as the speaker reflects on the implications of her wisdom. But overall, the prophetic voice of Dickinson is teacherly, insightful, and quotable, even if it may be unconventional in its vision. We find this voice even in many of those poems that show shifts in mood.

Sometimes the ambivalence or uncertainty will lead the speaker to revise the initial proposition in the (implicit or explicit) application given in the last lines of the poem. Poem #501 stands as a well-known example. "This World is not Conclusion," the speaker declares in line 1, the authority so weighty that, in the original manuscript, the line ends with a period, one of the very few times we see a period in Dickinson's poetry. But after reflecting throughout the poem on the meaning of that assertion, the speaker ends with a nuanced response: although a "Species" apparently does "stand beyond," that species is "invisible," "baffling" in its transcendence and mystery (lines 2, 3, 5). Evidence can consist only of a "twig" (line 15); that transcendent other-world cannot be examined analytically. In fact, the faith needed to believe in that "species" itself "slips—and laughs, and rallies—" (line 13). The "gesturing" and pronouncements from the pulpit (lines 17–18) are not enough to relieve the speaker's doubt and uncertainty about that "species" that "stands beyond"; the realm is so profoundly other. Hence the poem can end only with a response to that otherworld that includes acknowledgment of the effects of the mystery of that world: "Narcotics cannot still the Tooth / That nibbles at the soul—." The "Tooth" is the skepticism or uncertainty that the mystery invites. The implication of the last lines—or, we could say, the application of the "prophecy" of the poem—is that the idea "This World is not

Conclusion" leads one inevitably to doubt, and one simply has to live with the doubt associated with the mysterious otherworld. No philosopher (line 6), scholar (line 9), or even preacher (line 17) can relieve one's "tooth" of uncertainty about that world. Dickinson here challenges easy notions of spirituality, a characteristic stance she adopts as a prophet.

As we will see more pointedly in Chapter 3, in #501, Dickinson also continues the rhetorical structures of prophecy; but the propositional opening and the application of the last lines of this poem fit into a larger pattern of sermonic rhetoric. The end is jarringly emotional, a quality of both scriptural prophecy and traditional sermons; indeed, the poem seems to invite an emotional response, which the speaker herself captures in the last lines. Yet the poem itself proceeds, in one sense, like a syllogism, just as the sermons do with their logical progression in a context of intense emotionality. At the risk of being simplistic, we could summarize the logic of the poem like this: (1) some realm lies beyond this earthly existence, (2) but it is so mysterious, so profoundly "other" (indeed, a different "species"), (3) that one must live with doubt and uncertainty about it (presumably because it is one's possible destiny). The emotionally charged tone in which this spiritual vision is given, along with the implicit challenge of an easy practice or outward religiosity, further distinguishes the poem as prophecy. What is also striking is that although Dickinson begins the poem sounding quaintly conventional, she ends the poem with a surprising revision of traditional notions about the afterlife. Certainly, Dickinson successfully functions as a prophet in showing us a complex spirituality that demands a heartfelt response to the terms of faith.

Like the biblical prophets, Dickinson wrote with a sense of mission, purpose, urgency—not for mere entertainment or aesthetic craft— believing that her poetry had a sacred function to perform. Her poetic "Occupation" was, after all, "to gather Paradise"; it was a religious calling (#657, "I dwell in Possibility," lines 10–12). Like the prophets' Hebraic poetry, Dickinson's poems are concerned with literature not so much as an art or an aesthetic, as was Greek and Roman poetry, but as the vehicle to right thinking and acting, to the ability to distinguish between good and evil and choose the good.

Dickinson wanted her audiences to be able to discern truth. But unlike many of her female poet contemporaries, she revealed truth not with didactic intent, focused on narrow moralisms, but with visionary authority. In #1043, for example, she muses:

> Lest this be Heaven indeed
> An Obstacle is given
> That always gauges a Degree
> Between Ourself and Heaven.

In a reversal of conventional religious rhetoric that would have us seek to escape this world to gain heaven, Dickinson offers a fresh version of life, one that celebrates this world while acknowledging its imperfections, or "obstacle." Perhaps spoken out of some frustration, #1043 nonetheless is concerned with correct perspective and vision as opposed to right dogma.

The difference in focus between Dickinson's poetry and that of her female contemporaries is obvious when we juxtapose the verse. Her friend Helen Hunt Jackson, in a poem addressing an angel, gives a more conventional view:

> Thou knowest that in grasping
> The bright possessions which so precious seemed,
> We lose them; but, if clasping
> Thy faithful hand, we tread with steadfast feet
> . . . .
>
> There waits for us a treasury of sweet
> Delight; . . .
>
> Oh things
> Of Heaven, Christ's evangel
> Bearing, call us with shining face and poised wings,
> Thou sweetest, dearest angel![5]

While Jackson, too, is interested in right action and perspective—her focus suggests the appeal of the prophetic to Dickinson's female contemporaries—ultimately, she cannot offer a fresh, vital perspective on living. Jackson's speaker seems attracted to some of the things this life offers ("bright possessions"), but the poet cannot affirm that desire. The poem ends by offering right dogma: that greater treasures lie beyond this life. Curiously, the speaker urges the angel to call her away from this life, suggesting life's strong appeal. But unlike Dickinson's persona, who speaks with the daring voice of the iconoclastic prophet, Jackson's poetic voice ultimately cannot acknowledge the riches of this life. Dickinson, in contrast, offers a fresh vision that recognizes the complexity of life.

Dickinson drew on the various roles of the prophet—traveler to eternity, indictor, consoler, and wisdom sayer—as she spoke her poetic prophecy. Often questioning norms, she was more concerned with spiritual vibrance than with outward forms. Indeed, as she adopted the roles of the Judeo-Christian prophet, even contemporary readers sensed an authoritative voice that challenged their conceptions of faith, shaking them loose from forms and traditions that could deaden, as Dickinson exposed the paradoxes and difficulties of Christian dogma.

In the figure of the prophet, Dickinson found a persona who was privileged to speak despite cultural restrictions on female public expression and whether or not an audience listened to her. In the Judeo-Christian tradition, the importance of the prophet as an inspired visionary who focuses on speaking that vision was so great that the audience became subordinate. Indeed, the prophet often lost an awareness of audience; John of Patmos in the Book of Revelation stands as a typical example. Absorbed in the details of their revelation, prophets might minimize the presence of a listening "you." Because the most important element of a prophetic voice was the articulation of a divine truth, the prophet's effectiveness and worth were measured not in terms of an audience's reaction but in whether he or she had carried out the role of spiritual visionary. As a prophet, Dickinson could focus on her visionary message and choose her own form of publication, the fascicles, envisioning her ultimate audience as posterity, an anagogic audience of eschatological dimensions.

Indeed, scholars are discovering more and larger nineteenth-century audiences of Dickinson's poetry. Dickinson had a select audience of her friends, critics agree; she also had a public audience in her lifetime, larger than most twentieth-century critics have acknowledged until fairly recently.[6] Equally important, the readership of her published works in the decades just after her death was vast. From the multitude of reviews that Willis J. Buckingham has compiled, it is evident that nineteenth-century critics found much value in Dickinson's art, and their remarks are striking in the implications for Dickinson's prophetic voice. Over and over, those early readers cited the poetry as being "pleasingly quotable, spiritual, didactic." They frequently compared her to the poet-prophet William Blake for her "strangeness," which they liked, and also for her depth of "insight."[7] Certainly, those readers sensed a prophetic, preacherly voice speaking to them, one that taught truths and revealed new visions as the poet made innovations upon poetic and religious traditions. While twentieth-century scholars have been uncomfortable in calling Dickinson "didactic"—and certainly, she is not bluntly didactic or moralistic in the ways that many of her poetic contemporaries were—nonetheless, her readers in both centuries have sensed a communicative voice that has revealed insight and truth.

A specific example of this response to Dickinson occurred in 1890. In that year, a volume of poems arrived at the home of a sixty-year-old British poet, a woman known in part for devotional poetry (and prose) and who was, in many ways, a literary sister of Emily Dickinson. Christina Rossetti said this to her brother William on receiving that volume, December 6, 1890: "There is a book I might have shown you. . . . Poems by Emily Dickinson lately sent me from America—but perhaps you know it. She *had* (for she is dead) a wonderful Blakean gift, but therewithal a startling recklessness of poetic ways and means."[8] The comment is significant for its indication that Emily Dickinson indeed had an audience for her wisdom—even an international one— and that that audience recognized her for her prophetic voice. Here, Rossetti associates Dickinson with William Blake, the British poet renowned for his unearthly prophetic poetry. Rossetti's identification of Dickinson with Blake is absolutely typical also of Dickinson's American audience (as indicated by critics' reviews) in the years just after her death. Like those readers, Rossetti calls Dickinson's prophetic gift "wonderful," even as she notes the poet's "recklessness," which apparently appeals to her for its "startling" qualities. Early readers did like the disarming aspects of Dickinson's verse, as we do today, finding in the poems a daring attempt to break with poetic convention (the "recklessness") and, at the same time, to speak "Blakean" wisdom.

Modifying the public voices of biblical prophets such as Isaiah and Jeremiah, Dickinson adopted an intermediary position between "public" traditions of prophecy—those expressions in which the "you" is specifically invoked—and a retreat into privacy or a refusal to prophesy. Experiencing a compulsion to speak, as the abundance of her poems and letters attests, Dickinson expressed her spiritual vision to an audience of her own invention, one appropriate to her time and gender. She rejected commercial publication and the demands of editors who would have modified the form and content of her vision to have her speak more conventionally, less prophetically. Instead, she sent poems to readers who apparently responded to her wisdom— Susan Gilbert, the Norcross cousins, the Hollands, and others. Those letters constituted what Paul Lauter has called her "major form of publication": as he points out, fully a third of Dickinson's poems found readers during her lifetime within the context provided by letters. Indeed, Dickinson redefined "the public" as the largely individual recipients of her letters, according to Lauter.[9]

Dickinson also apparently had in mind posterity as her reading public, as her decision to preserve some poems in fascicles indicates. The fascicles as a form of publication were unconventional, but, as Lauter suggests, with the letters they served as a valuable means for a nineteenth-century woman to bridge private and public worlds. Through those forms of publication, Dickinson could assume the prophet's stance as one commissioned to speak to readers of her own time or of a future generation. At the same time, she could preserve her often startling messages from the tinkering of editors. Certainly, in Dickinson's art the private has become public: we know that, at least to twentieth-century audiences, Dickinson has been a spiritual visionary of sorts, showing us a new understanding of religious devotion.

In creating her own strategies to express her vision, neither quite public nor yet quite private, Dickinson participated in the historical shift in conceptualizing prophetic poetry that occurred during the nineteenth century. She shared the conception of Emerson, who described poets as prophets who should refuse to enter the marketplace or political arena and thereby remain private in their prophecy. "Thou shalt lie close hid with nature, and canst not be afforded to the Capitol or the Exchange," Emerson admonishes poet-prophets at the end of "The Poet." In rejecting the marketplace and political arena, poets must renounce worldly fulfillment and even go unrecognized in their prophetic role, Emerson warns, to the point that the poet-prophet even passes for "a fool and a churl for a long season."[10] Dickinson likewise believed that commercial publication and commercial consumers of poetry could cheapen poetry of prophecy. "Publication—is the Auction / Of the Mind of Man—," she declares in #709, calling commercial publication "so foul a thing" (lines 1, 4). She preferred to find less public expressive strategies, rather than allow her wisdom to be "reduced" to "Disgrace of Price—" (lines 15–16).

Dickinson generally shunned Emerson's polemic, insistent tone in her art, but she shared his strategy of preaching to an audience of the poet-prophet's own making. In doing so, she shaped a paradoxical conception of a prophetic poet: one who adopts the structures and stances of the biblical prophets yet who does not speak the way they do, to a public or national audience. Dickinson "commits" her poems to "hands" she "cannot see," envisioning a receptive audience, one of her own choosing (#441, "This is my letter to the World"). The relative privacy of her expressive strategy does not limit her prophetic voice, although it reached only a small readership of her friends and a few other readers in her lifetime.

Dickinson's poems often imply an audience, and she at times addresses that audience directly. In poems such as #610, "You'll find—it when you try to die—," and #1322, "Floss wont save you from an Abyss," she directly invokes her audience as "you." In #634, "You'll know Her—by Her Foot—," she even identifies for "you"—her audience—the signs by which to know the poet-prophet, presumably herself, whom she describes through the metaphor of a robin. "You'll know Her—by Her Foot—," she points out, punning on the word "foot" as a poetic term; and "You'll know Her—by Her Voice—," which, although it "At first [has] a doubtful Tone—," nonetheless comes to "squander on your Ear / Such Arguments of Pearl" (lines 21–22, 25–26).[11] "Pearl" is Dickinson's frequent metaphor for her own poetry. In choosing the word "squander," she expresses frustration at readers' inability to receive her wisdom. She takes seriously Christ's prophetic directive not to "cast your pearls before swine, lest they trample them under their feet" (Matt. 7:6). Yet she indicates, too, the power of her "squandered arguments of pearl" to stimulate her audience, representing her audience as "beg[ging] the Robin in your Brain" to keep the "other"—presumably herself, the poet-prophet— "still" (lines 27–28).

More often than speaking to a "you," Dickinson invokes an audience by speaking in terms of "we" or "us." "We learn in the Retreating," she states aphoristically, in the preacherly tone of the Judeo-Christian prophet (#1083, line 1). Similarly, in #1411, she declares, "Of Paradise' existence / All we know / Is the uncertain certainty—," speaking to her audience as people who share her concerns and experiences (lines 1–3). In employing the first-person plural pronouns, Dickinson revises the prophetic voice of the biblical prophets, who most often separated themselves from their audiences by juxtaposing the "I" against the "you." She comes to her audience as a wisdom giver, but she acknowledges the humanity she shares with that audience. The pronouns serve to bring her closer to the audience she invokes. Her use of "we" and "us" may have been a rhetorical strategy to create an audience she longed for but could not find, an audience who shared her perspectives.

Despite Thomas H. Johnson's statement that "in later years almost all poems were intended for enclosure in letters to friends," the occasion of writing to friends seldom or never prompted the initial composition of the poems, as Brita Lindberg-Seyersted points out.[12] Often the poem did not fit the content of the letter in which it was enclosed. Dickinson's impulse to write was greater than a passing desire to send an elegy or a flower. Her letters and poems were created out of a need for communication; she was a transmitter of a "Message" addressed to her "Sweet—countrymen—" (#441, "This is my letter to the World"). She always felt a deep gratitude to her editor T. W. Higginson for listening, saying he had saved her life by doing so (*L*, 2:460). Having prophetic drive, she felt compelled to speak, recognizing, with the biblical prophets and preachers, the power of words. Her poems were not private, idiosyncratic messages to herself but a vital message "to the World." Like the prophet-preacher, Dickinson believed in the power of words to affect her audience, even an audience she could not see— posterity. As Cynthia Griffin Wolff has pointed out, "Millions of Americans feel that they *know* Dickinson—not merely that they know and read her poetry, but that there is, somehow, somewhere, a *person* who voices insights and emotions that are directed sympathetically to us." Higginson himself asked Dickinson for a picture because, Wolff indicates, he wanted to see the person whose voice he had heard speaking to him.[13]

The scriptural prophets believed in the power and perseverance of their messages; their prophetic articulations of God's word "will not return—empty," God declared in Isa. 55:11, a famous text that Dickinson surely knew. Like the scriptural prophets and the nineteenth-century preachers—and despite her reticence to publish her poetry commercially—Dickinson apparently believed in the spiritual weight and longevity of her own verse. In the spirit of the biblical prophets, she affirmed that "A Word that breathes distinctly"—presumably hers— "Has not the power to die" (#1651, lines 9–10). She differed from such male counterparts as Thoreau and Whitman, who spoke to a broad, national audience; she obviously visualized her relationship to her audience differently. But we need to note that here, historically, the definition of prophecy has been established almost exclusively by male divines and scholars who focus almost totally on male prophets. Thus, we do not yet have an adequate definition of prophecy, one that also considers women. In the Bible, female prophets often appear to speak to smaller audiences than their male counterparts have—Miriam sings her prophecy only to women (Exod. 15:20), and Huldah is described as prophesying only to a small delegation of men (2 Kings 22:14). In her own time, Dickinson had before her the historical precedence of Angelina Grimke, a Quaker, who quit her public speaking as a female prophet but nonetheless continued to speak to private audiences. Her sister, Sarah Grimke, moved to an even more private mode by expressing her vision in letters (of course, the letters were eventually published). It may be that this conception of a small audience is a feature that defines female prophecy—and which Dickinson shared as she offered her poems to select friends. Her audience was a "fit audience though few," to use Milton's phrase.

Significantly, feminist scholars for the most part presume that Dickinson was speaking to an audience, despite her rejection of commercial publication. Given the importance to women of the concepts of relationship and communication, as Nancy Chodorow, Jean Baker Miller, and other feminist scholars have pointed out, it is not surprising that feminist and female readers presume Dickinson to be fundamentally communicative with and directing her words to an audience beyond herself.[14] The feminine identity of the persona may further affect these readers' understanding of Dickinson's audience as they sense that the voice, because it is female, speaks to a listening audience, not to the poet herself. As Allen Tate and R. P. Blackmur exemplify, it seems to be the nonfeminists who tend to call Dickinson private and eccentric, a poet who simply talks to herself.[15] Indeed, a more accurate assessment is perhaps that only her personal habits were private. Her manipulation of imperatives, exclamations, and questions suggests a listening audience: "I'm Nobody! Who are you?" she conversationally asks an audience in #288. In #704, she similarly questions a listener: "No matter—now—Sweet— / But when I'm Earl— / Won't you wish you'd spoken / To that dull Girl?" (lines 1–4). In the future, an analysis of female prophetic strategies and female prophets' audiences may help us to understand Dickinson's adoption of the prophet's stance as inspired visionary, the central, defining feature of Judeo-Christian prophecy, even as she rejected a wider, commercial audience.

Dickinson's prophetic-poetic "word" does "breathe distinctly," and she offers us a very particular prophetic voice, but her decision as a woman poet to adopt a prophet's stance in fact is not so distinctive. To be sure, in Dickinson's day, for a female poet to speak on public matters, let alone engage in social protest, was to challenge Victorian aesthetics and conventional ideas about women, as Elizabeth Helsinger, Robin Sheets, and William Veeder point out. Yet a poet whom Dickinson admired, Elizabeth Barrett Browning, had begun doing just that. Called by Helsinger, Sheets, and Veeder "the most important [woman] poet to write explicitly about child labor, slavery, and prostitution," Browning at mid-century became increasingly concerned with women's problems and challenged the status quo through her poetry. She is also notable for her acceptance, in her poems, of the legitimacy of women's anger expressed in literature, an emotion that we also observe in Dickinson's art.[16] Of course, political and social indictments, especially as they emerge out of spiritual convictions, have historically remained an important focus of prophets since the time of Jeremiah and Amos. Browning was undoubtedly an important example for Dickinson of a female poet who adopted a prophetic stance and who expressed anger directly.

But Dickinson would not follow Browning, for the most part, in that poet's political and social emphases. In concentrating on expressing a spiritual vision that could include social statements but also more, Dickinson did not have to look farther than the female prophetic models from her own country and religious tradition. She had easy access to these through the anthologies her family owned and the magazines she read. And those models, in their focus on religious messages, could show her peculiarly American forms of female "prophecy"—as well as the ways the poets overcame or simply avoided the obstacles set before would-be American female prophets. But before we examine the legacy of female American prophets, let us consider Dickinson's prophetic rhetoric.

3. "Captivating Sermons" and Dickinson's Rhetoric of Prophecy

"**H**AD BUT THE TALE a warbling Teller— / All the Boys would come— / Orpheus' Sermon captivated— / It did not condemn—," Dickinson insists in #1545 (lines 13–16). In contrast to the enchanting message of Orpheus, she points out, "The Bible is an antique Volume—" (line 1). Dickinson had surely heard enough sermons in her childhood and young adulthood to recognize the qualities that make one sermon "captivating," another "condemning." By 1855, she had been exposed to a variety of preaching styles, "ranging from the comfortably orthodox," which biographer Richard Sewall thinks "bored her," to "the hell-fire, which frightened her."[1] These sermons were her first and most immediate link to the prophetic tradition. The preaching she heard offered her personal models of the prophet in the figures of the preacher as well as examples of prophetic rhetoric, which she would exploit for her own art.

Dickinson took the rhetorical forms and tonal features of the sermon and crafted them into a poetry of prophecy that truly captivates. Voicing in #1545 her impatience with dead forms and simplistic ideas about religion, she shows throughout her corpus her own revitalization of the traditional sermon. That form needs a "warbling Teller," a role she could claim through her own innovations upon the sermon. "I shall keep singing!" she states in #250, even if it is "too loud" and "shuts Me out of [a conventional] Heaven" (#248).

Dickinson knew well the sermon tradition of the Connecticut Valley. These were sermons profoundly influenced in their style and form by Jonathan Edwards, who had attempted to stay close to the Bible in his method and rhetoric. "No single minister," Harry S. Stout declares, "did so much to alter preaching or set the tone for pulpit discourse as Jonathan Edwards."[2] Williston Walker, in his history of Congregational churches, made the same point more than a century before Stout, pointing out that by the beginning of the nineteenth century, Connecticut and western Massachusetts were "thoroughly leavened" with Edwardsian views and methods.[3] Although Unitarianism had grown in eastern Massachusetts since the beginning of the nineteenth century, the Puritan legacy retained a powerful presence in Dickinson's locale, even into her adult life. As Thomas Le Duc puts it, Dickinson's hometown, Amherst, remained one of the last frontiers of Connecticut Valley Puritanism, "where the teaching of Thomas Hooker and Jonathan Edwards still held sway."[4]

Although Edwards and his homilectical heirs changed Calvinism profoundly from the earliest Puritan understandings, their influence in western Massachusetts is noteworthy for the ways in which they attempted to continue, rhetorically and theologically, an emphasis on the biblical writings. Dickinson surely understood the rhetorical potentials and weaknesses of this tradition and recognized that it bore distinctive connections to biblical prophecy that other oratorical and literary traditions did not. One link was historical: the conservative ministers saw themselves as continuing the prophetic tradition that extended from the Old Testament beyond the New Testament Pentecost by functioning as speakers for God. Another connection was rhetorical: the sermons, at their best, replicated the visionary, spiritually vital content of the biblical prophecies, their religious and emotional intensity, and their colloquial, imagistic style. As an early means by which she learned of prophetic empowerment, the sermons motivated and inspired Dickinson. They offered her a prophetic voice to imitate, and they enabled her to develop her own wise poetic voice as she shaped her poems to be brief homilies that communicated truth as she saw it.

Connecticut Valley preaching had significant similarities with biblical prophecy, the homiletics featuring important aspects of the scriptural writings. Perhaps most important, both the scriptural prophets and the Edwardsian preachers saw themselves as commissioned by God to speak a divinely inspired spiritual vision. They included among their tasks warning their audiences about sin, giving consolation, and providing divine wisdom, instruction, and insight. As divinely commissioned speakers, they understood themselves to be set apart, both in terms of having a special, elevated status and in being called to a life of renunciation of personal gain. Such renunciation could even include suffering for the prophet-preachers, who experienced real costs of their self-denying holiness.

The sermons rooted in the late Puritan, Edwardsian tradition reflect a distinct style and approach toward expressing religious vision, and they are particularly important for giving Dickinson direct access to a contemporary prophetic expression. They showed her how prophets could structure their intense religious visions into ordered, crafted presentations that still retained an emotional character. In style, the sermons offered Dickinson a model of colloquial, plain language; vivid imagery appealing to the senses; and an emotionally charged tone with an intensity of feeling. In form, they offered her a logical, four-part structure through which she could appeal to her readers' intellects: presentation of text, introduction of doctrine, elaboration, and application. We can see her drawing on this form, or variations of it, in more than half of her poems, adopting the sermon's emphasis on reason and evidence. Employing some of the same rhetorical strategies and forms as the traditional preachers used, Dickinson is able to achieve some of the same effects: she influences both the minds and the hearts of her audience in her attempts to express her own version of religious faith.

Dickinson's rhetoric and the effects she achieved are only some of the aspects that she adopted from the evangelical sermons. The sermons also provided her with metaphors and themes and showed her a literary form concerned with ultimate questions, such as truth, death, and the world lying beyond time. And through that form she found that she could expound her prophetic criticism of the inconsistencies she saw in nineteenth-century Christianity. She could offer her own perspective on spiritual truth, the ultimate goal of prophecy.

Having heard well over fifteen hundred sermons during her period of regular attendance at church, Dickinson was exposed to a steady stream of visiting preachers and reverend professors of the Puritan legacy in Amherst and at Mount Holyoke.[5] She herself was "capable of being transported by a good" sermon; Sewall points out that "the effect on her of these weekly (at Mount Holyoke more frequent) invasions of her spirit . . . was profound."[6] At Mount Holyoke, she also had the model of headmistress Mary Lyon, who gave sermonic lectures to her students three times a week. Although Dickinson eventually rejected the content of Lyon's "sermons," the headmistress served as an important early model of a female prophetic "preacher" for her, speaking so powerfully that many of Dickinson's classmates were eventually converted.

In Amherst, Dickinson heard biology professor Edward Hitchcock preach in the village church, insisting on the wonders and meaning of the created world. At Mount Holyoke she heard Professor Henry Boynton Smith of Amherst College, who, as Dickinson described in a letter to her brother Austin, preached "such sermons [as] I never heard in my life." Indicating Smith's power as a speaker as well as her own ambivalence toward the Christianity she heard preached, she remarked that "we were all charmed with him and dreaded to have him close" (*L*, 1:64). But when Professor Edwards Amasa Park of Andover Theological Seminary preached in the First Church in Amherst on November 20, 1853, Emily Dickinson spoke with enthusiasm to Austin about his preaching: "I never heard anything like it, and dont [*sic*] expect to again. . . . And when it was all over, and that wonderful man sat down, people stared at each other, and looked as wan and wild, as if they had seen a spirit, and wondered they had not died. How I wish you had heard him" (*L*, 1:272). Park, a noted preacher of his day, spoke as one prophetically inspired, as Dickinson indicated, preaching with the intensity characteristic of the biblical prophets.[7] Commenting many times on how "beautifully" and "wonderfully" the Reverend Edward S. Dwight preached, Dickinson indicated that preaching was, for her, an aesthetic activity. Thus it is not surprising that she would incorporate this prophetic form into her poetry. One sermon of Dwight's, she told the Hollands, "scared" her (*L*, 1:309).[8] Certainly, she appreciated both the beauty and the verbal force of a well-crafted, well-delivered sermon.

One of the most influential preachers for Dickinson was the Reverend Charles Wadsworth, pastor of the Arch Street Presbyterian Church in Philadelphia from 1850 to 1962. Having met him in 1854 while she was visiting her friend Eliza Coleman in Philadelphia, Dickinson soon began a correspondence with Wadsworth that lasted over two decades, and she collected his published sermons beginning in 1858 and perhaps also heard him preach. Dickinson undoubtedly read and reread his sermons, probably often in pamphlet form as they were issued, and she eventually owned a volume of his sermons. Perhaps more than any other person, Wadsworth influenced her development of a prophetic voice in the manner of a preacher, giving her immediate contact with the Christian prophetic tradition.[9]

Dickinson came from a family with a tradition of oratory, one that inlcuded Christian themes: her father, Edward, was one of the most famous orators in Hampshire County, and her grandfather Samuel Fowler was also known for his oratorical power. Through her father's readings of Scripture to the family and his presence as an orator, the prophecy of preaching and of other oratory became linked to the domestic sphere. For Dickinson, life at home meant less the experience of "a helpless agoraphobic, trapped in her father's house," as

Sandra M. Gilbert and Susan Gubar would have it, than an experience of domesticity that saw the home as a forum for prophecy.[10] She learned that prophecy—usually regarded as a public genre, proclaimed from the public platform or pulpit—could originate in the private setting of the home yet retain its power and authority over audiences. With the home as a field for her father's oral deliveries, Dickinson saw the breaking down, to some degree, of the "separate sphere" ideology of the day by her experience of a father-preacher, father-orator, within the home. Through her father, Dickinson directly experienced the power of the prophetic word and the possibilities for speakers in the home.

New England congregations of the Puritan tradition, even more than secular oratorical audiences, assumed the centrality of the preached word, situating the sermon—the "ministry of the word"—as the climax of the worship service. Through the lasting power of the sermonic word, nineteenth-century preachers as prophets were thought to have great influence on their hearers, shaping their intellect, taste, morals, and even their "literary character"—that is, their style of conversation and writing—as, for instance, Edwards Amasa Park in "The Influence of the Preacher" (1857) attests. Preaching is "a prominent agency," he says, "attended with consequences peculiarly extensive, and meliorating the state of man more directly than is done by other causes—more universally and more radically." Such consequences may be produced "by [the preacher's] printed works long after his death," Park points out. "As the author of written sermons," he continues, the preacher "sometimes gives an impulse to more minds than he affected by his spoken words. Many a clergyman never dies."[11] Indeed, through their written words, Park suggests, preachers can gain a literary immortality more lasting and more important than that of the authors of other kinds of texts. His view is absolutely typical of the era.

Dickinson's own belief in the power and longevity of the word is clear from poems such as #8, "There is a word"; #952, "A Man may make a Remark—"; #1261, "A Word dropped careless on a Page"; #1409, "Could mortal lip divine"; #1467, "A little overflowing word"; and #1651, "A Word made Flesh is seldom." Poem #1212 succinctly states her most persistent view:

A word is dead
When it is said,

Some say.
I say it just
Begins to live
That day.

She recognized with the preachers and biblical prophets the power of words: "We used to think, Joseph," she wrote to friend Joseph Lyman, "when I was an unsifted girl and you so scholarly that words were weak & cheap. Now I dont know of anything so mighty."[12]

As Dickinson's readers are aware, her poetry has an oral effect, which, I argue, she sought to achieve in part as an aspect of the power of the word she admired in the prophecy of sermonic oratory, often drawing on the same strategies as those used in sermonic practice. The pulpit oratory captured the verbal power of the biblical prophets as the ministers and prophets expounded their spiritual vision. In style the traditional sermon paralleled the biblical prophets' colloquial, conversational character; the nineteenth-century ministers valued simplicity as their antecedents, the biblical prophets, had. Preachers maintained a forceful, earnest tone, the best ones employing pauses to emphasize points and to convey the seriousness of their messages.[13] In fact, Dickinson's unique notational system may be rooted in nineteenth-century elocution, particularly those principles and symbols found in Ebenezer Porter's *The Rhetorical Reader; Consisting of Instructions for Regulating the Voice, with a Rhetorical Notation . . .* , which was one of Dickinson's textbooks. According to Jack L. Capps, Porter, a Congregational clergyman and educator, was particularly interested in pulpit eloquence.[14] His book gave Dickinson a specific way to capture the oral quality of the sermons.

With her use of dashes, Dickinson follows the practice that *Rhetorical Reader* and other homiletical rhetoric books advocate, using pauses to slow down lines that move quickly, a technique as valuable for her as a poetic prophet as it was for the sermonic prophets in facilitating the reception of the lines. Pauses help to effect slowness and solemnity, to give weight to a good thought, and to awaken the attention of one's audience, the homiletical rhetoric books point out. These are practices that Dickinson adopts throughout her poetry with similar effects, as in, for instance, "Truth—is as old as God— / His Twin identity / And will endure as long as He / A Co-Eternity—" (#836, lines 1–4). The dash separates the important word "truth" from the rest of the clause, giving weight to it, and dashes draw our attention to the two separate thoughts of line 1 and lines 2–4. They help us better to hear and remember the point of the lines. Although dashes may perform other functions as well (for example, serving as ellipses in other cases), they are part of the oral, even homiletical quality of her verse. Her use of other devices, such as a first-person plural pronoun, exclamatory language, colloquial diction and rhythm, imperatives, and questions, also contributes to a tone of spokenness and colloquial simplicity, as was modeled by the preachers.

Like the Connecticut Valley preachers, Dickinson's poetic speakers often indicate their awareness of an audience. In #668, " 'Nature' is what we see—," the speaker cautions her audience that "So impotent [is] Our Wisdom / To her [Nature's] Simplicity," offering a moral application clearly intended for a first-person plural audience and following the sermonic structure (lines 11–12). Likewise, in #314, "Nature—sometimes sears a Sapling—," she warns, "We—who have the Souls— / Die oftener—Not so vitally—" (lines 7–8). And in #1286, "I thought that nature was enough," she gives a hortative application, suggested in the imperative verb that creates an audience: "But give a Giant room / And you will lodge a Giant / And not a smaller man," she prophesies, after explaining to her audience the dynamics of nature, human nature, and the divine (lines 10–12). Like the prophet-preacher, Dickinson believed in the power of words to affect an audience, which her poetry clearly intends in its rhetorical constructions, no matter what her ambivalent attitudes toward her actual readers.

Yet the addressee constructed by the poems, like a congregation listening to a sermon, never becomes a speaker; the authoritative "I" is always at the center of interest, speaking to a "you" or a "thee" who, in many of the poems of the 1860s is urged to action, as in #158, "Dying! Dying in the night!"; #177, "Ah, Necromancy Sweet!"; #181, "I lost a World—the other day!"; #182, "If I should'nt be alive"; #186, "What shall I do—it whimpers so—." The same strategies characterize the sermons of the traditional preachers, including those whom Dickinson heard. As in the sermons of Dwight (1820–1890), W. S. Tyler (1810–1897), Aaron Colton (1809–1895), and other ministers she heard in Amherst, the imperatives, exclamations, and questions in Dickinson's poems help create a tone of immediacy and a situation of direct address of an audience. A characteristic sermon on evangelism that Tyler preached in the Amherst College chapel typifies this tone of immediacy: "In thick succession, fast as the strokes of the pendulum, they pass out at the gate of death and drop—must we say so? into the burning lake! Fain would we disbelieve it. But we cannot. . . . Is it not inhuman as well as unchristian, to withhold the gospel from the heathen? Oh, the heathen! the heathen!!"[15]

Tyler's language is conversational; his tone is urgent personal, qualities that even the written text of his sermon captures in its punctuation. Dickinson was much closer in voice to this kind of sermon than she was to the poetry of her contemporaries. "Life—is what we make it— / Death—We do not know—," she cautions in #698, even continuing one of Tyler's themes (lines 1–2). Compare these lines to lines from Helen Hunt Jackson: "Dost know Grief well? Hast known her long? . . . / So long, thou barrest up no door / To stay the coming of her feet?" (lines 1, 9–10).[16] Jackson's language is archaic, her tone, languishing. Dickinson, in contrast, employs the diction and syntax of speech in her poetry, even when she also experiments with sentence style and structure.[17]

The contractions Dickinson used, as well as such signals as "you know" and "you see," further heighten the effect of spokenness in her verse. And Dickinson's elliptical syntax contributes to the directness and emphasis of her messages; she omits superfluous words. Any abruptness we may experience is due to her locating the reader "immediately inside an experience, as if she were speaking to one whom she knew for certain was present."[18] The spoken and the written converge in her poetry as they do in a written sermon. Indeed, David Porter's conclusion that "there has existed no stronger will *to say*" than that of Emily Dickinson highlights not only the context that the nineteenth-century oratory provided but also the prophet's compulsion to speak, which Dickinson shared with the preachers.[19]

As a rhetorical form, the sermon identified with the Puritan legacy had specific features that Dickinson would have easily recognized. both its formal structure and its doctrinal content appear in a variety of modifications throughout the corpus of her poetry. The traditional sermon of Dickinson's era typically followed a four-part structure, emphasizing an orderly arrangement of ideas as it appealed to the listener's reason. Rhetoric textbooks of 1830 to 1860 (devoted to traditional preaching and important for their description of the culturally dominant forms) advocated the Puritan four-part pattern of organization: the presentation of the text, a brief introduction in which the doctrine is stated, the development or elaboration of the doctrine, and a conclusion in which the doctrine is applied and restated. The sermons of this tradition emphasized a colloquial simplicity rather than the exalted style of an earlier era or the literary elegance of the Unitarian sermons. But nineteenth-century Congregational sermons were also vivid, with the ministers employing figurative language to engage their listeners' senses and dramatizing biblical narratives with pointed imagery in the tradition of Edwards, who, "more than anyone else" of his time, had "supplied a stock of images and metaphors that evangelical ministers could draw from to engage their listeners' affections."[20] Giving close exegeses of their texts, the Congregational preachers strove, as had Edwards, to engage their listeners in the immediacy and ultimacy of their message.

Nineteenth-century homiletical rhetoricians of Edwards's tradition stressed plain, compact diction and verbal force; they valued brevity, beauty, and energy in the sermon. Structure and organization remained paramount; as Ebenezer Porter emphasized in his book on homiletical rhetoric, the good sermon was both brief and well planned.[21] Stylistic qualities (the colloquial diction, vivid imagery, plain and compact presentation, and urgent, forceful tone) as well as the four-part structure distinguish the traditional sermon from the Unitarian form, which tended toward eloquence and literary ornateness as well as a seven-part structure or a loose mode of presentation.[22]

In drawing on the traditional sermonic style and structure, Dickinson also adopted the very purpose of this type of sermon. For Edwards and his theological heirs, the sermon was to appeal to both the "will," which Edwards identified with the emotions, and the mind, since inclination involved both of these. Religion involved the heart—it was experiential, engaging the "affections" or emotions, as Edwards argued in "A Treatise Concerning Religious Affections," but not at the expense of the intellect. For Edwards, understanding was the integral experience between the heart and the will. The structure and style of the traditional sermon in the nineteenth-century still emphasized both the emotions and the intellect, as the sermon moved audiences logically and emotionally to an experience of conversion. Dickinson's adoption of the sermonic rhetorical techniques speaks of her similar interest in both the emotions and the intellect. We see in her poems a mind at work, constantly giving reasons and arguing, even while the poet engages readers' emotions, confronting her audience with experiential, jarring reality. As in the traditional sermons, Dickinson shows that she wants to persuade, instruct, even disarm—to give a spiritual vision, not a rationalist exposition on morality, a practice often followed in the Unitarian sermons.

As exemplified by Wadsworth, the sermon of the Puritan legacy
shares major stylistic features with the biblical prophecies, although
the two forms differ notably in structure. Wadsworth's sermons as
prophecy clearly exemplify the traditional Puritan homiletics, with
their four-part structure, colloquial diction, vivid imagery, and urgent,
forceful tone. Critics have noted parallels between the diction, figurative language, and themes of Dickinson's poetry and Wadsworth's sermons. "There is no doubt," Richard Chase asserts, "that Wadsworth
supplied Emily Dickinson with certain verbal usages and with certain
poetic images." Chase and others have pointed out that Dickinson
often imitated Wadsworth's diction, which shows Edwardsian vividness and drama as Wadsworth coined new forms of verbs. According
to Chase, Dickinson apparently replicated from Wadsworth's sermons
the practice of using such words as "complicate" as if they were past
participles and of ending words with "-less"—for example, "strength-
less" and "resistless." She also derived Wadsworth's vivid images of
jewelry, involving gems, carbons, and diamonds, as well as those of
royalty—for example, thrones, robes, and diadems—all of which are
also found in the prophetic Book of Revelation, a text that probably
influenced both writers.[23] The Reverend George Burrows's general
description of Wadsworth's preaching—a description that highlights
traditional features—could likewise be applied to Emily Dickinson's
poetic discourse: "His argumentation is peculiar, close, compact, and
strong, with a powerful condensation, till it glows like a diamond."[24]
As a practitioner of the homiletical strategies in her letters and poems,
Dickinson probably also had an influence on Wadsworth's sermons, as
David Higgins and Jay Leyda suggest, given the apparent intimacy
between Wadsworth and Dickinson for many years.[25] Not merely a
passive receiver of a male tradition, Dickinson refined the strategies of
sermonic-prophetic writing in interaction with Wadsworth, another
practitioner.

Dickinson adopted not only certain diction and images from Wadsworth, her personal favorite among traditional preachers, but the style
and structure of the Edwardsian sermon as the tradition was continued by other preachers she liked. Indeed, the style of this preaching thoroughly informs Dickinson's verse. The best of nineteenth-
century traditional sermons—and the ones that Dickinson found most
engaging—rejected the formal, excessively elaborate, and stereotyped
method of a former period in favor of a well-defined, clear presentation shaped with reference to cumulative effects. The return to the

colloquial, plain style moved the sermons closer to the style of the biblical prophetic writings.

One sermon preached by a minister whom Dickinson knew in Amherst exemplifies this style. In "Integrity the Safeguard of Public and Private Life," preached in the College Chapel in 1857, W. S. Tyler uses personification to intensify the dramatic effect, which reaches a peak in his exposition of his final point. A curious detail for our study here is that Tyler personifies the conscience as female even when he describes it as speaking as the voice of God; he thus (perhaps unwittingly) suggests possibilities for female voices. "She" is God's "vice-regent in the human soul," the highest authority on earth and in the soul.

Even more notable are the other ways in which Tyler achieves his dramatic effects. In plain, direct language, he pleads with his audience, summarizing his three-point argument: "The voice of God is in the storm. It bids us remember, that integrity and uprightness alone can preserve us . . . and that it is the only security for the favor and blessing of God." The conversational quality of the rhetoric is unmistakable. Like his Puritan predecessors, Tyler relied on language to move the wills of his listeners, not to impress or to entertain. When he closed his sermon in a direct exhortation to act, he compressed language even more into clipped, short imperatives. The earlier female gendering of conscience to produce a personal image adds even more drama to Tyler's plea that the conscience should never be "violated":

> Therefore suffer no stain to rest upon your character. Never violate your conscience. Never do a dishonest or dishonorable act. Do right in little things. . . . Not only wash your hands of all corruption; but keep your heart pure, and your conscience tender, and your will ever obedient to its slightest whisper. Then will your whole spirit and soul and body be full of light, and your whole life a track of light along the earth and upward through the sky.[26]

When he moves beyond imperatives, Tyler's syntax is almost Hemingwayesque in his choice of simple constructions joined with "and." Rejecting participles, elaborate dependent clauses, and qualifiers, Tyler opts for rhetoric immediately accessible to his audience. One- and two-syllable words prevail; the number of function words is minimal in his attempt at an intensified language. We see the argumentative quality of the sermon in the "therefore" of this exhortation, yet

Tyler also includes metaphor—the "track of light" into which the conscience-abiding individual is transformed. Clearly, Tyler's interest is in the cumulative effect of his message. He attempts to move both the mind and the emotions of his audience.

Tyler's sermon epitomizes typical Congregational preaching of Dickinson's day. As Lewis Brastow described in his 1906 study of nineteenth-century homiletics, such preaching featured "compactness, directness of diction, quiet philosophic reflection; facile, offhand homiletic suggestion," and was "not rhetorically elaborate."[27] The description obviously characterizes Tyler's sermons; and we could apply it to Dickinson's poetry, in spite of her verse's complexity and innovation. She clearly adopted the plain style, the "compactness," the forceful tone, and the syntax of conversation in her art. Her use of concrete nouns to make metaphysical abstractions comprehensible— such as "still volcano" for life (#601, "A still—Volcano—Life—") and "insect / Menacing the tree" for death (#1716, "Death is like the insect")—is similar to the traditional ministers' practice (Tyler compared a life to a "light"); they all relied on simple yet pointed diction to communicate spiritual truths.[28] Edwards likened the reality of sin and his listeners' need for repentance to a spider suspended over a fiery pit; Dickinson draws on similarly immediate images to concretize abstract reality. "'Hope' is the thing with feathers— / That perches in the soul—," she describes in #254 (lines 1–2).

Replicating features of biblical prophecy, the stylistic influence of the traditional sermon on Dickinson's art extends beyond simplicity and compactness in diction. Dickinson's poems, in their structured presentation of ideas, intellectual strength, striking imagery, and emphasis on a sense of ultimacy, have much more in common with the sermons of Tyler and others of the Connecticut Valley preaching tradition than with the liberal, Unitarian sermons to which they have been compared. The latter sermons emphasized the reasonableness of faith, not the immediacy of religious experience. In fact, the earliest examples of Unitarian preaching established it as a homiletical tradition focused on the primacy of reason; the early sermons tended to be very cogent, rationalistic orations, having few metaphors or literary allusions. In the 1820s and 1830s, the Unitarian sermons began moving away from their older form of announcing the arguments, exegeting Scripture, and applying the text, as the Edwardsian sermon had done, to a more freely flowing presentation; but although the new presentations showed great literary effect and eloquence, they still captured the reasonableness of the faith in their themes. The intellectual power of their themes paled, however, beside that of the traditional sermons.

Basically, then, we have in Unitarian preaching rationality as theme, with eloquence and literariness in style; in the New England evangelical sermon, we see an emphasis on the primacy of experience and the importance of action in theme, with an appeal to the senses and the intellect in style.[29] Edwards undoubtedly had seen that the older Puritan manner of preaching, with its rationalistic presentation, would not shock people into change. He and other figures after him, including Dickinson, urged people's need to change by weaving an intellectual appeal with attempts to touch the heart. In a pattern that Dickinson also followed, Edwards and his heirs marshaled evidence with intellectual strength to support their propositions at the same time that they confronted listeners' senses to vivify truths. In doing so, these preachers replicated the strategies of the biblical prophets, who reasoned with their audiences even as they spoke with dramatic intensity, as is witnessed by the books of Isaiah, Jeremiah, and Amos.

The nineteenth-century Congregational ministers continued the emphases that made Edwards memorable, as we see, for example, in this passage from Edwards's pastoral sermon "The Excellency of Christ," which urges his audience to envision Christ: "Look on him, as he stood in the ring of soldiers, exposing his blessed face to be buffeted and spit upon by them! Behold him bound, with his back uncovered to those that smote him! And behold him hanging on the cross!"[30] Certainly, in emphasizing an orderly, logical presentation, the Edwardsian sermon did not sacrifice vividness or even sensationalism. The New England revival sermons coming after Edwards, as opposed to frontier revival sermons, continued the attempt to challenge the intellect even as they engaged the senses.

We see this dual focus also in a sermon by Tyler. He reasons with his congregation on the biblical justification for missionary work and also passionately implores them, through vivid images, to become missionaries:

> The points of light [of Protestant Christianity], of which we have spoken, are scarcely enough to make the darkness [of heathenism] visible. . . . Six hundred millions of heathen living without God, dying without hope, and entering eter-

nity unprepared? In thick succession, fast as the strokes of the pendulum, they pass out at the gate of death and drop—must we say so? into the burning lake![31]

Despite the century or so lying between Edwards and the ministers whom Dickinson heard, the sermonic strategies are surprisingly similar. Taking their congregations point by point through a carefully constructed argument, complete with subpoints and appeals to the biblical texts, these ministers enhanced their rhetoric with clear and forceful imagery. They characteristically culminated their sermons in an urgent exhortation, replete with metaphors and moving descriptions, directed at each person in their audience. These sermons could be powerful in their effect, as demonstrated by the great numbers of people converted during the Second Great Awakening.

This is the preaching that influenced Dickinson from her earliest years. Her personal favorite among these ministers, Charles Wadsworth, pointedly exemplifies the historical change away from dry, formal presentations to a style closer to that of the biblical prophets. He absolutely typifies the preaching tradition of the Edwardsian legacy, even taking it to new heights in some of his finest sermons. An article in the newspaper *Metropolitan* (September 8, 1875), for example, described him as "remarkable for his force of argument, beautiful imagery, and impressive manner," a preacher who is "earnest," "clear," and "concise and powerful as a logician." The *Springfield Republican* reprinting an article from *The New York Evening Post*, included the observation that "Wadsworth's style . . . is vastly bolder, his fancy more vivid, and his action more violent" than one of his contemporaries.[32] Here is one example of the vividness of Wadsworth's style, a passionate exposition on the efficacy of the Lord's Supper:

> All the works of God, all the riches of God, all the attributes of God, all the persons of God [are] *consecrated unto us!* "All things present" . . . "All things to come"—all that higher economy of the eternal world—thrones, crowns, white robes, heavenly mansions—all—all consecrate to us![33]

Obviously, the rhetorical effect is powerful. Like Edwards, Wadsworth engaged his listeners with vivid description, relying on plain, colloquial, familiar language and employing exclamations and imperatives while he worked within a logical structure. Like Edwards, Wadsworth did not rely so much on delivery, gesturing, or modulations of voice for effect as on content and style. Perhaps even more than Tyler, Colton, and other ministers whom Dickinson heard, he could (as a fellow minister described) find "hidden manna" in the pages of Scripture where others could not and bring forth "sweet," living truths.[34]

Dickinson achieves the same dynamic of intellectuality and intensity of emotion that Wadsworth and the other preachers she knew did. The intellectual strength of her poems—which, we will see, she in part accomplishes through the sermon structure borrowed from the preachers she heard—is not at the expense of an appeal to the sight and hearing of an audience. Within a reasoned discourse, Dickinson relies on vivid, striking images, engaging the senses of her readers even as she engages the intellect. In one characteristic poem, Dickinson presents a reasoning speaker—"The Savior must have been . . ."—as well as vivid imagery, describing eternity as the "Road to Bethlehem" (#1487, lines 1, 5).

Likewise, in #915, the basic image of faith as a bridge is intellectually conceived:

> Faith—is the Pierless Bridge
> Supporting what We see
> Unto the Scene that We do not—
> Too slender for the eye
>
> It bears the Soul as bold
> As it were rocked in Steel
> With Arms of Steel at either side—
> It joins—behind the Vail
>
> To what, could We presume
> The Bridge would cease to be
> To Our far, vacillating Feet
> A first Necessity.

The idea of a bridge without piers joining what we do see to what we cannot see and bearing the soul is difficult to visualize; without piers or connections, the structure can hardly be called a bridge. Indeed, the analogy entails our thinking more than our seeing in order to understand. Arguing her analogy within the structure of the traditional sermon, Dickinson, in the body of the poem, musters convincing details to support her initial proposition and to show the aptness of the image. At the same time, also in the manner of the traditional preachers, she employs vivid details to engage the senses and emotions of her readers. She suggests that the soul is "rocked in Steel / With Arms of Steel at either Side," joining "behind the Vail" to "what," we cannot "presume" to know. Although we may not be able to visualize a "pierless" bridge, we do experience the emotional power of the idea that faith entails mystery and uncertainty—even struggle, as Dickinson suggests in the last stanza. We need faith, difficult as it is, because we cannot see. Our alternative to struggling with faith is to struggle with "vacillation," the uncertainty surrounding our inability to see and to know what we cannot. Dickinson may be uneasy with the "necessity" of faith, yet the implicit application of her "prophecy" seems apparent: one should not be troubled that she or he cannot know what can be known only by faith, for faith, by its very nature, involves struggle and effort. Like many of her poems, this one is an articulation of Dickinson's thoughts and emotions, the images often intellectually conceived yet presented in a context of intense emotionality.

Many poems, like the traditional sermon on which they are modeled, vivify a situation by drawing the reader into the experience through specific, sensual detail. Examples include many of the poems on death (such as #280, "I felt a Funeral, in my Brain") and poems describing other intense experiences (such as #510, "It was not Death, for I stood up," and #1099, "My Cocoon tightens—Colors teaze—"). Dickinson proclaims truths through sharp, lively imagery, not dry, abstract reasoning. She often translates the spiritual into the emotional. "Longing is like the Seed / That wrestles in the Ground," she describes in #1255 (lines 1–2). As in #915, in this poem she draws an intellectually conceived analogy for her sermonic proposition, dramatizing the abstract and elaborating on it with concrete detail. In #501, she employs synesthesia to vivify the world beyond this one in arguing the reasonable assertion of line 1: "This World is not Conclusion. / A Species stands beyond— / Invisible, as Music— / But positive, as Sound—" (lines 1–4). Through pointed description and focused imagery, her sensual appeal occurs alongside an intellectual emphasis.

Dickinson adopted the style and voice of the prophet-preacher throughout her art, and she even adopted the sermonic form, or variations of it, in as many as half of her poems. As in the sermons, this four-part structure helps to establish the intellectual quality of her verse, the speaker arguing and reasoning with the audience within the logic of the organizational scheme. Dickinson undoubtedly was impressed by the structure of the traditional sermons, since the success of Edwards and his homiletical heirs—Wadsworth, Tyler, Dwight, and others—lay especially in the structure and style of the message, rather than in the delivery or dogma.

Dickinson revised the sermonic form for her own needs, characteristically omitting the citation of a biblical text yet continuing with the opening–reasons–application structure. Writing to exposit not an established text, as the ministers did with the Bible, but rather her own prophetic vision, Dickinson created her own "text," a body of beliefs underlying her poems. In the tradition of the evangelical sermon, then, the pattern discernible in much of her poetry includes an opening proposition or statement of the situation, development or elaboration of the proposition, and an application or final comment. Dickinson often used the sermonic pattern to confront her readers with a striking truth, then challenged them with its experiential and jarring reality.

Critics have attempted to describe the structures of Dickinson's poetry, noticing the orderliness of her lines yet not explaining how the structures work alongside her other rhetorical choices—her diction and imagery, her parallelisms, or even her distinctive dashes, to name only a few. For example, Carroll D. Laverty has pointed out eight structural patterns in Dickinson's poetry, all of which seem to be variations of the sermonic structure discussed by Suzanne Wilson. I claim, more explicitly, that all these patterns replicate the conventions of the traditional sermon and that Dickinson's decision to draw on them, as well as on the other devices, was very purposeful, as she attempted, like the preachers, to speak as a religious visionary.[35] Dickinson's imitations of this sermonic pattern when she adopts the prophetic voice in its spiritual and emotional intensity incorporate not only the sermon's characteristic structure but also its tone. We hear the authority of her voice most strikingly in the frequently aphoristic quality of her initial proposition or "doctrine." Dickinson achieved this quality by working the conventions of the sermon with the devices in the scriptural prophecies, as we will explore in Chapter 6.

The sermon form shaped Dickinson's imagination early on and, as we will see, so deeply that it is evident throughout her oeuvre. We see it as early as 1858 in Poem #1, the valentine poem, which Barbara A. C. Mossberg has identified as a parody of a sermon. Specifically, Dickinson's pattern in this poem is an Edwardsian one, and the parody lies in her manipulation of the pattern as she mocks a belief of her time through the sermonic structure. Complete with text and application, the speaker, as Mossberg has described, in the manner of the Edwardsian preacher "exhort[s] God's faithful to mate in accordance with natural, social, and spiritual laws."[36] Dickinson follows the complete four-part sermon structure, even drawing attention to her poem as "sermon" when she points out her "application" in line 23, the most important part of this sermonic valentine.

We can find Dickinson's "text" in #1 in the first four lines, a text she seems to have inferred from Scripture (in passages such as Gen. 2:18; 7:15–17; Eccles. 4:9–12) and the world around her. "Oh the Earth was *made* for lovers, for damsel, and hopeless swain," the speaker jests; "God hath made nothing single but *thee* in His world so fair!" (lines 1, 4). In the next six lines she gives her opening, the "doctrine" of mating, reading in experience a "proof text" for scriptural revelation. Playfully experimenting with the structure, she notes briefly some examples of "twos" in nature and society and, in good humor, articulates her doctrine, a parody of Matt. 7:7–8 ("Seek, and ye shall find; . . . For every one that asketh receiveth"). For her own doctrine, Dickinson applies the biblical statement about seekers of spiritual truth to those who seek mates: "The life doth prove the precept, who obey shall happy be, / . . . None cannot find who *seeketh*, on this terrestrial ball" (lines 7, 10). For the argument of her "sermon," she elaborates on this precept in the next twelve lines, citing example after concrete example of creatures that pursue and gain their "beloved"—the bee "courts" and gains the flower, the wind "woos" the branches, the wave "makes solemn vows" with the moon. She couches all of her examples in the rhetoric of courtship, providing a logically persuasive, albeit parodic, argument.

Dickinson draws special attention to her application and thus to the sermonic form that structures the poem: "*Now* to the *application* . . ." (line 23). Her witty application consists of the last sixteen lines. Since "Thou art a *human* solo," her reader ought to "seize" a lover and thus fulfill the scriptural injunction to mate (lines 25, 34). Like the preachers of the Puritan legacy—but in a teasing voice—she urges action on her reader in these last lines: "Approach that tree . . . then up it boldly climb, / And seize the one thou lovest. . . . / Then bear her to the greenwood" (lines 33–35). The poem thus follows the text–opening–reasons–application structure of the sermon, even if the tone lacks the seriousness of most of the Amherst preachers. Dickinson's playful application stands as a parody of what could seem to be humorlessness. Apparently one of the first poems she wrote, the work is significant because of what its structures and tonalities may have suggested to her poetic mind. Yet even her more characteristic poems, the ones distinctive for the shortness of the lines, the frequent dashes, and the Dickinsonian rhythm, often follow the four-part pattern, varying it at times to suit her interests and purposes.

Following the structure of the sermon in many of her poems, Dickinson proceeds logically through the "doctrine," "reasons," and "application," usually omitting the citation of a text since her text characteristically originates in the poem. Dickinson's basic structure can be seen clearly in #1317, in which she alludes to a scriptural text (Gen. 22:2) in her propositional opening: "Abraham to kill him / Was distinctly told—." In the next eight lines, the poet elaborates on the proposition, interpreting Abraham and Isaac's situation as it appears to her:

> Isaac was an Urchin—
> Abraham was old—
>
> Not a hesitation—
> Abraham complied—
> Flattered by Obeisance
> Tyranny demurred—
>
> Isaac—to his children
> Lived to tell the tale—

The last two lines give an application: "Moral—with a Mastiff / Manners may prevail." In the stance of the preacher—and again, exploiting the structure to achieve humor—Dickinson extends the significance of the text, and her reading of it, to all humanity. The sermonic structure can prevail even when Dickinson is most at odds with Scripture's prophetic moral lesson; the poet here gives an unconventional reading of Scripture and offers her own figure for God. Obviously, too, she draws on the terse, compact style of the traditional form, compressing biblical narrative in these few lines. Written in the 1870s, the poem shows that Dickinson's fascination with the sermonic form continued at the same time as she experimented with other poetic structures.

In her use of the sermonic structure, Dickinson may present the initial statement through a simile or metaphor (as in #319, "The nearest Dream recedes—unrealized—," and #889, "Crisis is a Hair") or without a figure focusing on a proposition or image (#444, "It feels a shame to be Alive—"; #1116, "There is another Loneliness"; #1138, "A Spider sewed at Night"). Sometimes she presents the statement with a story that elaborates on it—a technique that traditional ministers such as Park and Wadsworth used when they retold a biblical narrative in fuller, more vivid detail.[37] We have seen this approach in #1317, "Abraham to kill him," and it occurs also in, among other poems, #986, "A Narrow Fellow in the Grass," and #83, "Heart, not so heavy as mine." The elaboration is not so much a series of reflections but a narrative. In other poems, Dickinson modifies the sermonic pattern by omitting the final, explanatory statement or application to allow her opening proposition and elaboration to stand with no final comment, in a deductive approach (as in #477, "No Man can compass a Despair—"; #478, "I had no time to Hate—"; #809, "Unable are the Loved to die"; #1498, "Glass was the Street—in tinsel Peril"); or she may omit the initial proposition, simply listing examples and concluding with a generalization, thus adopting an inductive strategy (as in #12, "The morns are meeker than they were—"; #167, "To learn the Transport by the Pain—"; #169, "In Ebon Box, when years have flown"; #1189, "The Voice that stands for Floods to me").[38] By omitting the first or last elements of the form—rarely, if ever, both—the poet heightens the impact of the wisdom she speaks.

Thus, Dickinson does not rigidly follow the sermonic method; she works it in flexible ways to serve her purposes of confronting, arguing, reflecting, even wondering, as she explores the prophetic voice. The rhetorical principles of the evangelical sermon operate even in poems that contain these revisions of the sermonic form, because the rhythm and the logic of the retained elements recall the basic structures. The revised patterns often work well for her when she wants to challenge her audience to deduce the main point or application themselves.

This is the case, for example, in #59, "A little East of Jordan." Dickinson alludes to a scriptural text in the first four lines, as she gives her opening statement:

> A little East of Jordan,
> Evangelists record,
> A Gymnast and an Angel
> Did wrestle long and hard—

In the next three stanzas, she retells the story of Jacob wrestling with and overcoming a "man" whom he discovers to be God (Gen. 32:22–30). But Dickinson ends the poem with only the exposition of the text: "And the bewildered Gymnast / Found he had worsted God!" (lines 15–16). She omits the application. She knew that a reader of her day would recall the biblical passage and how it explained the significance of the event. But instead of concluding the poem as her culture might expect, by explaining how God blesses those who acknowledge God as source of blessing (as Jacob does in Gen. 32:30), she let her exposition stand without further comment. The effect is an unorthodox challenge to doctrines of God's omnipotence. Dickinson uses the sermonic form to prophesy the truth of Scripture, which is, in her reading of it, contrary to Judeo-Christian doctrines of the godhead. Thus the poem becomes a complex combination of the engaged yet disengaged, conventional yet unorthodox religiosity that characterizes Dickinson's verse.

Another variation on the basic sermonic pattern involves Dickinson's presentation of only the initial proposition, with no further development; one single statement runs through one or two stanzas (#105, "To hang our head—ostensibly—"; #183, "I've heard an Organ talk, sometimes—"; #481, "The Himmaleh was known to stoop"; #1008, "How still the Bells in Steeples stand"; #1510, "How happy is the little Stone"; #1676, "Of Yellow was the outer Sky"). Often the very short poems follow this pattern, as in #1707: "Winter under cultivation / Is as arable as Spring." Developing her proposition within the structure of a single sentence, Dickinson rejects a longer exposition in favor of a presentation that makes her point implicitly and, in the case of the very short poems, in the form of a proverb, a form that the biblical poets favored. In #1510, "How happy is the little Stone," the development occurs in the phrases of the sentence (lines 3–8), with the last phrase giving her application implicitly: "Fulfilling absolute Decree / In casual simplicity—" (lines 9–10). In its omission of a long exposition, the poem stands as an extreme example of the homiletical precept of simplicity and brevity of form, which Dickinson adopts here in both the form and the content. Aware that she implies rather than states her application, readers realize that Dickinson in fact is urging as a value "casual simplicity" in lifestyle (lines 3–4) and in appearance (lines 5–6), as well as—fitting for her as a prophet—a nonconformist spirit (lines 7–8). In this and the other short poems, she gives her audience freedom to reflect on the implications of her proposition, appealing to their reason in the tradition of the Edwardsian sermon.

An awareness of the sermonic form and its potential for Dickinson's poetic structure can help readers both to discern her thought patterns and to experience the full weight of her messages. In #675, for example, the implied conclusion is actually an application of her opening proposition, "Essential Oils—are wrung." The elaboration in the body of the poem illuminates her proposition, suggesting the dual meaning of "essential" as she hints at her unstated application, which we sense as a completion of the thought of the poem:

> Essential Oils—are wrung—
> The Attar from the Rose
> Be not expressed by Suns—
>
> It is the gift of Screws—
>
> The General Rose—decay—
> But this—in Lady's Drawer
> Make Summer—When the Lady lie
> In Ceaseless Rosemary—

The pun in the proposition, as it is explained in the elaboration, is important to the application and thus to our reaction to the poem. "Attar" (line 2) is "essence," in the sense of perfume; thus the phrase "Essential Oils" of line 1 suggests sweetness of smell, an aesthetic image. But the "Essential Oils" are also juxtaposed with the "General Rose" of line 5, suggesting "necessary" or "fundamental" as meanings for "essential," given the opposition of the undifferentiated "general" rose. Significantly, these oils are "wrung," the speaker states unequivocally. The image is one of violence, elaborated in lines 3–4 in terms of the attar's being produced by "Screws," not "Suns"—a strenuous, even brutal process. But although the rose decays, the attar survives long after its owner (the "Lady") dies, and it continues to "Make Summer" or bring delight by its fragrance. The poet's structure of thought illuminates her conclusion, an unstated application: a process of brutality, even agony, is necessary for one to attain "essential oils"—the fundamental and beautiful elements. Yet those "oils" will survive long after their owners' death, having "Ceaseless" effect (line 8). Presumably, the agony and brutality of the process will be worth it.

Dickinson may have had in mind as the "essential oils" her own art, mindful of the strenuous, even agonizing poetic process through which she achieved the essential and the beautiful, her brief and pointed poems. In offering the poem without a specific, stated application, she allows an audience to interpret the poem in ways particular to its own circumstances. Dickinson confronts us with startling reality, this time playing on a pun and relying on metaphor, with the effect of provoking readers to reflect on the symbolic significance of natural phenomena as they sense the implied concluding application.

Dickinson also varies the four-part sermon structure by engaging additional homiletical and prophetic devices. She may repeat the statement and elaboration two or more times before stating the application or conclusion, drawing on the biblical prophetic-poetic technique of parallelism or amplification, as in #324, "Some keep the Sabbath going to Church—." In this poem, the second stanza parallels the first. Both stanzas give a proposition in the first two lines and elaborate on contrasting kinds of church services and church architecture in the second two lines:

> Some keep the Sabbath going to Church—
> I keep it, staying at Home—
> With a Bobolink for a Chorister—
> And an Orchard, for a Dome—
>
> Some keep the Sabbath in Surplice—
> I just wear my Wings—
> And instead of tolling the Bell, for Church,
> Our little Sexton—sings.

The effect is to drive home her proposition—in this poem, one that draws attention to the opposition of traditional forms of worship to the forms practiced by the speaker.

The third stanza, continuing the comparison of particulars of religious observance, contains a commentary on the relative merits of institutional and personal ritual. It also functions to model the moral applications of the body of her text, just as the traditional sermon concluded with moral application:

> God preaches, a noted Clergyman—
> And the sermon is never long,
> So instead of getting to Heaven, at last—
> I'm going, all along.

Staying at home within the natural order of an orchard can result in an encounter with the divine, the speaker suggests, an encounter that is never boring or uncomfortable. In fact, that encounter does not consist of a single moment—"getting to Heaven"—but is ongoing, a state of being: "I'm going, all along." The sermon form in this poem structures Dickinson's thought into reasoned reiteration as she drives her point home about the merits of her own kind of worship.[39]

In adopting the sermonic form, Dickinson often gives her initial proposition in the shape of a definition, which gives the lines a proverbial effect. Her use of the proverbial form, which the biblical prophets often used, shows her drawing on biblical prophecy to enhance the sermonic structure. In the poems employing definition, the lines are declarative and give a short saying of a spiritual truth, as in the biblical proverb. Sometimes the poem may be brief, consisting only of the definition. Poem #1002 is one example:

> Aurora is the effort
> Of the Celestial Face
> Unconsciousness of Perfectness
> To simulate, to Us.

More often, the definition is achieved through statements of development and a final comment expressing its significance, an Edwardsian application, as in #668, which has the definition in the first line:

> "Nature" is what we see—
> The Hill—the Afternoon—
> Squirrel—Eclipse—the Bumble bee—
>
> . . . .
>
> Nature is what we know—
> Yet have no art to say—
> So impotent Our Wisdom is
> To her Simplicity.   (lines 1–3, 9–12)

Other definition poems include #254, " 'Hope' is the thing with feathers—"; #744, "Remorse—is Memory—awake—"; #976, "Death is a Dialogue between"; #983, "Ideals are the Fairy Oil"; #988, "The Definition of Beauty is"; #1118, "Exhilaration is the Breeze"; #1472, "To see the Summer Sky"; #1763, "Fame is a bee."[40] The definition expresses the proposition of the Edwardsian sermon, a wise saying that recalls the preacher-prophet's role as sage.

In a small portion of her poetry, Dickinson also gains from the Edwardsian sermon tradition the practice of focusing on a biblical text, staying close to the text in content, if not in interpretation, as she borrows and shapes that form of prophecy. The similarity of her practice to that of the evangelical preachers of New England is more apparent when we consider the strategy of the Unitarian preachers of her time. The Unitarian preachers, although they, too, chose a particular text to preach on, did not maintain the close exegesis that the evangelical Protestants did; they often used the scriptural texts to provide subject matter, but they neither dramatized scriptural narratives at length nor analyzed texts closely for the Christian principles they provide (as the sermons of, for example, William Channing show). In contrast, like the conservative Amherst preachers she heard, when Dickinson focuses on a biblical text, she dramatizes a narrative through pointed descriptors or comments on a scriptural passage or even builds a message around short phrases or key words from a scriptural text. Wadsworth, the preacher she most admired, exemplifies these practices. For instance, in one sermon, "The Great Watchword," he chose one verse of Scripture on which to focus and provide comment—the single statement "Go forward!" from Exod. 14:15. He brought it to life through literary devices such as dramatization and metaphor, retelling the story of the Israelites' exodus. Like other traditional preachers, Wadsworth offered his own interpretation and application of the single biblical line, a strategy Dickinson would have liked since, ironically, it would allow her to interpret with prophetic license and abandon the preachers' conventional Christian interpretations.

Dickinson's practice of vivifying biblical narratives is apparent in, for example, #1317, "Abraham to kill him," in which she retells the story of Abraham and Isaac (Genesis 22), and #59, "A little East of Jordan," her famous rendition of Jacob wrestling with the angel (Gen. 32:22–30). Like the evangelical preachers (and unlike the Unitarians), she stays close to the text, offering a concluding remark on the significance of the passage according to her own interpretation. Such biblical retellings abound in her poetry, as scholars have pointed out (though they have not recognized this strategy's connection to other traditional sermonic features in her verse): in #597, "It always felt to me—a wrong," she discusses Moses' narrative of his seeing Canaan without being permitted to enter the Promised Land (Deut. 34:1–4), and in #1254, "Elijah's Wagon knew no thill," she describes Elijah's ascent into heaven on the whirlwind (1 Kings 2:11).

Poem #1459, "Belshazzar had a Letter—," offers an exegesis of the narrative of the handwriting that appeared on King Belshazzar's wall, which Daniel interpreted:

Belshazzar had a Letter—
He never had but one—
Belshazzar's Correspondent
Concluded and begun
In that immortal Copy
The Conscience of us all
Can read without it's Glasses
On Revelation's Wall—

In this poem Dickinson retells the story of Daniel 5 in eight brief lines, giving her proposition in the first two lines and her application in the last three. She maintains her focus on the biblical text throughout. In the manner of the preachers she heard, she uses a figure of speech, the "Letter" to King Belshazzar, to signify the writing that mysteriously appeared on his wall. And she adopts colloquial diction to vivify the biblical passage and engage her readers. Dickinson's point in her proposition is that Belshazzar was given only one divine message concerning his status before God—that is, that he had offended God and would be destroyed (Dan. 5:27). She prophetically "applies" the text by extending its significance to a contemporary audience, in the manner of the preacher; she indicates that they, too, are inadequate before God, and their "Conscience" knows it full well, not needing "Glasses" to read "the writing on the wall."

In a related strategy, sometimes Dickinson offers poems that are commentaries on a single verse of the Bible, as in #1492, the opening line of which is taken directly from 1 Cor. 15:35: " 'And with what body do they come?'—." In these commentary verses, as in her lines that dramatize scriptural narratives, she still follows the technique of the evangelicals in closely analyzing and interpreting the text according to her vision of spirituality. Poem #62, " 'Sown in dishonor'!" is a comment on 1 Cor. 15:43, which she cites as her first line. Sometimes she conflates two biblical texts in one poem, as in #168, "If the foolish, call them *'flowers'*—." The poem deals with the biblical narrative of Moses seeing the Promised Land, as well as a passage from the Book of Revelation. Dickinson draws a parallel between God's denying Moses the land and—the main thrust of the poem—the possibility of her readers being denied a heavenly home. Likewise, #1342, " 'Was not' was all the Statement," explicates Gen. 5:24 ("and he was not; for God took him"), the assumption of Enoch; the poet expands one-half of the Genesis verse into an eight-line poem.

Poem #573, "The Test of Love—is Death—," draws on John 15:13 (line 1), John 3:16 (line 2), and perhaps Phil. 2:8 (lines 11–12). In this poem, as in others, the allusion is subtle, consisting of only one or two words ("Last—Least—" in line 11 of the poem). Dickinson retains her focus on the biblical text of John 15:13 even as she paraphrases it ("The Test of Love—is Death—") to drive home the larger point that one who loves will sacrifice all. Although the biblical context in #573 suggests that Dickinson derived her precept from the example of Christ, we cannot help but wonder if she intended her unstated application to extend to all lovers, divine and human, including, perhaps, her own.

In this kind of poem, Dickinson clearly expects readers to supply the context for her biblical references, as Jack L. Capps points out.[41] Still, she maintains a close exegesis. Like a traditional preacher, she focuses on the implications of the biblical text or uses the text to support an argument, rather than simply using the text to provide subject matter as a point of departure, as Unitarian preaching tended to do. She acts as a "warbling teller" (#1545) in considering the Gospels, prayers, and sacraments and responding with her own versions. She maintains the expository method of the Edwardsian preachers, but ultimately, she is interested in spiritual vitality, not in the status quo.

Dickinson's manipulations of the sermonic style and structures work together to give her the authoritative, prophetic voice that she heard modeled for so many years in the traditional sermon. Like those preachers, her tone is forceful and earnest, yet it is not melodramatic, as was that of the frontier revivalist preachers or the sentimental poets of her day. Dickinson speaks colloquially and with emotional intensity, in the tradition of the Puritan ministers and the biblical prophets. The authority of her voice, notable even when she is at odds with the dogma of her homiletical tradition, is perhaps most apparent in the aphorisms that frequently form her opening propositions: "Who has not found the Heaven—below— / Will fail of it above—," she states unequivocally in #1544; "The Spirit is the Conscious Ear," she asserts in #733. It is the aphoristic quality of many of her propositions that makes much of her poetry memorable. The stance of a poet who speaks wise prophecy gave Dickinson access to an authoritative voice that she would make memorable through her innovations on the prophetic strategies and devices.

The traditional ministers of Dickinson's time, mindful of their authoritative role as prophetic speakers of spiritual truth, continued the public functions of the scriptural prophets into nineteenth-century America: they exhorted, edified, and, alternately, consoled their listeners. In doing so, they adhered to the Old and New Testament stipulations and models for prophet-preachers (as in 1 Cor. 14:3) and followed the example of Edwards, who had preached hortative sermons such as "Sinners in the Hands of an Angry God" and pastoral, consolatory messages such as "The Excellency of Christ." As the homiletical tradition to which Dickinson was continually exposed in her early years, the Connecticut Valley preaching offered her a prophetic voice to imitate as it stressed the power of the word to penetrate and influence the hearts of an audience. Like those homiletical speakers, Dickinson spoke confidently in her poems as a visionary speaker of truth, moral chastisement, or consolation, as she appropriated the preacher's prophetic role as exhorter, edifier, and comforter.

We see Dickinson drawing on her prophetic authority to adopt the preacherly role of chastising her audience when she recorded some of the follies and pretensions of the people of her day. As Charles Anderson pointed out in 1960, her poems about her contemporaries have largely been neglected because of a concern with her "grander" poetry, and because of the assumption that a recluse could know little of the life around her. This practice still continues to some extent, although currently, various critics—feminists, New Historicists, and others—are working to read Dickinson in her historical context. When all of her poems are read as a group, they provide an unexpected commentary on her culture. In Anderson's words, "Her portrait gallery of village and national types comprises a fairly wide range: hollow men and hedonists, lost drunkards who 'cannot meet a Cork / Without a Revery,' urbane but shallow bankers, gossips and genteel females, several types of preachers and that man of the 'Appalling Trade,' the undertaker."[42] In the four short lines of #185 ("'Faith' is a fine invention"), she criticizes her culture in the tradition of the Judeo-Christian prophets for inconsistencies and hypocrisy as, when "In an Emergency," it substitutes science—or even social propriety—for the Christian faith it touts from its pulpits. And in #401, "What Soft—Cherubic Creatures—," her target is the women of the leisure class; Dickinson exposes the shallowness of their Christian faith, representing the women as more concerned about manners and dress than true redemption. Although Dickinson perhaps most often adopted the edifying voice of the prophet-preacher, offering wise statements on human living and faith, in poems such as these we hear the chastising tone modeled by the prophets of the Scriptures and, more immediately, by the preachers of her time.

If Johnson's numbering of the poems is more or less correct in its chronology, Dickinson's prophetic focus shifted in her later poetry. By the end of her life, she moved away from the directives of the preacher to the consolation of the biblical prophets and the preachers she heard in Amherst. Although those ministers typically turned even a funeral sermon into an opportunity to exhort and direct, they did express comfort to their saddened audience in language that was tender, clear, and concise. "Religion hath an exceeding great reward," Aaron Colton reminded his congregation at one funeral. "Faith, hope, joy, peace; an approving conscience and a smiling God; comforted in all trials; . . . having a good name while living; leaving precious memories when gone; and then—Oh! transporting prospect,—'shall shine as the brightness of the firmament and as the stars, for ever and ever.'"[43]

Dickinson adapted this mode for many of the poems of her later life, the poems becoming shorter, the sermonic structural pattern often disappearing. We find that, beginning in the 1870s, the poems increasingly focus on human suffering, until in the 1880s, most of the poems have an anonymous persona speaking in a meditative tone, addressing human despair in a consolatory voice. "The stem of a departed Flower / Has still a silent rank," she offers in #1520, seeing in nature an example applicable to human disappointment (lines 1–2). In #1639, she focuses on one of the small comforts in life: "A Letter is a joy of Earth— / It is denied the Gods—" (lines 1–2). Often the persona speaks for a universal "us," as in #1493 and other poems about suffering: "Could that sweet Darkness where they dwell / Be once disclosed to us / The clamor for their loveliness / Would burst the Loneliness—" (lines 1–4). In these poems the speaker characteristically reaches out to all fellow sufferers in a shared grief over loved ones—the stance of the consolatory prophet Isaiah, whose writings formed one of Dickinson's favorite books of the Bible. Dickinson considers the subject of death more frequently in the late poems than in the earlier ones; she also adopts a personal and tender, not self-pitying, tone in messages of comfort, when she plays the role of the consolatory prophet and preacher. She moves away from the confident confrontation of the sermon tradition to its comforting sympathy.

It is important to recall that the traditional preachers' delivery and style paralleled those of the biblical prophets, both figures relying on plain, simple, colloquial language with vivid imagery and giving their speeches with inspired energy and force. In their personal involvement with God, all derived a sense of divine urgency, expressing this in emotional fervor and earnestness. But often they chose to speak in indirect ways, because they wanted to direct their messages only to the spiritually attuned. In these cases, they characteristically chose paradox, parable, or, as is seen in the sermons of the traditional preachers, allegory. We will explore the biblical strategies of indirection and Dickinson's interest in them in Chapter 6. What is important to note here is that into the nineteenth century, the tradition of Puritan preaching had retained many of the qualities of scriptural prophecy as that prophetic tradition had been interpreted by the Reformers and by Calvinist preachers such as William Perkins, Jonathan Edwards, and the evangelical Protestants of the Connecticut Valley.

Yet, as we will see in the next two chapters, the differences between the biblical and homiletical traditions rendered both of them appealing to Dickinson as sources for her poetry. More so than the homiletical tradition, the scriptural prophetic tradition emphasized dreams and visions as modes of divine transmission and the importance of liminal experiences, with bizarre juxtaposition of time frameworks. Another obvious distinction is in the rhetorical structures of the two traditions. While the homiletical tradition of prophecy offered Dickinson cogent models of a rhetorical structure and style appropriate to it as an oral, contemporary expression of prophecy, the scriptural tradition showed her particular devices and kinds of parallelism, peculiar to the biblical prophecies as poetry. Dickinson would have seen that the scriptural tradition offered a more complete expression of prophecy, with its range of prophetic genres and voices. And that tradition drew on poetry for its literary expression. As a female poet and prophet, Dickinson would have seen in the scriptural tradition ways to develop an authoritative prophetic-poetic voice, even as she worked those ideas with the models of prophecy she discovered in the nineteenth-century sermons.

4. Speaking for "Infinitude": Dickinson and Poetic Inspiration

"THE LORD THY GOD is a consuming fire," the prophet Moses warned the people of Israel when he gave them the Deuteronomic law (Deut. 4:24). Later, when Moses wanted to inspire the people to place their confidence in God, he used the same sort of imagery: "Understand therefore this day, that the Lord thy God is he which goeth over before thee; as a consuming fire he shall destroy them" (Deut. 9:3). Over and over in the Scriptures, the prophets speak of God as fire, energy, light. Moses described God's appearance at Mount Sinai as fire and smoke (Exod. 19:16–19); similarly, Amos warned that the Lord might "break out like fire" if the people failed to return to God (Amos 5:6).

In a yet sharper description, Isaiah speaks an oracle from the Lord:

> Behold, the name of the Lord cometh from afar, burning
> with his anger, and the burden thereof is heavy:
> his lips are full of indignation,
> and his tongue as a devouring fire:
> And his breath, as an overflowing stream, shall reach
> to the midst of his neck, to sift the nations.
>
> (Isa. 30:27–28)

Isaiah returns to the imagery throughout his long prophecy: repeatedly, he speaks of the divine presence as a fire and the voice of God as sounding like wind or rushing water. Or he may portray God as coming in a storm, associating God's power with the thunder and "consuming fire" of lightning: "And the Lord shall cause his glorious voice to be heard," Isaiah warns, "and shall show the lightning down of his arm, with the indignation of his anger, and with the flame of a devouring fire, with scattering, and tempest, and hailstones" (Isa. 30:30).

In what is perhaps the most specific description of the divine, John in the Book of Revelation offers a picture of the returning Christ that draws together the Old Testament images:

> His head and hairs were white like wool, as white as snow;
> and his eyes were as a flame of fire;

73

And his feet like unto fine brass, as if they burned in a
furnace; and his voice as the sound of many
waters.

And he had in his right hand seven stars: and out of his
mouth went a sharp two-edged sword: and
his countenance was as the sun shineth in his
strength.   (Rev. 1:14–16)

Indeed, although the prophets describe God at other times as a compassionate shepherd (Psalm 23; Isa. 40:11) or caring parent (Ps. 68:5; Isa. 9:6; Matt. 6:9), more often, the prophets present the divine as a terrifying and awe-inspiring presence. John's response to the Christ he encounters in his vision is to fall down "as [though] dead," so awesome is the Christ.

This portrayal of the godhead is relevant to our reading of Dickinson's poetry in several ways. It affected both her conception of her relationship with the divine and the ways in which she spoke to her audience, influencing the genres she chose within her poetry and also the thrust of the prophecy itself—her emphasis on wonder as key for living. It is significant that, although Dickinson had available to her a number of different conceptions of God, she returned most often to this understanding of the divine—as a presence associated with fire, energy, and wonder. She might have adopted a Unitarian or transcendentalist vision—William Ellery Channing's understanding of God as an eternal being of love, or Ralph Waldo Emerson's conception of the divine soul that potentially inspires all people. The evangelical conception of God as a caring father or, alternately, a wrathful parent might also have served her. But Dickinson's figures suggest a being both personal (unlike the transcendentalists' image) and wonderful, a mysterious deity that commands authority and evokes awe.

In Poem #564 ("My period had come for Prayer—"), for example, Dickinson's speaker attempts to visit God at "His House," "step[ping] upon the North / To see this Curious Friend—" (lines 9, 7–8). The poet's images suggest God to be both a distinct and personal being. What the speaker learns is that this being is also a faceless, invisible "Infinitude" (line 15). Her response to what she discovers indicates that the "Silence" she has found on the "Vast Prairies of Air" is to be understood not as an absence of God but as a powerful spiritual Presence: "awed beyond my errand— / I worshipped—did not 'pray'—" (lines 19–20). Her reaction is strikingly similar to John's in Revelation—and strikingly unlike that of Thoreau, Emerson, or others of their cohort. For Dickinson, an encounter with the godhead is a humbling, amazing experience.

Yet Dickinson rarely described direct encounters with God; "My period had come for Prayer—" is unusual in that sense. More often, her speakers make comments about God or only allude to God. Perhaps a direct meeting with God was too amazing, too overwhelming, for Dickinson to envision. We can derive the poet's sense of God only by reading poem after poem and noticing the ways that the divine, as a unifying center of her poetry, looms behind the texts. What we find when we examine Dickinson's figures for her relationship with the godhead is a poet who experiences a powerful sense of divine inspiration that often becomes the subject matter for the poetry. Her imagery both for her inspired speaker and for the inspirer himself (the figure is always male) seems to derive from the biblical portrayals of the inspired prophet-poet. But in her characteristic manner, Dickinson offers a view of inspiration distinctive for the ways in which it is shaped by her awareness of her gender and by her historical situation, as well as her understanding of truth itself.

To be sure, the wonder that Dickinson's speakers experience in their encounter with the divine has its dark side—the terror, fear, or confusion we often find in the poetry. But at other times, her apprehension stimulates ecstasy. In either case, Dickinson's sense of a wondrous God who speaks words through her gives us personae in the inspiration cluster who are at once empowered but also humbled in the prophetic task. Rarely in any of her poems, for instance, does Dickinson adopt the self-satisfied, strident tone of Emerson or the sometimes arrogant voice of Whitman. Her confidence seems to emerge not from an egotistical sense of self but from an awareness of the spiritual magnitude of her poetic endeavor. When she claims a "title divine" or a position as "Empress of Calvary," as in #1072, she tends to associate her confidence with the divine itself. In #1072, for example, the "Acute Degree" is "conferred" on her, presumably by the godhead; her status is not self-generated or assumed. Dickinson, like the biblical prophets, speaks as one sent. Her confidence emerges from the encounter with the divine.

Isaiah, Jeremiah, and the other biblical prophets—as well as the Protestant ministers—in their inspiration spoke unequivocally and with divine force in their weighty pronouncements. They looked to a divine Other to validate their authoritative proclamations: "Thus saith the Lord," the Old Testament prophets reiterated. So their prophetic messages, having divine endorsement, carried an importance and a sanctity not experienced by other speakers. Dickinson's speakers often call on an inspirer, usually nocturnal, to authorize their words, one who also raises the persona to a royal status as sanctioned speaker. That status Dickinson could have through no human inspirer; it takes a transformation of the mortal to find a voiceless Other who depends on her to speak.

In #1005, "Bind me—I still can sing—," a poem claiming the undying power of the poetic voice, we see operating the biblical prophets' understanding of inspiration when the speaker lays aside her own claim to power in the last line:

> Bind me—I still can sing—
> Banish—my mandolin
> Strikes true within—
>
> Slay—and my Soul shall rise
> Chanting to Paradise—
> Still thine.

The speaker claims nothing less than a true and eternally chanting voice; but she is in the service of a distant love or God: "still thine." The attribution of individual prophetic authority—her soul's "chanting"—to a source in the Other may be "an attempt to make a poem that claims voice and ego less powerful and more conventional," as Charlotte Louise Nekola reads it, but this convention of the prophetic tradition paradoxically sets the speaker apart as one having special status.[1] The prophet's voice is not obliterated; it is validated, even immortalized. The poem suggests the authorization of an eternal, regenerated inspiration. And because of the inspiration of a higher power, the prophet can and must claim the authority of a bard and more. That higher power needs the prophet to speak; the inspirer is nothing without her. Dickinson's figuring herself as divinely inspired is both a claim to poetic-prophetic authority and a testimony to her creativity in claiming a role that her culture associated with men.

As in #1005, Dickinson's speakers frequently abdicate their own authority or voice by naming an inspirational Other as the agent of that voice, thus laying claim to a higher authority. The abdication is a positive strategy for Dickinson and can be regarded as a decisive challenge to the authority hoarded by the male divines of her day, who claimed that only they, as publicly ordained "prophets," could speak divinely sanctioned words. In claiming an inspirer, Dickinson put herself on a level with the biblical prophets and preachers. Scholars, most recently feminists, have debated the significance and identity of Dickinson's inspirer, some feminists rejecting the possibility of a male inspirer because they see it as implying that a man had a position of importance in Dickinson's life. Suzanne Juhasz summarizes one such argument: "Both positions are phallocentric," she points out, "that (a) Emily Dickinson wrote poetry because she did not have a sex life or (b) the only explanation for such poetry was an active (albeit secret) sex life. Both interpretations lodge the male at the center of a woman's creativity."[2] But that perspective fails to consider the scriptural pattern, in which prophetic speakers, male and female, are not diminished by a "male" inspirer. Dickinson's speakers go farther than the biblical ones in ultimately transcending the inspirer, but the scriptural pattern nonetheless offers a model of inspired speech that focuses less on the gender of the prophet than on the special authority conferred on him or her.

Sandra M. Gilbert and Susan Gubar come closer in describing an accurate picture of Dickinson's relationship to her inspirer when they consider the identity of the "Master": "Mothered by Awe, [Dickinson] might sometimes abase herself to her distant Master in a fever of despair, but she could also transform into a powerful muse to serve her purposes."[3] Indeed, although Dickinson may have looked to a man (or men) as a real or imaginary lover, it was through her own creative energy that she could transcend him to find a divine inspirer who would remain voiceless while she spoke empowered words. The Judeo-Christian connection to Dickinson's poetry justifies our sense that Dickinson's creativity did not spring from emotional dependence—or worse, from some neurosis—but from her own imaginative ability to seize visionary authority.

Unlike those readings that attribute the source of her inspiration to some classical or romantic figure of a daemon or to some exclusively internal, psychological aspect of her personality, the association of Dickinson's inspiration with the Christian tradition fits into a larger, more comprehensive understanding of her art.[4] Even if, at times, she does figure her inspirer as a male lover, we can go beyond the (potentially) distressing conclusion that she needed men to motivate her art. She "needs" the male only as much as he needs her to voice the divine words. Indeed, unlike modern readers, Dickinson was concerned not with where her audience would perceive her center of creativity—in an inspirer gendered male or otherwise—but with the justification to express her imagination.

In the seven "Master" poems, Dickinson frequently turns to address the inspirer; the divinity that she associates with the figure suggests the weight that the Other could lend to her poetic pronouncements. In the final line of #461, "A Wife—at Daybreak I shall be—," "Master" is the alternate word for "Savior." Although "Savior" appears in the fair copy, perhaps sent to a friend, "Master" is the word in both the draft and packet copies and may even have been her preferred word, since she chose it for the fascicle version. In the packet version, then, it is "Master" who is the heavenly bridegroom and whose face she has seen before. Similarly, in #96, "Sexton! My Master's sleeping here," "Master" also seems to be Jesus, with the poem dramatizing Mary Magdalene's visit to the tomb. Of course, "Master" is not necessarily used in precisely the same way in all seven "Master" poems (and in her letters, Dickinson used the word to refer to different people). Yet it seems absurd to suppose that there is no consistency of meaning in the poems, since all are believed to have been written in a relatively short period of time, between 1858 and 1863. In the poems the "Master" often takes on divine importance.

Adapting Christian tradition to her own purposes, Dickinson often associates "Master" or her Jesus figure with poetry, as we see in the Jesus cluster, which consists of as many as seventy poems. In #488, "Myself was formed—a Carpenter," she figures herself as a carpenter whose art is "the Art of Boards" (line 6). She works for a master builder, presumably Jesus, the carpenter from Galilee; she is his "little 'John,'" as she calls herself in #497, "He strained my faith—" (line 15). Poetry seems to be Jesus' earthly emblem, spoken through her. For Dickinson, the creative act is a reverential one, the poet figuring herself as inspired by the Jesus figure or "Master." Addressing the master or inspirer in #336, "The face I carry with me—last—," she indicates that it is the master's favor (the biblical meaning of "face") which will guarantee her being crowned in heaven. She will gain that favor when the angel "scans," or scrutinizes, the "face," her verse (line 9). Here the poet equates Jesus and poetry: the divine Other is master and owner of the poet's earthly and heavenly life, the poet bearing his "name" (line 15) as she speaks his poetry. And that "name," presumably, will set her apart from more ordinary poets or public speakers.

In #754, "My Life had stood—a Loaded Gun—," the speaker affirms that she is speaking for the Other, her "Master" (line 14), at the service of him and loyal to him. In the first stanza she describes herself as waiting, full of potential to speak, until her "Owner" empowers her:

> My Life had stood—a Loaded Gun—
> In Corners—till a Day
> The Owner passed—identified—
> And carried Me away—
>
> And now We roam in Sovreign Woods—
> And now We hunt the Doe—
> And every time I speak for Him—
> The Mountains straight reply—   (lines 1–8)

Although there are no overtly religious referents—and indeed, the poem seems to work against assuming them, with its ostensible theme of hunting—an emotional-psychological structure replicates that of the traditional Christian or Old Testament prophet in relation to the prophet's source of truth, power, and authority. The "Owner" is separate from the speaker, "other," and the speaker has been "identified" or chosen by him, as the biblical prophets were chosen by Yahweh. This "Owner" is the poet's inspirer, real to Dickinson as One who gives her words power and force.[5] Yet in the figure of the Other as owner of the gun, the relation is complicated: Dickinson gives her inspirer's words force as she "speaks" for him (lines 7–8). Such is the complex relation between Yahweh and the biblical prophets, whose words derive from Yahweh yet whose own verbal force communicates the divine messages. That the speaker's inspirer is silent is not "strange," as Gilbert sees it, when we consider the poem in the context of the prophetic tradition.[6] Like Yahweh who speaks to his people through the vehicle of his prophets, Dickinson's "Owner"—as she sees him—gives her authority. Expressing less humility and awe at her empowerment than in some other poems, the speaker acknowledges the rewards of speaking for the voiceless one by smiling ("And I do smile," line 9).

Also in #754, Dickinson reveals her knowledge of her power as a prophet—the power of her inspired words to "kill":

> To foe of His—I'm deadly foe—
> None stir the second time—
> On whom I lay a Yellow Eye—
> Or an emphatic Thumb—   (lines 17–20)

Disturbing in its juxtaposition of pleasure and the power of killing, the poem shows the verbal power of the biblical prophets transformed and magnified into destructive power in the poet's celebration of prophetic authority. The poem suggests the concepts of the Old Testament God of power and might and the prophet-poet as agent of that power. In the gun image, we see the potential of the poet as a prophetic speaker, who "explodes" with potent words on the discovery of her vocation. In this poem, her power as a prophet is power unharnessed and destructive. She carries prophetic power to new heights.

Yet despite this revision of the biblical models, like the scriptural prophets, Dickinson ultimately speaks as one intimately related to the inspirer. Her words may have longevity (she has not "the power to die"), but he must "longer live" than she or she will be only a "Loaded Gun," a prophetic voice full of potential but incomplete without a master to "speak for." Serving her master, her inspirer, gives her a task and fulfillment, satisfaction at her "good Day done—" (line 13). Without a master to speak for and to empower her speech, her gift of prophetic expression would lie dormant, her life standing still "in corners" without a source of empowerment.

This inspiring presence is sometimes identified by Dickinson's speaker more specifically in the Judeo-Christian tradition, through figures of king or Christ, alternately possessing the more conventional attributes of potential lover, companion, wise counselor, and husband. Sometimes she conceives the presence less as a "person" and more as a natural force. Even given the variety of Dickinson's imagined sources of inspiration, she repeatedly presents the inspirer as enabling her to convey the weighty messages of nature and God, both of whom, in Dickinson's mind, sought her out to be the receiver of messages that they wished to transmit to humanity. Thus, in one innovation upon her scriptural models, Dickinson figures her inspirer most often as playing a mediatory role between God and herself, a presence who enables her to speak for an opaque or lost God.

At times, the inspirer figure is identified as Christ, whom Dickinson seems to have regarded as more accessible, gentler, perhaps less intimidating than the inhumanly powerful God the Father, figured in one poem as a "distant—stately Lover—" (#357, "God is a distant—stately Lover—"). Dickinson's godhead is distant, aloof, and unknowable—except through nature, poetry, the soul, and Jesus. For her, Jesus represents the accessible member of the Trinity, the Logos or "Envoy" (#357, line 6), who is a means of coming to know something of an "illegible" God (#820, "All Circumstances are the Frame," line 8). Through the inspirer, she acquires insights into "immortality"; the source of her power, in turn, finds a means of expression through the poet's voice, in the tradition of the prophets. She undoubtedly found the power of insight that the mediator wielded tempting, since through his arcane knowledge and her access to it, she could envision a role and a future for herself that promised to be much more gratifying than her life in Amherst had ever been. The prophetic role offered her an authoritative voice and thus a means of powerful self-gratification, which she celebrated in the image of the gun in #754 and in more conventional images of religious reward elsewhere, as in poems #215, "What is— 'Paradise'—," and #1153, "Through what transports of Patience."

But how could Dickinson gain audience with her inspirer? When does inspiration occur? If God is a mysterious power too awesome for humans to encounter directly, then a confrontation with the mediator might itself be dangerous, and the occasions of inspiration could be wondrous events. Not surprising, for Dickinson the shroud of darkness offered by night invited the appearance of the inspirer; night, after all, is the time when the division between mortal and divine is not so pronounced. Several poems speak of the nocturnal appearances of the visitor, a mysterious "shapeless friend" known only by his presence, as in #679, "Conscious am I in my Chamber." The visitor does not seem to be bound by physical laws, for he is invisible. In fact, in poems such as #679, the speaker suggests that the meeting between the mortal and the divine needs to be indirect, so as not to present injury to the human party: "Presence—," the speaker states, "is His furthest license—" (line 9); his appearance alone is powerful. Dickinson may have gleaned her conception of inspiration from romantic writers such as Nathaniel Hawthorne, who suggests the imaginative possibilities of moonlight; chances are, however, that the broader association of nighttime and dreams with inspiration derives originally from the Scriptures.

In both the Old and New Testaments, God often visits prophets and other individuals at night. The prophets Samuel, Daniel, and Zechariah, along with the apostle Paul, all name night as the time of their visitations, with Daniel and Zechariah reporting several nighttime visions or dreams.[7] Dickinson would have known the biblical texts which indicate that some dreams communicate to the sleeper a message from God.[8] The idea that prophetic inspiration comes through the form of graphic pictures from an unearthly world no doubt explains a biblical synonym for prophet, as a text from 1 Samuel assumes: the person "that is now called a Prophet was beforetime called a Seer" (1 Sam. 9:9).[9] The prophet John in the Book of Revelation exemplifies the intimate connection between seeing, on the one hand, and prophetically and poetically speaking for God, on the other; that figure's visions constitute his prophecy, which he also imagines as a scroll that he eats. Visions become words; they are divine truth as visual or as rhetorical expressions.

Moreover, the visions and dreams that the prophets of the Bible describe sometimes include auditory experiences (auditions); often the dreams are a combination of vision and audition, as in the account of the call of Isaiah. With neither visions nor auditions are the physical eyes or ears involved. Dickinson suggests about her own visionary eyes that they are not so much those "without our Head" (#1284) as those able to see beyond temporality and appearances. As we also see in Dickinson's poems, the visions and auditions seem so real and vivid to the receiver that they carry more significance than any event in the everyday world.

In Poem #1335, Dickinson affirms the power of dreams to teach her truth:

> Let me not mar that perfect Dream
> By an Auroral stain
> But so adjust my daily Night
> That it will come again.

The period of dreaming and visions is nighttime, a "purer" and more truthful state that is free of the "stains" which mar our perception by day. In #939, "What I see not, I better see—," daylight is a "jealous . . . interrupt[er]" (line 11) that mars the "perfectness" of the dream (line 12). It is important to understand that the dream is not merely a psychological part of Dickinson but a source of inspiration, understood as separate. For Dickinson, dreams are perfect not only because they present the poet ideal scenes of truth but because they depict with accuracy and power; they are more trustworthy than one's own thoughts.

In #939, the speaker asserts her preference for the dream state over her ordinary eyesight and for its aspect of encounter with an empowering Other:

What I see not, I better see—
Through Faith—my Hazel Eye
Has periods of shutting—
But, No lid has Memory—

For frequent, all my sense obscured
I equally behold
As someone held a light unto
The Features so beloved—

And I arise—and in my Dream—
Do Thee distinguished Grace—
Till jealous Daylight interrupt—
And mar thy perfectness—

If we read the poem as if there were a period after the first line (because lines terminated by dashes are not normally enjambments in Dickinson's verse), the poem expresses the speaker's choice of "Memory," acting through her dreams, over "Faith," mainly because memory here is involuntary and does not suffer from lapses of doubt, as faith does. In fact, the dream seems so real that the speaker actually turns in the last stanza to address the One (the inspirer?) who has "Features so beloved—" to her, calling him "Thee" in line 10, so imminent does he seem to her. As she describes, it is as if "someone held a light unto" him (line 7); the vision has yielded a figure more real to her than anything communicated by her "sense" (understood as either "senses" or as "common sense"), which she describes as "obscured" (line 5). Certainly, dreams in their perfectness and vividness can serve for this speaker as a source of inspiration. Poem #1670, "In Winter in my Room," similarly recounts an incident that seems so vivid and real to us that the last line comes as a surprise: "This was a dream—." In #518, "Her sweet Weight on my Heart a Night," the persona—this time, male—is unsure whether his desire was physically embodied or whether he was given a dream of his bride; the line between dream and reality is blurred.

For Dickinson, the dream world is so vivid that it even replaces faith, which must subsist on hope alone; this is also made clear in #518. A "Fiction"—that is, a dream—"supersed[es] Faith," the speaker asserts (line 11). This speaker points out that God is the author of both faith and "fiction," charitably giving "to All" what they need to believe, whether it be the faith or the dream (lines 9–10). Dickinson's speaker affirms the need for the dream: in this poem and others—such as #531, "We dream—it is good we are dreaming—"; #1376, "Dreams are the subtle Dower"; #1755, "To make a prairie it takes a clover and one bee"—the dream offers perfection, accuracy, power to the imagination. It offers inspiration.

Sometimes in this large cluster of poems, the divine visitor himself appears in the speaker's dream. Again, apparently, nighttime is the most conducive time for these visitations. But in #103, the speaker is only "half glad" when she experiences the dreams and the "peeping" emblematic of a vision (lines 4, 5). Such an experience brings her the din of stanza 2. Her inspirer or "King" may be mute, but he has powerful effects:

> I have a King, who does not speak—
> So—wondering—thro' the hours meek
> I trudge the day away—
> Half glad when it is night, and sleep,
> If, haply, thro' a dream, to peep
> In parlors, shut by day.
>
> And if I do—when morning comes—
> It is as if a hundred drums
> Did round my pillow roll,
> And shouts fill all my Childish sky,
> And Bells keep saying "Victory"
> From steeples in my soul!
>
> And if I dont—the little Bird
> Within the Orchard, is not heard,
> And I omit to pray
> "Father, thy will be done" today
> For my will goes the other way,
> And it were perjury!

The speaker may have access to the kingly figure at all times, but apparently, she cannot elicit information from him until nightfall, when she can see and hear him in her dreams. Curiously, there is a forbidden aspect to the speaker's acquisition of the king's knowledge: the opposition seems to come from the will of a conventional God the Father, who permits her to peer into divine matters or not as he pleases, including the experience of hearing a bird sing. And when she does not have a dream or vision, she has little motivation to pray, to acknowledge God's existence. In this poem and in others, the power behind her own prophetic power is depicted as parental, distant, even opaque, sometimes even as One who is frightening and inaccessible.[10] But the speaker has access to that power through her mediating "king," who is often, when she names him, Christ—gentle, accessible, both human and divine, enabling her to speak, and allied to the poet in his special treatment of her.

Still, Dickinson's speakers must be ever vulnerable to her inspiring mediator, always ready to receive his revelations. As is characteristic of the scriptural portraits of prophets, Dickinson's sense is that the poet does not so much choose to be inspired as she is assaulted by a sudden influx of divine signification. As she writes in #1055:

> The Soul should always stand ajar
> That if the Heaven inquire
> He will not be obliged to wait
> Or shy of troubling Her

In another poem, #1335, "Let me not mar that perfect Dream," the moment of inspiration is less polite; "the Power accosts" in a sudden, unexpected encounter (line 5). These two poems indicate that one must remain perpetually open to the sudden revelation of heavenly significance.

As all of these poems suggest, to speak under the auspices of an inspiring presence means to be chosen, singled out, given special status. Like the biblical prophets, the voice in Dickinson's poems presents itself as having a special relationship to this inspiring higher power. But Dickinson focuses on the idea of selection far more often and in more glorious terms in her poetry than the scriptural prophets do. It is in the cluster of poems that refer to her sense of selection that Dickinson comes closest to the self-congratulatory voice of her more secular romantic contemporaries, such as Emerson (but, as we also will find, she has a more profound sense than he does of the affliction she bears, a pattern that recalls the biblical prophets). For example, Dickinson describes her special selection as being "Baptized . . . Unto supremest name" as she is "Called to [her] Full"; she chooses with her "Will"—not involuntarily—to accept her prophetic task, she suggests in #508, "I'm ceded—I've stopped being Their's" (lines 8–11, 18). In some poems she portrays the special selection in the imagery of a nun set apart in her white garb (#271, "A solemn thing—it was—I said"). Quite often, she is a bride, "baptized" to this special status (#473, "I am ashamed—I hide—," line 27).

Unlike the biblical prophets, Dickinson portrays the king's calling of her in terms of heavenly marriage, not simply in terms of the prophet as a special servant of God, as we see in a marriage-to-divinity cluster of her poems: #473, "I am ashamed—I hide—"; #493, "The World—stands—solemner—to me—"; #506, "He touched me, so I live to know"; #508, "I'm ceded—I've stopped being Their's—"; #528, "Mine—by the Right of the White Election!"; #616, "I rose—because He sank—"; #1072, "Title divine—is mine!"; #1737, "Rearrange a 'Wife's' affection!" Through her speakers, she assumes a status for herself even higher than that of the biblical prophets and also, obviously, appropriate to her gender. She is the "betrothed" of the Emperor of Calvary, the ordinary self metaphorically dying to the higher prophetic self, which is "wed" to the Emperor whose truth she speaks:

> Title divine—is mine!
> The Wife—without the Sign!
> Acute Degree—conferred on me—
> Empress of Calvary!
> Royal—all but the Crown!
> Betrothed—without the swoon   (#1072, lines 1–6)

Although she demonstrates scorn for marriage in the temporal world (#199, #1737), she portrays her own divine, royal marriage to the king not in terms of dutiful subordination but as an elevation in rank. In her prophetic role, she has "the Right of the White Election," a status that is hers "by the Royal Seal" of the king, "here—in Vision—," that is, by virtue of her vision (#528, lines 1–2, 5). She is "Titled—Confirmed— / . . . long as Ages steal," assured of her place alongside her king for eternity (lines 7, 9).

Yet for some reason, unlike either her contemporaries or the male biblical prophets, Dickinson feels she must keep secret this status of "empress." One might speculate that her gender is the cause. After all, few people in her day would have encouraged either female prophecy or a woman's seizure of special status. Dickinson indicates in #1737, "Rearrange a 'Wife's' affection!" her sense both of burden and of triumph, at the same time framing those in a context of secrecy. In this poem and in others, in signifying her sense of selection she also employs metaphors that call our attention to her gender. Here, she is a wife, with particular female characteristics:

> Rearrange a "Wife's" affection!
> When they dislocate my Brain!
> Amputate my freckled Bosom!
> Make me bearded like a man!
>
> . . . .
>
> Burden—borne so far triumphant—
> None suspect me of the crown,
> For I wear the "Thorns" til *Sunset*—
> Then—my Diadem put on.
>
> Big my Secret but it's *bandaged*—
> It will never get away
> Till the Day its Weary Keeper
> Leads it through the Grave to thee.   (lines 1–4, 13–20)

It is only at "sunset," the time of dreams, that the speaker can begin to assume her rightful place as the wife of her inspirer. The poem is a defense of her betrothal to the king, a spiritual state that she feels called to maintain, renouncing marriage in the temporal world. Like Jesus the suffering servant, she endures the pain of thorns, which are transmuted to the glory of a "Diadem." She exchanges the pain of thorns for a diadem each night at sunset, passing from a state of suffering to one of chosenness and power. The freedom she enjoys in the nocturnal period of visionary inspiration portends the experience of absolute freedom she will know after death. As other scholars have pointed out, the diadem is her metaphorical badge of rank, a token of her marriage to the king, but most important, it is evidence of the transferral of information taking place between herself and the inspirer—between the physical and metaphysical worlds, the earthly and the heavenly.

Similarly, in another poem Dickinson figures herself as a "Queen" "wed—to Him—," with the effect that "the World—stands—solemner—to me—" as she feels the weight of being chosen (#493, lines 12, 2, 1). The symbol of her rank this time is "that perfect—pearl—," the sign of her "whiter Gift—within—" (lines 6, 10). As in "Conscious am I in my Chamber" (#679), the male figure in #493 is too beautiful to have a specific shape or posture: the similarity between the guest of #679 and the bridegroom of #493 would indicate that the kingly figure she hoped to marry through death—perhaps a symbolic death of renunciation of self—and her nocturnal informant are one and the same. The speaker in #493 indicates that she hopes the pearl will "prove" her "more angel" (line 9), or angelic, in the sense of being close to the godhead.

In the marital imagery in this poem and in others, we find a possible motivation for Dickinson's habit of wearing white. The angelic voice she finds herself possessing in #493 is the "whiter Gift." White is also the color of God's chosen, as figured in the Book of Revelation, in which marriage is also a dominant figure.[11] Like the biblical prophets who enhanced their messages by means of acted oracles—such as walking naked (Isaiah), smashing a potter's vessel (Jeremiah), or eating locusts and honey (John the Baptist)—Dickinson may have seen herself as demonstrating with her white clothing her eternal betrothal or marriage, a sign of her having been specially selected for her prophetic task. Whiteness is indicative of purity, of being set apart; the "pearl" in this poem and others signifies her betrothal—an appropriate gem to unite a pure king and queen—as well as her gift of poetry. Her poetic expression was her "pearl of great price," pursued at cost to herself as she, like the biblical prophets, endured misunderstanding, lack of appreciation or fame in her own lifetime, and even isolation. For Dickinson, to be a poet was to be a seer into the heart of things and a translator of these insights into words, which she indicated in #448, "This was a Poet—It is That," and #449, "I died for Beauty—but was scarce." To be this seer was to be the "Queen" chosen to experience the "munificence" of the inspirer, a special status indeed (#493, lines 11–12).

But, as I mentioned earlier, Dickinson's experience of prophecy led her to suggest continually that dedication to vision has its costs. It can be both terrifying and lonely. As the biblical prophets made plain in passages such as Jer. 20:7–18, the call to prophecy can mean both special calling and affliction. The biblical prophet typically bore scorn and reproach, "stigmatized as a madman by his contemporaries, and by some modern scholars, as abnormal," as one scholar describes it— a description also applicable to Dickinson.[12] Indeed, loneliness and misery are part of the prophetic task. Even Emerson, who rarely described his own suffering publicly, in "The Poet" wrote of the poet's isolation among his contemporaries by virtue of the truth he speaks and his art. This isolation was the classic situation of the Old Testament prophets in the midst of a hard-hearted Israel, and such was the situation of Christ. Dickinson's sense of empathy and identification with Jesus may well have been strengthened by this bond.

The price Dickinson sees as her payment for her elevation is solitude, the seclusion of her special selection. At times she champions solitude, as in #306, "The Soul's Superior instants," and #383, "Exhilaration—is within—." But she also knows what it is like to be seen as mad, to have the "madness" of the prophetic "sense" misunderstood. "Much Madness is divinest Sense," she counters in #435. In a later poem, she assents to the idea that perhaps, after all, she does not "have her senses"—"perhaps 'tis well they're not at Home," she says, because her inspirer is "liable with them," that is, the inspirer can manipulate them to give her a vision (#1284, "Had we our senses," lines 2, 4). Yet despite the affliction and loneliness she might suffer, she seems as compelled to speak as the scriptural prophets were.

Perhaps her compulsion to speak derives, at least in part, from a sense that her poetic gift or even her life itself will come to an end. If God ultimately is the fiery presence that keeps her poetry of prophecy alive, that energy might be withdrawn at some point, and she no longer would be able to speak. Yet she seems to believe that her poetry, like the prophecy of the Scriptures, will survive. Dickinson describes poets in an image that she perhaps derived from Emerson but that also carries biblical, prophetic associations, the light shining in the darkness:

> The Poets light but Lamps—
> Themselves—go out—
> The Wicks they stimulate—
> If vital Light
>
> Inhere as do the Suns—
> Each Age a Lens
> Disseminating their
> Circumference—   (#883)

Here, Dickinson identifies poets with their own "Light," or wisdom, which eventually will "go out." But she focuses on the hope that her poetic messages will shine like a light in the world, never dying. As a prophet, she can stimulate "Wicks," her listeners, with "vital light." She expresses confidence that the light, or wisdom, will persist in some form, reflected through the different lenses of succeeding "ages" or audiences. The wicks, or audiences, will themselves "disseminate" the light of her poetic wisdom into "each Age." It is no wonder that Dickinson sewed her poems into fascicles: they might be read one day by posterity, passed on to more and more readers.

A sense of divine inspiration is distinctive to the poet who understands her literature as prophecy. While experience may teach common wisdom, only a meeting with the divine can enable one to speak profound and lasting spiritual truth. But before we examine the genres that Dickinson favored for her transmission of wonder and wisdom, we should note that inspiration alone does not guarantee an audience's recognition of the truth-telling mode. A prophet requires an able audience to receive the transmission of truth. For the Old Testament prophets, Christ, and even the Protestant preachers, the prophetic stance not only involved the prophet's perception of truth but also oriented the listener to a position of spiritual receptivity to the prophecy.

Dickinson's understanding of audience recalls that assumed in the Bible. In a key cluster of poems, she indicates that her messages are, in a phrase Christ often used (Matt. 11:15; 13:43; Luke 14:35), for those "who have ears to hear":

> The Spirit is the conscious Ear.
> We actually Hear
> When We inspect—that's audible—
> That is admitted—Here—
>
> For other Services—as Sound—
> There hangs a smaller Ear
> Outside the Castle—that Contain—
> The other—only—Hear— (#733)

Merely "hearing" her words is inadequate, Dickinson suggests; one needs to listen with "the Spirit," the "smaller Ear" that "inspects" as it listens. She desires an able listener with "a rare Ear / Not too dull—" (#842, "Good to hide, and hear 'em hunt!"), for although it is "Good to know, and not tell" the truths illuminated to her by her kingly inspirer, it is "Best, to know and tell" the proper listener (#842, lines 5, 6). Some people hear, others do not, she points out in #1048, "Reportless Subjects, to the Quick." In this poem she contrasts the "Quick" and "the rest," that is, those who hear "Reportless Subjects" only as a foreign dialect. Whether the message is understood depends on the ability of the hearer, not the teller, a principle affirmed continually by Christ and the Old Testament prophets.[13] For Dickinson, poetry of prophecy is a gift recognized by the wise; it is a holy object, a communication from God. Poem #733 begins with an association of understanding with the spirit, but the location of the poem within the particular hearer is her conclusion.

The enigmatic and ambiguous qualities of Dickinson's poetry, such as the dashes that function as ellipses, obscure referents, and metaphors that are left unexplained, all serve to suggest a body of poetry directed to an audience attuned to listening closely. Her wisdom is not for the faint of heart who want only easily deciphered pronouncements. Envisioning herself as poetically inspired by a wondrous (if sometimes opaque or frightening) presence that looms behind her poetry, Dickinson seems to care less about her audience's appropriation of her art than about her own calling to speak wisdom. As we will see in the next chapter, that inspiration could result in prophetic genres both bizarre and uncannily appealing in their descriptions of experience beyond human ken.

5. Constructions of Genre and Self

As DICKINSON READERS have readily noticed, the poet's speakers assume a variety of voices, from the sarcastic to the doubtful and from the playful to the longing. Surely, the richness of Dickinson's poetry is due in great measure to the authenticity and immediacy of her voices. Not wanting to tamper with them, scholars rightly have resisted the temptation to try to reconcile the voices when they seem contradictory, opting instead to allow for the different moods and modes of the poet. Nonetheless, when we consider some of those patterns as genres instead of as individual voices carried through a number of poems, we discover a poet far less arbitrary in her selection of a voice and far more focused on a particular conception of poetry than may have been assumed. In both their formal and their tonal qualities, the biblical prophetic writings once again showed Dickinson, and show us, ways to think about poetic expression—this time, in terms of the genres that prophetic poetry can assume. Specifically, they may help explain Dickinson's interest in the voices of the traveler to eternity, the indictor, and the consoler, which together form a large portion of her poetry.

Let us first consider Dickinson's poems on pain and death. These poems provide an expansive portrait of nineteenth-century experiences of suffering alongside idiosyncratic commentaries on the afterlife. Viewed in another way, however, many of the poems can operate to provoke readers to consider their own position in the universe, especially as that position relates to God. When attuned to receive them as wisdom, we observe a genre deriving from the Scriptures: what we might call the travel literature of the Bible (travel through either time or space), which warns audiences of what may come. Most notably in the Book of Revelation but also in the writings of Isaiah, Ezekiel, Daniel, and other Old Testament figures, the prophets recorded experiences of visions that turned out to be narratives of their surreal travels. Their stories are not merely assertions about the future, although sometimes the prophets did such foretelling; rather, I refer here to dramatizations that include the prophet as a player in the events and scenes described.

Ezekiel, for example, records a visitation by "a likeness as the appearance of fire," who looks like fire from his waist down and glows like amber in his upper body (Ezek. 8:2). This individual, says Ezekiel, lifted the prophet up by his hair and carried him to Jerusalem (Ezekiel's home was in Babylon), where he touched ground by the north gate of the temple. Ezekiel goes on to recount in vivid detail both conversing with the mysterious figure and witnessing startling events in the temple—its desecration; the killing of idolaters; the glory of the Lord leaving the temple, accompanied by the departure of strange living creatures that had multiple faces and eyes (Ezekiel 8–10). The vision is one of several given to Ezekiel to warn and direct his contemporaries, whom the Lord describes to the prophet as people who have "eyes to see, and see not" and "ears to hear, and hear not: for they are a rebellious house" (Ezek. 12:2). Like Isaiah in chapters 40–66 and John in Revelation 4–22, Ezekiel recounts an experience of being projected into the future and returning from eternity to tell about it. His description is a prediction of the future, but it also functions as a warning and as wisdom to his audiences. In this particular case, Ezekiel is told by God at the end of his vision what to say to the people about his experience, but they would pay him little heed: he prophesied in 592 B.C., and the temple was destroyed in 586 B.C., just six years later.

Equally graphic are the eschatological experiences of Isaiah and John. Both speakers recount in compellingly sharp detail pictures of events to come, but neither prophet interprets his vision. We can see the same pattern in Dickinson's poetry. Isaiah speaks as one who has both conversed with the Lord and is himself filled with the Lord's voice, but he leaves pronouns undefined (for example, the "he" of Isaiah 52 and 53) and enigmatic images uninterpreted (such as "the wolf and the lamb shall feed together, and the lion shall eat straw like the bullock" in Isa. 65:25). In contrast, John's prophecy seems even more mysterious for its strong visual component. Dickinson favors John's method. Offering image after image of things to come, John describes visions that are essentially narratives about highly symbolic creatures, places, and objects—for instance, a throne in heaven surrounded by a rainbow, more thrones, and four strange living creatures that recall Ezekiel's vision (Revelation 4); a dragon whose tail sweeps stars out of the sky before he falls to the earth (Revelation 12); a woman who sits on a scarlet beast in a desert (Revelation 17). The pictures are vivid and the symbols recognizable—trumpets, horses, people—yet they are otherworldly in their details and in the contexts in which they occur. The prophet speaks of them with little emotion;

he describes them with a matter-of-fact tone that heightens their strangeness. Like Isaiah, John figures much more as a witness than as a player in his unearthly experience; it is as if he stands on the edge of mundane reality, looking over at a world beyond.

A number of Dickinson's poems capture these prophets' visionary emphases. Like her biblical models, Dickinson's speakers sometimes report from the extremities of experience; usually, they seem to come back from a place beyond death. In this sense, they offer a notable revision of the biblical pattern: instead of identifying the visions with the future of a community (the people of God, for the biblical prophets), Dickinson's speakers associate the visions with individual experience, usually death. Still, her travel literature can be as otherworldly and as vivid as that of the biblical prophets. Both her speakers and theirs are what Victor Turner discusses as "liminal *personae*"—they are "neither here nor there" but stand "betwixt and between the positions assigned and arraigned by law, custom, convention, and ceremonial."[1] From the position of liminality, these personae receive special information.

Like John and Isaiah in describing an eschatological vision, Dickinson's visionary speakers report in specific, concrete detail and focused imagery but do not try to interpret or make sense of the strange events. In #465, "I heard a Fly buzz—when I died—," the speaker rather matter-of-factly describes her death experience, including the odd association of color with the acoustical revelation ("Blue—uncertain stumbling Buzz—," line 13). As in the Book of Revelation, she allows her weird experience to stand unexplained, the strangeness of her perception gaining power from the reversal of the conventional, expected associations. For the liminal speakers of this poem and others such as #378, "I saw no Way—the Heavens were stitched"; #470, "I am alive, I guess"; and #800, "Two—were immortal twice—," the event is almost beyond the telling. Dickinson's speakers are absorbed in their experiences and seem to have little awareness of audience. Yet the poems, functioning like the Book of Revelation, serve as powerful reminders of the mysteriousness of life, death, and God; they call their readers to consider what lies beyond the visible world.

When Dickinson's figures speak from the extremities of experience, they often exhibit the biblical prophets' sense of time: the present is collapsed into the future.[2] As we saw in the books of Ezekiel and Revelation, the prophets sometimes adopted a backward-looking perspective. They would visit the future and then report on their experience, with the effect that the future would become the past. Likewise, in many poems Dickinson's speakers visit and report on what David T. Porter has called "the place of aftermath"—a term suggestive of the prophet's unique perspective, which we see in #378, "I saw no Way— the Heavens were stitched"; #414, " 'Twas like a Maelstrom, with a notch"; #470, "I am alive, I guess"; #599, "There is a pain—so utter"; #721, "Behind Me—dips Eternity"; #761, "From Blank to Blank"; #802, "Time feels so vast that were it not"; #856, "There is a finished feeling"; #963, "A nearness to Tremendousness"; #1046, "I've dropped my Brain—My Soul is numb"; #1231, "Somewhere upon the general Earth."[3] These poems, often understood as rejecting Christian notions of immortality because of their focus on death, may in fact closely approximate scriptural constructions of immortality. Both the scriptural prophets and Dickinson refused the exactions of synchronous time, which lends an enigmatic quality to the descriptions.

Dickinson celebrates the genre in Poem #160, "Just lost, when I was saved!" in which she unabashedly presents the paradoxes and ambiguities of the prophets' travel literature:

> Just lost, when I was saved!
> Just felt the world go by!
> Just girt me for the onset with Eternity,
> When breath blew back,
> And on the other side
> I heard recede the disappointed tide!
>
> Therefore, as One returned, I feel
> Odd secrets of the line to tell!
> Some Sailor, skirting foreign shores—
> Some pale Reporter, from the awful doors
> Before the Seal! . . .

There is an air of confidence in the verse, a tone of entitlement and privileged insight. She, like the biblical prophets, has returned from her near "onset with Eternity" with "odd secrets of the line to tell"— the "line" being the boundary between time and eternity, a measure of circumference where the two hemispheres meet. The speaker approaches the line from this side, the side of mortality, and returns safely. Like the biblical prophets who exposed the alternatives of human destiny, Dickinson may see the line as a "plumb line," the speaker "exploring the recesses of human possibility with John of Patmos in the Book of Revelation at 'the awful doors / Before the Seal!' "[4] Yet, although the speaker feels compelled to tell what she has learned about the line, she does not tell her "secrets" but allows the paradox of the first stanza to stand. Her wisdom is for those who have ears to hear the spiritual truth of the paradox, of being "lost" when one is "saved." The poem is a celebration of the journey to and from the "line," where there are "things to see . . . / Unscrutinized by Eye—" and things "by Ear unheard" (lines 13–15). And it is here that we see another departure from the biblical prophets' treatment of the genre: Dickinson's speaker has been so moved by the experience that she vows, "Next time, to stay!" (line 12). Her travel literature does more than communicate warning or wisdom; it flaunts the wonder of traversing the boundaries of ordinary human experience.

As Sharon Cameron points out, the most eschatological indication of boundary is death, which "epitomizes the problem of boundary" because it is the "severest manifestation" of boundary and of its potential obstacles to a poet.[5] But the very existence and shape of the biblical travel literature gave Dickinson an opportunity (and perhaps even encouraged her) to consider experiences of crossing the border. If death is understood as the edge between time worlds, then Dickinson, seeing herself as a prophet, may have felt an obligation to envision a trek to the other side—even when that experience may have terrified her.

Poem #414, "'Twas like a Maelstrom, with a notch," offers us a glimpse of such an experience. It takes on the visionary qualities of the biblical prophets' poetry in the vividness of the details, the strangeness of the imagery, and the perspective that is all at once from the past, present, and future:

> 'Twas like a Maelstrom, with a notch,
> That nearer, every Day,
> Kept narrowing it's boiling Wheel
> Until the Agony
>
> Toyed coolly with the final inch
> Of your delirious Hem—
> And you dropt, lost,
> When something broke—
> And let you from a Dream—
>
> As if a Goblin with a Gauge—
> Kept measuring the Hours—

Until you felt your Second
Weigh, helpless, in his Paws—

And not a Sinew—stirred—could help,
And sense was setting numb—
When God—remembered—and the Fiend
Let go, then, Overcome—

As if your Sentence stood—pronounced—
And you were frozen led
From Dungeon's luxury of Doubt
To Gibbets, and the Dead—

And when the Film had stitched your eyes
A Creature gasped "Repreive"!
Which Anguish was the utterest—then—
To perish, or to live?

In the first stanza, the concreteness of the experience suggests a present time frame, the "Agony" of the speaker remaining very immediate despite the metaphoric description. The agony even "toys coolly" with her "Hem," a detail of present, immediate experience. But at line 9, we immediately are plunged into a different time and world: goblins and fiends are not of temporality but of a time beyond life, immortality. Indeed, the poem is an exploration of the border between life and death, the pain of the temporal world contrasted to that of the atemporal, as the final question indicates. The speaker collapses the boundaries between present and future, refusing, as did the biblical prophets, to identify life with synchronous time. Death is not the terminus of experience, Dickinson affirms in so many of her poems on death and immortality, but a middle ground from which the speaker can look into another world and time. In poems such as #414, Dickinson rejects the boundaries between experiences, something rarely done in the evangelical poetry of her period; she blurs the distinctions between the now and the yet-to-come, or the eternal. The strategy gives her poetry, as it does the biblical prophetic writings, an enigmatic quality and forces the reader to sort out the temporal and atemporal referents.

Yet, the poem is not an exercise in solipsism. As a poem of her prophetic literature, #414 also calls audiences to wise reflection. In this poem, we are left to ponder for ourselves the boundary—or lack of it—between life and death. We are invited to consider that the atemporal world may present its own "anguish"—an idea that directly challenges easy conceptions of the afterlife as a pie-in-the-sky existence after death.

Genre can work to challenge audiences to achieve greater insight, even when the voice in the poem is uncertain, even fearful, and altogether absorbed in the immediacy and emotion of an experience. The mere telling of the experience can be an occasion for wisdom; but the biblical prophets offered Dickinson an even more pointed means to call audiences to vital faith: they showed her a poetic genre that emphasizes indictment. When Dickinson adopts this mode, we discover a voice impatient with the hypocrisy and superficiality she detected in the people around her. Her experiments with this genre spawned poems strikingly unlike much of the women's poetry of her time, which often did not go beyond conformist lyrics or simple moral statements. "To simulate—is stinging work— / To cover what we are . . . / For their—sake—not for Our's—," Dickinson writes in #443, "I tie my Hat—I crease my Shawl—" (lines 19–20, 24). Obviously, Dickinson found "simulation" of expected cultural role models difficult, but the biblical poetry gave her access to a conception of the poet different from the nineteenth-century one she knew to be constrained by gender and dogma. The Old and New Testament models gave her justification to try out imaginative poetic personae that were radically unconventional for a nineteenth-century woman.

When the biblical prophets spoke as indictors, they exposed and condemned the corruption they saw, giving little regard to the possibility (or the reality) of their audience's rejection of them. Their prophetic purpose was not self-expression or the purgation of emotions but communication of warning and true spirituality. Characteristically, the style that they employed was charged with agitation as they confronted nonacceptance and indicted their audience. The prophet, as Abraham J. Heschel describes, is "an iconoclast, challenging the apparently holy, revered, and awesome. Beliefs cherished as certainties, institutions endowed with supreme sanctity, [the prophet] exposes as scandalous pretensions."[6] The prophet may even sound blasphemous, Heschel points out, citing Jer. 6:20. Jeremiah, Isaiah, Amos, Hosea, and Micah, to name a few, as well as Christ, all condemned the substitution of conventional religious practices for true spirituality: of rite and ceremony for justice and kindness, of sacrifices and offerings for personal holiness.

For the prophets, the rituals of worship, however costly and splen-

did, could never be an acceptable substitution for obedience to ultimate moral demands. Isaiah, for example, frequently lambastes his
audience for worship that is hateful to God; he rails against people's
hollow pretensions, for instance, women who are obsessed with dress,
decked with costly ornaments, and enamoured of luxury. When Dickinson adopts this role of iconoclast, she, too, challenges standard cultural expressions of religion. She exposes the lack of spiritual vitality of
her day as it is expressed by "ladies" obsessed with dress and manners,
not redemption (#401, "What Soft—Cherubic Creatures—"); in the
dry sermons of preachers who fail as "warbling tellers" of spirituality
(#1545, "The Bible is an antique Volume—"); and even in the un-
examined use of an antique religious text "Written by faded Men"
(#1545, line 2). Like the biblical prophets, she evaluated the terms of
conventional religion and found them lacking, pointing out the short-
comings of nineteenth-century worship, even at the risk of sounding
blasphemous.

Poem #241 stands as a sharp comment on the hypocrisy Dickinson
saw in her contemporaries. The speaker expresses preference for the
truth that shows itself in human pain and death, truth that often
indicates the falsity of people's everyday demeanor and actions. She
declares:

> I like a look of Agony,
> Because I know it's true—
> Men do not sham Convulsion,
> Nor simulate, a Throe—   (lines 1–4)

as if to say that she can be certain of one's sincerity only when that person is in the throes of pain. One might guess that she saw hypocrisy
running rampant in her culture; she could believe only the experiences
of pain and death, which are "Impossible to feign" (line 6). She could
not trust the practitioners of Christianity, as #243, "I've known a
Heaven, like a Tent—," suggests. In that poem, the revivalists with
their "Shows" are here one day, gone the next. Religion seems like a
traveling circus, a carnival that "pluck[s] up it's stakes, and disap-
pear[s]" (line 3). For Dickinson's speaker, heaven should be permanent, not transient like a migratory bird (line 14). Over and over,
Dickinson exploited the genre to speak out, directly or by suggestion,
against the inconsistencies and superficiality of her culture.

Able to see beyond appearances and the shallowness of much of
nineteenth-century institutionalized religion, Dickinson could write

99

Poem #324, "Some keep the Sabbath going to Church—," asserting her preference for the pure religion she found "at Home." In this poem she speaks against the confusion of rite and ceremony with true religion, as the Old Testament prophets did. The speaker's religion does not depend on maintaining conventions or proper appearance—going to church or wearing a "Surplice"—but on listening to the preaching of God, whom she comically identifies as "a noted Clergyman" as if to say that her contemporaries regard Him as being only on a par with the most eloquent, interesting preachers of her day (lines 5, 9). For her, the sermon of the God who resides in her orchard, although it be short, results in redemption if it is properly attended to. Her redemption is of the here and now, not the otherworldliness that her more conventional Christian contemporaries look forward to "getting . . . at last" (line 11): the speaker is in "heaven" already, Dickinson implies, the heaven constructed by her orchard and bobolink as she listens to "God's sermon." Her religion is unconventional to the point of unorthodoxy, but its purity is enough to get her to her own kind of "heaven."

Such purity contrasts sharply with that of one kind of preacher she found in her day, as she describes in #1207: the minister whom she describes as "preaching on 'Breadth' till it argued him narrow." In contrast to the pure Sabbath that she keeps staying at home underneath her orchard, the worship that the preacher of #1207 exemplifies is artificial, lacking the simplicity and purity of Jesus. This preacher's sophistication would dazzle simple, innocent Jesus. Like the false prophets of the Old Testament, the preacher's own messages "proclaim him a Liar—," giving him away as one not to be believed (line 3).

Yet, like the emphases of biblical prophets, Dickinson's focus is not exclusively chastisement. Behind the austerity of the biblical prophets lies compassion for humankind: "almost every [biblical] prophet," Heschel describes, "brings, consolation, promise, and the hope of reconciliation along with censure and castigation."[7] The biblical prophets typically began with indictment, yet they concluded with messages of consolation and statements of simple truths. Similarly, the major part of Dickinson's prophetic message does not consist in indictment but in speaking consolation and truth as she sees it. Certainly, consolation for our ignorance in a fallen world is an art in which Dickinson has had few equals. Like Isaiah with his "Comfort, comfort ye my people," Dickinson's prophetic voice is one that is compassionate because "acquainted with grief" (Isa. 40:1; 53:3). Her verse is frequently able to console because she has confronted the extremities of experience and the realm beyond the grave. Like the biblical prophets, she does not sentimentalize the horror and emotional pain of death; death is real, an end to life as we know it. Yet, consolation is possible because, although she may question and doubt, she also hopes and desires, the encounter with death enabling her to return to her actual, living moment with an enhanced perception of life's value. Dickinson may risk despair in her perception of death, but it is seldom ultimate despair. Death points her toward life, causing her to cherish life.

In this view of death, Dickinson adopted the role of the consoling prophet who has suffered yet can offer wisdom, insight, and hope, even in the midst of pain and suffering. Consolation literature was an important part of nineteenth-century American culture, but Dickinson's conscientious production of consolation went beyond the conventions pursued in her time, as she avoided trite sentimentality and shared the pain of the sufferer. Although in some poems she revealed only the simple truth that pain and suffering can obliterate any other reality for the sufferer—as in #341, "After great pain, a formal feeling comes—," and #599, "There is a pain—so utter—"—in other poems she looked past the tragedy of the moment to offer encouragement, as in #548, "Death is potential to that Man," and #561, "I measure every Grief I meet."[8] In these poems she often maintained faith for others, for instance, saying to the Norcross cousins with firmness in her role as consoler, "God made no act without a cause" (#1163, line 1). Porter, drawing attention to Dickinson's "lifelong role as a consoler," postulates that "the words of consolation, if not in fact the faith itself, by sustaining others was no doubt a way of assuaging her ignorance."[9] Dickinson's role as wisdom giver led her to insights that rendered her less "ignorant" than empathetic, as she attempted to comfort even herself with her prophetic words.

As early as Poem #2, "There is another sky," we see Dickinson adopting the prophetic role of consoler, in this poem providing consolation in a context of humor. Here, she tries to lure her brother, Austin, back to Amherst from the harsh environs of Boston, where he had gone to study law. Deliberately setting up the expectation of a conventional, heavenly consolation, she writes:

> There is another sky,
> Ever serene and fair,
> And there is another sunshine,
> Though it be darkness there;

Never mind faded forests, Austin,
Never mind silent fields—
Here is a little forest,
Whose leaf is ever green;
Here is a brighter garden,
Where not a frost has been;
In its unfading flowers
I hear the bright bee hum;
Prithee, my brother,
Into *my* garden come!

As Douglas Anderson points out, the strategy of consolation here "is roughly the same as that which Bradstreet employed in 1666," in, for example, "Verses on the Burning of Our House": "a permanent world waits to comfort us for the losses we experience in the present, painfully mutable one."[10] Dickinson's poem, of course, turns at line 7 to humor Austin. Yet, by inviting him into her own garden, she shows us the deep importance she places on human affections, which she saw as consolatory, a heavenly refuge. She presents a lure for Austin that is not so much the beauty of the garden with its "unfading flowers" and leaves that are "ever green" but her own vision, as the creator of the garden. The "*my*" seems to point less to possession and more to the contrast of what her prophetic vision can imagine of eternity with the mutability of nature's garden. For Dickinson, earthly love is often interchangeable with transcendent or heavenly love.[11] While the (male) canonical prophets of the Bible base their consolation solely on God's comfort and love—and the divine ultimate vindication of God's people at the end of time—she, as a woman, sees sisterly comfort and love as equally consoling, if not more so.

This form of consolation appears often in her poetry, the speaker in #2 and in many other poems emphasizing the comfort of poetic vision, earthly love, and friendship as a replacement for faith. Dickinson's speakers, in both her letters and her poems, often adopt the consolatory role of offering their presence to the sufferer, sharing in the pain and even the doubt. She takes this theme of the biblical prophets and shapes it according to her own context and view of faith, rejecting the prophets' consolatory emphasis on a hopeful vision of a glorious time to come (as in Isaiah 66) but sharing their voice of comfort and concern for human pain. Her letter to the Norcross cousins on her mother's death remains one of her masterpieces of self-consolation, her strength emerging from her doubt:

> She was scarcely the aunt you knew. The great mission of pain had been ratified—cultivated to tenderness by persistent sorrow, so that a larger mother died than had she died before. There was no earthly parting. She slipped from our fingers like a flake gathered by the wind, and is now part of the drift called "the infinite."
>
> We don't know where she is, though so many tell us.
>
> I believe we shall in some manner be cherished by our Maker—that the One who gave us this remarkable earth has the power still farther to surprise that which He has caused. . . .
>
> I cannot tell how Eternity seems. It sweeps around me like a sea. . . . Thank you for remembering me. (*L*, 3:749–50)

Throughout her letters and poems, Dickinson struggled with an incomprehensible world, often arriving at a discourse of great consolatory strength, as in this letter to Louise and Francis Norcross.

We hear her consolatory voice in poems such as #610, "You'll find—it when you try to die—"; #993, "We miss Her, not because We see—"; #1308, "The Day she goes"; and #255, "To die—takes just a little while—," as well as in, among others, the two letters to Thomas Wentworth Higginson on the occasion of his wife's death; the series of letters to her friend Maria Whitney, who poignantly felt newspaper editor Samuel Bowles's death; and a letter each to Mrs. Bowles and her friend Richard Mather when their spouses died (*L*, 2:590–92, 594; 602–03; 599; 594–95). To Higginson she sent the first stanza of #1399 ("Perhaps they do not go so far") as a consolatory poem, later sending the entire poem to her cousins Martha and Harriet Dickinson after their father died. She consoles Higginson by saying that "to be human is more than to be divine, for when Christ was divine, he was uncontented till he had been human" (*L*, 2:592), and she points out her ability to console him: "The Wilderness is new—to you. Master, let me lead you" (*L*, 2:590). Like the biblical prophets, she has visited the extremities of experience and has come back whole, although she may still lack explanation for what she has seen, especially the mystery of the darkness of this world—the pain, the death, the suffering. Neither did the biblical prophets attempt to explain these mysteries. The belief that Dickinson and the prophets share is the idea that consolation *is* possible. She sees it as her role, as prophet and wisdom giver, to offer that consolation and comfort, as she suggests in Poem #544, "The Martyr Poets—did not tell." "Martyr Poets," she says—and we can infer her inclusion of herself in this category—" . . . wrought their Pang in syllable— / That when their mortal name be numb— / Their mortal fate—encourage Some—" (lines 1–4). Like the biblical prophets, she offers in her "Art—the Art of Peace—" (line 8).

As noted most clearly by Emerson in the "Divinity School Address," Dickinson's period in religious history appeared to be one ripe for prophecy—for both indictment and a renewed spirituality. In the Old Testament, prophets such as Elijah, Amos, Hosea, Isaiah, Ezekiel, and Zechariah spoke during periods of religious decline, warning people of the doom that would await them if they failed to repent of sin. Christ, too, spoke as a prophet in a time of spiritual deadness, presenting a vital religion at odds with the dry formalism of the pharisees, who were concerned more with rite and duty than with true devotion. Dickinson's nineteenth-century America paralleled those historical situations, as both Puritanism and Unitarianism were declining in their emotional force, leaving a spiritual vacuum with worn-out forms of religion. It is not surprising that Emerson would rise up as a prophet, speaking against shallow religious formalism in the "Divinity School Address" and calling at the end of the address for a preacher-prophet—or "teacher," as he styled the messianic figure. This "teacher," according to Emerson, would speak oracles of spiritual truth and revelation as the Hebrew prophets and Christ had done.[12] Dickinson shared the prophetic concern for spiritual vitality, speaking moral chastisement as well as messages of spiritual truth. Both Emerson and Dickinson seem to have seen preaching as vital enough to retain; that it need not be totally abandoned, as Emerson indicated in the "Divinity School Address" and Dickinson showed in her adoption of prophetic, preacherly rhetorical structures, as we saw earlier. Yet, other aspects of Dickinson's Judeo-Christian upbringing also revealed to her their potential for spiritual energy, including the less preacherly genres of traditional prophecy. Rising up as a prophet in a time needing spiritual revitalization, Dickinson evaluated the terms of her theological heritage and found them wanting, even when, ironically, she found in that tradition rhetorical devices, voices, and genres suitable for her own prophetic poetry.

Dickinson undoubtedly was aware of the theological implications of her literary revisions of Judeo-Christian prophecy. Exploiting the Bible to find models of spiritual legitimacy, she rewrote Scripture according to her own spiritual vision. She acknowledged the emotional force of the Bible through her adoption of its genres—the literature of the liminal personae and the roles of indictor, consoler, and, as Chapter 9 discusses more pointedly, truth teller. At the same time, like many of her literary contemporaries, she questioned the authority of the Bible. She reworked the biblical genres within a new theological and aesthetic framework to arrive at a wisdom or prophecy based on her own vision and authority (a wisdom we focus on in Chapter 9). As we have seen in this chapter, the categories of scriptural prophecy still had relevance for her. She would breathe life into them through her innovations upon the rhetorical techniques of prophecy, the subject of the next chapter.

6. Scriptural Rhetoric and Poetry

Dickinson's manipulation of aspects of the Judeo-Christian prophetic tradition necessarily led her to consider the possibilities inherent in the rhetorical strategies of the Bible. The idea that poetry, as opposed to oratory, could be a vehicle of prophecy she knew from her classical training. She also saw religious vision expressed in the poetry of her female contemporaries, however limited and conventional that literature appeared. But it was the Bible that offered her the most powerful model of the convergence of the roles of poet and prophet. To be sure, according to tradition, the scriptural prophets originally gave their wisdom orally, acting as preachers to their contemporaries; the spoken word was central to their task. But their oracles were recorded in the Scriptures in recognizable literary forms: "as a song or dirge, a hymn or a prayer, an argument or a dialogue, a parable or an allegory, an exhortation or a question, a vision or action"—always some "concise and rhythmical" form.[1] We find in the Bible models for the variety of forms in Dickinson's poetry: psalms or hymns (her poetry frequently following Isaac Watts's hymn meter, as in #712, "Because I could not stop for Death—"), prayers (#279, "Tie the Strings to my Life, My Lord"), dialogues (#417, "It is dead—Find it—"), stories (#59, "A little East of Jordan"), exhortations (#832, "Soto! Explore thyself!"), and visions (#414, "'Twas like a Maelstrom, with a notch"). But even more significant, we find in the scriptural prophetic writings models for some of the most important and distinctive rhetorical devices of her poetry, devices that contribute to the memorable, striking poetic voice for which she is known: the devices of parallelism, aphorism, and paradox. The rhythm and artistry of Dickinson's poems and of the biblical prophets' messages are attained in surprisingly similar ways.

It is not surprising that Dickinson would have seen the enabling possibilities for her poetry that the rhetoric of the scriptural prophetic writings suggested, when we consider that the Old Testament prophetic writings constitute the largest body of poetry in the Bible. Add to that portion the Gospels, which contain the wise sayings of Christ, and we have a very large part of the biblical canon that offers literary models of prophecy. Considered by Protestant theologians, as well as by Emerson and others, to be a prophet or wisdom giver, Christ continued in his sayings many of the rhetorical strategies adopted by the earlier prophets. Dickinson was a student of rhetoric, as we know from lists of her textbooks.[2] Since she was a poet, we can guess that she paid particular attention to the rhetorical strategies used by the poets of the Bible. One scholar mentions Dickinson's particular interest in the Book of Proverbs, Christ's parables, and the Book of Revelation—all writings in which wisdom and poetry converge.[3]

Dickinson's generation recognized the poetic nature of the biblical prophetic writings, because of the 1753 discovery of the Hebrew meter by Robert Lowth. Although biblical scholars before Lowth had noticed the paired lines in many of the biblical writings, it was he who established the general framework of the modern critical approach to the parallelism of biblical poetry, showing that the Hebrew meter lay not in a regularity of accented syllables but in a particular type of paired lines. Moreover, Lowth radically asserted the connection between biblical poetry (such as that found in the wisdom literature) and prophecy. Previous rhetoricians had argued a sharp distinction, but Lowth demonstrated that the prophetic writings shared many of the characteristics of biblical poetry. As he conclusively showed, biblical prophecy indeed was poetry, a notion that certainly appealed to Dickinson. Not only did the prophecy contain a kind of "meter" in its peculiar kinds of parallel lines, but these writings also included figurative language and showed "sublimity" in style, according to Lowth, the last of which was especially important in setting it apart as poetry. Such sublimity, he explained, is expressed in the "sententious" quality of the Hebrew prophetic poetry; one of the primary differences between classical and Hebrew poetry that Lowth emphasized was the brief, proverblike quality of the lines in the latter, a form ideally suited to inculcating wisdom. For Lowth, the proverbial form seemed so pervasive that "the sententious style . . . I define to be the primary characteristic of the Hebrew poetry, as being the most conspicuous and comprehensive of all . . . pervad[ing] the whole of the poetry of the Hebrews."[4] This aphoristic form obviously appealed to Dickinson, who used it constantly in her own poetry. She found it, as the Hebrews did, an apt means by which to express an intense, memorable thought aimed at the spiritual improvement of humanity.

"This World is not Conclusion," Dickinson's speaker asserts in #501. She ends the poem with another proverbial statement that subtly varies the initial proposition and thereby challenges readers to a more complex spiritual insight: "Narcotics cannot still the Tooth / That nibbles at the soul—." Dickinson uses the prophetic rhetorical devices to convey both orthodox and unorthodox messages, often, as here, in the same poem. The poem begins with a proposition that sounds like dogma—and the inclusion of the period at the end of the line adds weight to the sentence—but ends with an equally weighty epigrammatic application of the full implications of the introduction. The afterlife, Dickinson suggests, is so other, so mysterious, that one is left with doubt and uncertainty about the nature of it and perhaps even about one's own desire to go there. As in other poems, here she includes biblical images and allusions but turns them to her own ends. Dickinson finds the prophetic devices and voice empowering means to articulate a vision that goes beyond the simplistic (as she sees it) dogma of her day to include the emotional experiences of theological tenets. The device of the proverb, usually understood as a vehicle to transmit conventional wisdom, becomes a powerful expression of challenge.

Although it was not the nineteenth-century American rhetoricians but, rather, nineteenth-century German scholars who most effectively elaborated on the literary qualities of the biblical prophetic writings—such as paradox, which Dickinson also employs—the popular rhetoric books and theological treatises of Dickinson's day disseminated Lowth's findings in antebellum America and advanced the notion of the biblical prophecies as poetry. Hugh Blair's immensely popular *Lectures on Rhetoric and Belles Lettres* included a lecture on the poetry of the Bible, a summary of Lowth. Blair urged that "all writers who attempt the sublime, might profit much, by imitating . . . the style of the Old Testament [poetry]."[5] Commentaries on the prophetic books, such as Albert Barnes's *Notes, Critical, Explanatory, and Practical, on the Book of Isaiah* (1844), also perpetuated Lowth's work. Barnes even recommended to his readers Lowth's 1778 translation of Isaiah, which captured the parallelism of the lines in their arrangement on the page. By the time that Dickinson penned her first poem in 1850, the idea that the biblical prophecies were poetry was widely acknowledged in America, and the movement to study the Bible's literary qualities was well underway. Although the movement would not reach its pinnacle in America until the arrival of the twentieth century, Lowth and his successors did much to direct Dickinson's generation to reading the Bible as literature. As she listened to oral readings of Scripture by her father and the Amherst ministers and studied the biblical poetic prophecies on her own, Dickinson undoubtedly was sensitive to the particular literary qualities of the Bible, noticing the techniques of parallelism, proverb, and paradox in the Old and New Testament prophetic utterances as these served the larger goal of expressing a spiritual vision.

Dickinson regularly adopted the prophets' parallel structure and the pulsating rhythm that it gives to the biblical poetry. Central to the Old Testament prophetic poetry, the Hebrew parallelism establishes a rhythmic ebb and flow; it is the source of the simplicity of the biblical style. Separation of a larger idea into two half-verses that together represent a unit of rhythm demands a simplicity of structure. These two half-verses form two brief clauses of a relatively short sentence— "A is so, and what's more, B," James L. Kugel describes the pattern, as can be seen in Isa. 10:21: "The remnant shall return, / even the remnant of Jacob, unto the mighty God." Drawing on Lowth, Kugel summarizes biblical metrics thus: "B, by being connected to A—carrying it further, echoing it, defining it, restating it, contrasting with it, *it does not matter which*—has an emphatic 'seconding' character, and it is this, more than any aesthetic of symmetry or paralleling, which is at the heart of biblical parallelism."[6] Each biblical half-verse, if not a complete sentence, is at least a complete idea—a technique that encouraged the simple juxtaposition of ideas rather than subordination with participial phrases, subordinate clauses, and climactic periods. Dickinson's simplicity of style derives in part from this biblical style. The biblical prophetic poetry gains its rhetorical effect by abrupt, concise statements, as does Dickinson's poetry.

As Murray Roston points out, a significant effect of the simplicity of the prophetic parallelisms is the concrete suggestiveness of biblical imagery, "which rarely alludes adjectivally but draws, as it were, a tangible simile."[7] With only the few words of a half-verse to express an idea, Roston explains, the poet-prophet had to reduce the image to a vividly concise picture and compensate for the lack of detail by the sharpness of the comparison. The result is brilliantly focused imagery, as Lowth had noticed: "And in that day it shall come to pass, that the glory of Jacob shall be made thin, and the fatness of his flesh shall wax lean" (Isa. 17:4). Dickinson's short, rhythmic lines achieve the same effect: "The Soul selects her own Society— / Then—shuts the Door—" (#303). Following the model of the biblical prophets—and, subsequently, the orthodox preachers—Dickinson wrote condensed verse that contained vivid, distinctly focused pictures (in contrast to the generalized abstractions of much poetry written in her time—for instance, Emerson's poems or the evangelical verses of the gift books). Her verse, like that of the prophets, employs simple, direct images and the language of common people, free from artificiality of diction:

> Much Madness is divinest Sense—
> To a discerning Eye—
> Much sense—the starkest Madness—
> 'Tis the Majority
> In this, as All, prevail—
> Assent—and you are sane—
> Demur—you're straightway dangerous—
> And handled with a Chain—   (#435)

As in this characteristic Dickinson poem, which expresses the traditional idea of prophetic ecstasy or "madness" as yielding divine truth, the simplicity of style and the pulsating feel of the biblical poetry and of Dickinson's verses give the lines in each a distinctive emotional impulse. The emotional charge of Dickinson's poetry expresses a heartfelt intensity of vision that lies at the center of the prophetic tradition.

With its pauses and short, pulsing lines, often set in an antiphonal parallelism, the biblical poetry achieves a rhythm and an emotional intensity essentially closer to Dickinson's romantic poetry than to neoclassical poetry. The biblical prophet-poets provided Dickinson a model of poetry that expressed emotional involvement through the vivid, particularized images, the rhythmic parallelism admirably suited to the emotional intensity. "The mountains skipped like rams, and the little hills like lambs," the psalmist wrote, expressing the awe and fear of creatures in God's presence (Ps. 114:4). Dickinson's poetry achieves much the same effect, through the similarly vivid imagery and pulsating rhythm: "The Dust did scoop itself like Hands— / And threw away the Road" (#824, "The Wind begun to knead the Grass—," lines 7–8). The undulatory rhythm of the short lines with their necessarily precise images enhances the emotionality.

The parallelism of Hebrew prophetic poetry, occurring repeatedly in the oracles of Isaiah, Jeremiah, Amos, and the other Old Testament prophets, operates regularly in syntactic constructions to hold the verse together. Dickinson drew frequently on this technique of pairing to structure her own verses, as in #685: "Not 'Revelation'—'tis—that waits, / But our unfurnished eyes—." As David T. Porter points out (though without connecting the practice to scriptural prophecy), "The most basic of all Dickinson's units of construction is the two-line sentence, discernible when we look into the makeup of almost every poem. Two-liners are the way she makes her meanings."[8] In examining her scraps and fragments, Porter found that many contained two lines only; sometimes two such scraps were joined by a straight pin to form a quatrain. This practice suggests that she consciously composed in two-line units, the form of the biblical poetry. The pairings are omnipresent, and readers often parse syntax, movement, and meaning in her poetry by this arrangement.

Part of the rhythm of the Hebrew poetry—and, I argue, of Dickinson's poetry—derives from the brief pause that occurs between the two half-verses, the brevity of the pause reinforcing the connectedness of the two lines. The pause thus operates to give the lines both logic and rhythm, as the second line echoes, contrasts with, or carries further the first line. We see this pattern in Dickinson's poetry when she adopts the antithetical and the synonymous parallelism forms of the prophetic writings, which, along with synthetic parallelism, undergird the pulsating rhythm of the biblical poetry.[9] In the antithetical parallelism of the Bible, the second line completes the first by stating an idea that loosely expresses contrast, as in the song of the prophet Deborah:

> So let all thine enemies perish, O Lord:
> but let them that love him be as the sun when he goeth
> forth in his might. (Judg. 5:31)

Likewise, Dickinson often shapes her poetry with this device, as in #623, "It was too late for Man—." In a structure similar to the biblical poetry, the second line of each pair (lines 2 and 4) provides an idea contrasting with that of each first line (lines 1 and 3):

> It was too late for Man—
> But early, yet, for God—
> Creation—impotent to help—
> But Prayer—remained—Our Side—

We can see antithetical parallelism operating also in, among other poems, #244, "It is easy to work when the soul is at play"; #381, "A Secret told—"; #415, "Sunset at Night—is natural—"; #686, "They say that 'Time assuages'—"; and #698, "Life—is what we make it—."[10]

More frequently, as seems also to be the case in the scriptural prophetic writings, Dickinson uses synonymous parallelism. In the synonymous parallelism of the prophetic writings, the second line restates the main point of the first as it advances the idea:

> Seek ye the Lord while he may be found,
>   call ye upon him while he is near.   (Isa. 55:6)

This type of parallelism also appears in Dickinson's poetry:

> No Notice gave She, but a Change—
> No Message, but a Sigh—   (#804)

> Banish Air from Air—
> Divide Light if you dare—   (#854)

As in these examples, Dickinson sometimes arranges the parallelism between two lines, like the biblical models. She may also arrange a parallelism in four lines, treating a two-line phrase as if it were a single line, as #510, "It was not Death, for I stood up":

> It was not Death, for I stood up,
>   And all the Dead, lie down—
> It was not Night, for all the Bells
>   Put out their Tongues, for Noon.

The echoing of the lines is clear, the second pair repeating the syntax while reiterating and advancing the idea of the first. Synonymous parallelism occurs in two- or four-line pairings in such poems as #221, "It can't be 'Summer'!"; #222, "When Katie walks . . ."; #291, "How the old Mountains drip with Sunset"; #543, "I fear a Man of frugal Speech—"; #788, "Joy to have merited the Pain"; #893, "Drab Habitation of Whom?"; #1297, "Go slow, my soul, to feed thyself"; #1370, "Gathered into the Earth"; and #1375, "Death warrants are supposed to be." Dickinson's adoption of this aspect of Hebrew poetry gives her verse a pulsating rhythm and a simplicity similar to that found in the biblical prophetic writings.[11]

In the Bible, the synonymous parallelism structure also often occurs as a refrain, as in the many "woes" in the Book of Isaiah: for example, "Woe to the rebellious children, saith the Lord, that take counsel, but not of me" (Isa. 30:1). Similarly, Dickinson's parallelism sometimes operates as a refrain, achieving the symmetry of syntax found in the biblical refrains. Poem #23, "I had a guinea golden—," shows such parallelism:

> I had a guinea golden—
> I lost it in the sand—
>
> I had a crimson Robin—
>
> . . . .
> I had a star in heaven—

Another example showing parallelism between stanzas is #453, "Love—thou art high—," in which the syntax is repeated in the first lines of the stanzas: "Love—thou art high—," "Love—thou art deep—," "Love—thou art Vailed—." Other poems, among many, showing this use of parallelism are #549, "That I did always love"; #592, "What care the Dead, for Chanticleer—"; #668, "'Nature' is what we see—"; and #820, "The Only News I know."[12]

Dickinson's working of this technique of parallelism with the meter of Watts's hymns and, as we saw in Chapter 3, the structure and style of the Edwardsian sermon gave her poetry much of its distinctiveness. The example of neoclassical writers' parallelism as shown in Watts's hymns is the most obvious source for Dickinson; he even "seems to favor the 'synonymous parallelism' of the Hebrew poetry," as Brita Lindberg-Seyersted points out.[13] But if Watts drew on the Bible for his rhetorical patterns, he did so only in a general way. His poetry, as neoclassical verse, does not truly capture the parallelisms of the Scriptures with all their simplicity, focused pictures, and condensed verse, as Roston argues. For instance, according to Roston, Watts renders Ps. 121:1–2 thus:

> To Heaven I lift my waiting Eyes
> There all my hopes are laid.
> The Lord who built the Earth and Skies
> Is my perpetual Aid.

Roston asserts that "perpetual" and "waiting" are cumbersome and points out that the scriptural setting of the hills, a concrete image, is exchanged for heaven. As he explains, "The *hopes* laid in heaven are very different from the simple statement of the Hebrew, and the dependence on God for help, which is the central theme of the verse, is left to the last line of the stanza, almost as an addendum."[14] Dickinson's Authorized Version, in contrast, reads:

> I will lift up mine eyes unto the hills,
> from whence cometh my help.

> My help cometh from the Lord,
>> which made heaven and earth.

As romantic poetry, Dickinson's verse derives more directly from the biblical model with its particularized parallelism than from the neoclassical model of Watts; she owes a clear debt to Watts only in her choice of meter.[15] Even if she did draw the device of parallelism from Watts's hymns (and possibly from more indirect sources, such as the ballad, the nursery rhyme, and the literature of Sir Thomas Browne), she obviously looked beyond them for her inspiration regarding the fullness of the prophetic voice.

Steeped in the biblical poetry, Dickinson frequently uses the paired lines to communictate an aphorism or proverb. Her use of the aphorism—or, in Porter's words, her "abrupt wisdom"—was a strategy that arose from her reworking of patterns she found in the biblical poetry, as in the Book of Proverbs and the prophetic writings.[16] As scholars remind us, wisdom sayings and techniques characterize Old Testament prophecies to a significant extent, as in Amos and Isaiah, and also appear in the Psalms, which John Calvin and much of Calvinist tradition regarded as prophecy. The most notable prophet of the Bible who used wisdom sayings and techniques was Jesus Christ, commonly acknowledged in the Calvinist tradition as prophet, priest, and king.[17] Given her Calvinist heritage, as well as her familiarity with the Scriptures, Dickinson certainly knew Christ's identity as prophet and the great extent to which he and the other biblical prophets reflected the wisdom school in their utterances. The model that these prophets provided for her empowered her to write such aphorisms as that which appears in #1455, "Opinion is a flitting thing," with its antithetical parallelism; short, rhythmic lines; and simple, direct images:

> Opinion is a flitting thing,
> But Truth, outlasts the Sun—
> If then we cannot own them both—
> Possess the oldest one—.

As Dickinson's reading of the prophetic writings and the Book of Proverbs showed her, the aphorisms of the Bible are striking, memorable, and concise; the tone is authoritative, unequivocal. Their theme is wise living; the proverbs are stated as absolutes and are generalizations meant to be applied in specific situations. More than the ones containing exhortations, Dickinson favored the proverbs that give concisely summarized observations from experience, with the lesson in each implied and no direct exhortation given. Christ served as an important model for her as a prophetic wisdom sayer, particularly as he modeled the latter type of proverb throughout, for example, in his parables and his Sermon on the Mount (Matthew 5–7): "For where your treasure is, there will your heart be also," he declared aphoristically in his sermon (Matt. 6:21). The biblical prophets' short, balanced lines with their Hebraic parallelism prove to be well suited to wise sayings in aphoristic form, as Dickinson discovered. She even adopted some of their themes: "To lose one's faith—surpass / The loss of an Estate—," she says in a poem on belief (#377). The scriptural prophetic writings, along with the Book of Proverbs, gave Dickinson a catalogue of poetic wisdom sayings on which she could model her own prophetic, wise verse.

Inspired by the model of the wisdom prophecy, Dickinson saved aphoristic scraps of prose and worked up letters and poems out of them. Repeatedly in her poetry and letters, we come across proverbial sayings in which she adopted the structure, theme, and the tone of the biblical prophets, all of which #1163 exemplifies:

> God made no act without a cause,
>   Nor heart without an aim,
> Our inference is premature,
>   Our premises to blame.

Dickinson maintains the parallelism of the biblical prophetic poetry—in this case, synonymous parallelism—the prophets' interest in the spiritual significance of daily life, and their tone of earnestness and authority. Other examples include #254, "'Hope' is the thing with feathers—"; #539, "The Province of the Saved"; #764, "Presentiment—is that long Shadow—on the Lawn—"; #1106, "We do not know the time we lose—"; and #1116, "There is another Loneliness," to name only a few. Consisting of one or two lines, her proverbs imitate those of the Bible in their declarative form and their theme of wise living. When Dickinson arranges them in two lines, she makes use of the biblical parallelism—most frequently, synthetic parallelism, in which the second line syntactically completes the first, as in Prov. 18:9:

> He also that is slothful in his work
>   is brother to him that is a great waster.

We see the same pattern in, for instance, #799, "Despair's advantage is achieved":

> Despair's advantage is achieved
> By suffering—Despair— (lines 1–2)

The synthetic parallelism also occurs in, among others, #483, "A Solemn thing within the Soul"; #683, "The Soul unto itself"; #809, "Unable are the Loved to die"; #1376, "Dreams are the subtle Dower"; and #1544, "Who has not found the Heaven—below—."

Proverbs abound throughout Dickinson's poetry and letters. From these, Karl Keller has compiled a list of 271 of her aphorisms, yet I would claim even more, given the presence of proverbs in a great majority of her 1,775 poems. A brief overview of Keller's list reveals the similarity of the Dickinson proverbs there to the biblical wisdom techniques in form, theme, and tone. Yet Keller often omits the second line of the aphorism, or the aphorism is printed as one line when, in fact, it has two. Thus he obscures the scriptural form that Dickinson adopted. Reading the proverbs as she structured them in her poetry shows her adherence to the patterns more clearly. One aphorism, for example, Keller renders as "Who has not found the heaven below will fail of it above," while Dickinson, in the lines of her poem, shows the pattern of synthetic parallelism, the second line completing the thought of the first:[18]

> Who has not found the Heaven—below—
> Will fail of it above— (#1544)

Still, even Keller's partial list affirms the great extent to which Dickinson's work is laced with the generic convention of the wisdom sayings. Charles Anderson has pointed out that the poems after 1865 move increasingly in the direction of the epigrammatic, saying that "apparently she even came to talk, as she wrote, in aphorisms."[19] Her known letters reveal at least 150 more of these, according to William Shurr's count, demonstrating how profound was her sense of her prophetic voice.[20] Through all of these aphorisms, she speaks of abstract things with absolute conviction, describing in concrete terms generalized, even enigmatic precepts in the manner of Christ and other biblical wisdom givers. More than any other single device, the proverbs distinguish Dickinson as sage.

One final technique that the poet found modeled in the biblical prophetic and wisdom literature was paradox, or, more generally, indirection. For both Dickinson and the scriptural prophets, particularly Christ, paradox—the juxtaposition of contrasting ideas that ostensibly conflict—results in messages that are enigmatic, indirect, even puzzling. In Christ's prophetic exhortations, the paradox usually turns on some contrast between a scriptural truth and a more material or earthly understanding, as in Matt. 11:29: "Take my yoke upon you . . . and ye shall find rest unto your souls." Using indirection in his parables and in discourses relying on figurative language, Christ implicitly calls on his listeners to decipher the meaning underlying his puzzling statements. He himself points out his indirection in using figurative language in John 16:25: "These things have I spoken unto you in proverbs [or "figurative language," as a later translation, the New International Version, puts it]: but the time cometh, when I shall no more speak unto you in proverbs, but I shall show you plainly." Paradox and indirection are a kind of communication that characterize his preaching, related to the prophetic principle of speaking to "those who have ears to hear."

In Dickinson's verse, paradox and indirection form a powerful poetic principle, running through her whole poetry as a fundamental practice in expressing the thought content of the poems. Many commentators have pointed out the pervasiveness of indirection throughout her art, but without connecting it to the biblical rhetorical patterns. One aspect of the general technique of indirection, or "slantness," is paradox. Dickinson herself is explicit on the importance of paradox, with its juxtaposition of opposites, for her art: "'Tis Opposites—entice—," she says in the first line of #355. Her principle of slantness, or indirection, along with paradox, rests firmly in the biblical prophetic tradition she drew on in so many ways. Her enigmatic messages, like those of Christ and the Old Testament prophets, often prove difficult to distill.

Dickinson's articulation of her principle of slantness in #1129 sounds like the technique of the biblical prophets, who directed their wisdom to select audiences:

> Tell all the Truth but tell it slant—
> Success in Circuit lies
> Too bright for our infirm Delight
> The Truth's superb surprise
> As Lightning to the Children eased
> With explanation kind
> The Truth must dazzle gradually
> Or every man be blind—

As she indicates in this poem, direct proclamations of truth may be overwhelming, to the point of being rejected. A "kind" or indirect explanation of "Lightning"—an image that suggests abrupt light or vision—will be better received than the truth that "surprises" (line 4). The technique of paradox allows Dickinson the "slantness" she desires; in Lindberg-Seyersted's words, paradox is "a congenial device for slantness, and it is most distinctively a Dickinsonian feature."[21]

Dickinson expresses paradox in the form of enigmatic aphorisms as well as in short phrases, lines, and even whole poems, going beyond the scriptural practice in the degree of her innovation. For instance, paradox appears in short phrases and clauses in her poetry when she connects two contrasting nouns with a preposition, as in "Reward of Anguish" (#614), "Bliss of Death" (#648), "Dooms of Balm" (#1337); or, more often, she will pair an adjective with a noun: "Heavenly Hurt" (#258), "Confident Despair" (#522), "dear iniquity" (#1420), "a sumptuous Destitution" (#1382), "A piercing Comfort" (#561). We also see the paradoxical constructions in whole clauses: "The Cordiality of Death— / Who drills his Welcome in—" (#286); "Much Madness is divinest Sense" (#435); " 'Tis so appalling—it exhilarates—" (#281). Keller lists seventy examples of oxymoron in her poetry, succinct examples of her method of paradox.

Like Christ's parables, in which his indirection often baffled, even frustrated, his audiences, Dickinson's prophetic lines often have the form of riddle or enigma because she relies on paradox and indirection as basic techniques. Thus, although some scholars might read her poetry as "private" or "eccentric," the lines are no more private than the sayings of Christ and the other biblical prophets. Christ, the earlier scriptural prophets (if we take into account the oral tradition that lies behind the Bible), and Dickinson all focused on an audience of initiates; the prophetic tradition of writers presumes this kind of audience to be familiar with an indirection that rests most often on a contrast of spiritual reality with a more mundane experience of perception. Dickinson's poetry presumes this audience of initiates, an audience itself paradoxical in its simultaneous potential openness and resistance to prophetic revelations of spiritual truth.

The paradoxes important to the biblical prophetic tradition extend to the cultural position of the prophet, which Dickinson shared: isolated, yet speaking to the spiritual community; loving, consoling, even acting as potential savior of the community, yet rejected because of the confounding or painful nature of the prophecy; translating the familiar spiritual heritage of the religious community, yet resisted or rejected in part because of the seemingly radical expressions (called "eccentric" or "private" in Dickinson's case) in which that heritage is couched. Indeed, the prophetic voice of the biblical writers and of Dickinson speaks to those who are attuned to indirection, to the expression of truth in highly figurative, parabolic, and enigmatic ways, as the prophets play these paradoxical roles.

In Dickinson's poetry, we find whole poems that play on the paradoxically enigmatic, the prophetic voice speaking authoritatively as a sayer of truth even though that truth may be veiled to her audience:

> A Death blow is a Life blow to Some
> Who till they died, did not alive become—
> Who had they lived, had died but when
> They died, Vitality begun.   (#816)

As in this poem, paradox, aphorism, and parallelism often come together in a single poem, resulting in verse that is forceful in tone, rhythmic in form, and puzzling in theme. Dickinson here captures the life-in-death paradox that the biblical writers focused on, implicitly suggesting a spiritual reality lying beyond the mundane one of bodily life and death. But this truth lies embedded in the indirection of the poem, which is achieved through the clustering of generic features. It is precisely the clustering of features that marks scriptural prophecy and which connects Dickinson's poetry to that genre, as we see throughout her entire oeuvre.

The resemblance of Dickinson's aphoristic lines to the biblical ones in form, content, and tone becomes even more apparent when hers are contrasted with other forms of aphorism. Benjamin Franklin's aphorisms in *Poor Richard's Almanac*, for example, express the logic of rationalism, not the logic of biblical paradox. They rely on rhymed couplets for their form, showing triteness in theme and witty humor in tone:

> Women and wine, game and deceit,
> Make the wealth small and the wants great.[22]

Dickinson's proverbs, in contrast, have the emotional impulse of the biblical form, communicating not the pithy common sense of Poor Richard but revelatory truths on human living. She does not parade wit, as Franklin does, but expresses sober, thoughtful reflections. Her aphorisms achieve a provocative, sometimes enigmatic quality through her reliance on the biblical parallelism and paradox.

Like the aphorisms of the Old Testament prophets and Christ, Dickinson's wise sayings are communicative, didactic, and, for the most part, clear, more so than other forms her writing takes. They intend her contact with an audience, including her larger audience consisting of posterity. Her aphorisms give her a vehicle by which to console, criticize, or simply provide insight into life, both temporal and eternal, in the manner of the biblical writers. As Richard Sewall has pointed out, "Fully half her canon could be called 'wisdom pieces,' thoughts on life and living, sometimes exhortations, sometimes warnings, sometimes pure clinical analyses."[23] Through her "wisdom pieces," Dickinson continues the tradition of the prophet as wisdom sayer, a tradition that found its apogee in Christ. Whether speaking against conventional Christianity or as Christ's "little 'John'" (#497), her poetic voice stands firmly in the prophetic tradition.

The biblical prophetic tradition of paradox provided certain themes and tropes that we have already seen emerge in Dickinson's poetry. Not only life in death but also other paradoxes, set up by juxtaposing spiritual life and mundane existence, characterize both the biblical prophets' and Dickinson's poetry: the paradox of the dream as a more reliable source of truth than waking vision, the paradox of the time world beyond this life (at the edge of Dickinson's "circumference") providing knowledge more valuable than the visible world can provide. Like the biblical prophets, Dickinson as a prophet-poet discerned the paradoxes of human existence and presented them in enigmatic verse. She, too, saw her calling as being to reveal spiritual truth, whether in the form of exhortation, consolation, or proverbs about wise living. The biblical prophets provided her with a model of noble, inspired poetry, which, in her imitation of it, could vitalize her own poetry as prophetic verse.

For Emily Dickinson, to be a prophet meant to embrace many of the attributes of the biblical prophet: the inspiration, sense of calling, and special status; the ability to receive prophetic messages through dreams and visitations; the ability to move between time worlds; and the sense of compulsion to speak of these experiences, as well as to offer indictments and consolatory messages. The prophetic writings also gave her rhetorical devices to draw on—parallelism, aphorism, and paradox—which lent to her work a rhythm and tone shared by the biblical prophets. Assuming the stance of one who speaks truth to an audience that may or may not "have ears to hear," Dickinson wrote her verses not as a poet bent on being published but as a writer-prophet commissioned with a word to say, whether it was to be received by a select few readers of her own time or by a future generation. But female prophets in America had their own obstacles, ones that the biblical (and nineteenth-century male) prophets did not face. Patterns of female prophecy that Dickinson appropriated or shaped for her own ends form the subject of Chapter 7.

7. Female Prophecy in New England

T HROUGHOUT history, people have understood prophecy to occur when individuals claim an experience of divine inspiration and proceed to speak the will or message of the One who has inspired them. As the Bible testifies through its inclusion of Miriam, Deborah, and others, in Judeo-Christian history such an experience of inspiration and speech has been no respecter of gender. Yet, as Emily Dickinson and other Protestant women could testify, American prophetic women have faced a peculiar dilemma: divinely inspired to prophesy, they could not speak their prophecies because of the long-standing historical constraints on female public speech. Female prophecy in America undoubtedly began with the earliest Christian women to set foot on the New World soil. But because of their gender, when we look at one of the earliest and largest communities of American Christian women and their men, the New England Puritans, we find little public speech or writings that we recognize as obvious female prophecy. By the time that Dickinson began writing, the tide was starting to turn, but the situation had not changed significantly.

Still, prophets will prophesy. In Protestant America, those female speakers have found creative and subversive ways to articulate their spiritual messages. Dickinson continued many of the practices and patterns that her New England predecessors had tested—not the least of which was to explore poetry as prophecy. In this chapter, we look at two important early American women (of Dickinson's own Calvinist heritage) who prophesied—Anne Hutchinson and Anne Bradstreet—for the models they offered to women after them, including women of the nineteenth century. We also consider the obstacles that would-be female prophets faced and the ways in which some women overcame those barriers. Emily Dickinson, we find, emerged from a rich, albeit conflicted, tradition of American female prophecy that both contextualizes and magnifies her poetic achievements.

From the inception of the New England colonies (and in reaction to the religious practices in England), preachers had argued that the Bible was, in its entirety, normative for life, an idea that Dickinson's own Congregational tradition for the most part embraced. Western Massachusetts Christians tended to apply to their individual lives the biblical examples and exhortations, in a more or less literalistic reading of the Bible. That kind of interpretation and emphasis was grist for Dickinson's prophetic mill, giving her much dogma to challenge and much practice (which she would identify as hypocrisy) to expose in her poetry. But the conservative New England interpretive practice is notable, too, for another reason. Despite the claims that they were remaining "close to Scripture" in their interpretations, the traditional New England divines repeatedly revised the scriptural tradition when considering women as prophets. Privileging a few, isolated hortatory passages over the broader themes, examples, and patterns in the Scriptures, the conservative Calvinist circles disallowed women the office of prophet. Their ministers read 1 Tim. 2:12—which asserted that women should be silent—and similar verses as absolutely authoritative for all of women's public life, minimizing (or ignoring) the importance of the historical contexts of the verses and passing over the scriptural examples of women in public leadership roles.

Astute students of Scripture would have been able to see, and indeed did see, the possibilities for women's prophetic speaking that the Scriptures allowed. The Quakers of colonial America, along with Anne Hutchinson, stand as important examples. But even more "conservative" Christians, such as Anne Bradstreet and many of the female poets of Dickinson's day, found ways to claim religious authority in speaking their understandings of the faith despite the cultural constraints against them. Of course, many, perhaps most, of Dickinson's female poetic contemporaries sought to remain so firmly within their religious tradition that their poetry sounds conventional and tame. In contrast, other women religious speakers, especially the female orators, were bolder in their refusal to be limited by male ministers' interpretations of the Scriptures; they risked and often endured public censure, including official rebukes and harassment. Striking for the contrast to the common twentieth-century practice, many of those women more or less remained within an established Christian tradition even as they challenged aspects of that tradition.

Today, except for a small but growing number of evangelical women who continue the orators' practice, women who chafe against traditional views tend to reject, abandon, or transform Christianity beyond recognition; in contrast, the nineteenth-century public women for the most part sustained their commitment to the Scriptures and traditional Christianity. They believed that the Bible was a liberating doctrine for women. And while the female poets of Dickinson's day did not go as far as the orators in testing the limits of orthodoxy, they also found ways to claim power. Both groups of women offered Dickinson paradigms of power that could serve her own ends. As we will see, Dickinson's poetic strategies fit into long-standing patterns of American female prophecy, ones that began in colonial America and continued into her own time.

Indeed, both the nineteenth-century female orators and the female poets who adopted verse as their means of communicating spirituality could look back to America's colonial period. Anne Hutchinson, perhaps the most-remembered female prophet in American history, attempted to claim the oral tradition of female prophecy and was banished in part because of that stance. Excommunicated for her role in the Antinomian Controversy of the 1630s, Hutchinson represented the figure of a woman stepping out of her prescribed "womanly" role to speak as a prophet the religious truth transmitted to her, she declared, by immediate revelation. Hutchinson's strategy of submitting herself to the godhead worked to give her power to speak divinely inspired words. It became an assertion of autonomy from societal constraints, which the male religious establishment found to be so powerful a threat to the social order that it banished her. Such renunciation to the godhead had been the way of the biblical prophets to gain access to divinely inspired words, a strategy that, as we will see in Chapter 8, Dickinson also adopted.

Anne Bradstreet, claiming the voice of religious instructor to her children in the Andover Manuscript poems, helped to initiate a tradition of female prophecy that was also poetic. She drew on the scriptural prophetic tradition for rhetorical strategies and a poetic voice that empowered her verse. As other women would do after her, she looked to verse as a vehicle to express her religious devotion despite her milieu, which was at turns hostile and condescending to women poets.

In the centuries intervening between Hutchinson and Bradstreet's time and Dickinson's, a historical shift toward women gaining voice and power was well under way, though of course, it was only the beginning of a new struggle. The few women orators of Dickinson's time drew on scriptural arguments in their struggle for a voice; they showed Dickinson and others religious justification for female prophecy. Scriptural examples of women prophets, such as Miriam and Deborah, could serve as models for women who felt called to assume a public role as speakers of religious vision. Another group of female

124

religious speakers consisted of the women poets contemporaneous with Dickinson and deriving from the Bradstreet tradition. They "preached" the word of Scripture through their sentimental verse, adopting the didactic voice of a preacher. Dickinson could look to these female traditions of oral prophecy and poetry to empower her art, adopting and shaping their patterns for her own ends.

The public exclusion of nineteenth-century New England women from prophetic roles derived from Puritan theology and practice. Dickinson's New England had, after all, inherited the seventeenth-century Puritan model of the woman's role in the church—not the model of Quakers, Catholics, or any other Christian tradition (and there were several). The nineteenth century also compounded women's restrictions with a new economic system and accompanying ideology, which together separated men from the home and emphasized that the woman's sole place was the home, not the marketplace or public arena. But even with its traditional economic structure that kept men more involved in family life (as both women and men worked close to home), the Puritan model of the woman's role worked to keep females silent and subordinate.[1] Seen as occupying a position twice removed from God, Puritan women were to look to their husbands or fathers, not directly to God, for religious guidance, a tradition that more or less continued in Dickinson's time. In the Puritan mind, man was the "conveyance" between God and creation, with "creation" understood to include woman. Woman's mind was weaker or, conversely, her earthly ties were stronger, the argument went, so that she needed man to interpret God's will (as given in the Bible) and to struggle with the coils of covenant theology. Such a position precluded women's public role as prophets or speakers for God, because it kept them removed from God as a source of divine inspiration.

The case of Anne Hutchinson, whose story Dickinson likely knew, for it was retold throughout the eighteenth and nineteenth centuries, provides a pointed example of a New England response to a woman defying her culturally prescribed role: she assumed the role of woman prophet and was consequently censured. Hutchinson's case was one that any New England woman aspiring to the role of prophet and religious teacher, including Dickinson, had to confront. Nineteenth-century renditions of Hutchinson, such as a popular one by Hawthorne, were inescapable among Christian circles deriving from the Puritan tradition, Dickinson's included.

The details of Hutchinson's story are striking, let alone the distorted retellings of the tale. The initial charges against Anne Hutchinson had not been on issues of doctrine but on her stepping out of her "womanly" role in proclaiming religious truth. Hutchinson had ignored the tacit stipulations that women were not to expound their religious vision in public. The Puritans allowed women to teach under the conditions narrowly defined by the interpretation of the "rule" in the Epistle of Paul to Titus, that "elder women must instruct the younger about their business, and to love their husbands and not make them clash," as Massachusetts Bay Colony governor John Winthrop paraphrased it at Hutchinson's trial.[2] Hutchinson "failed" not only in her choice of subject matter—religious truth, as she saw it—but also by admitting men to her audience. And she had claimed immediate revelation, challenging the religious and social order, which had women look to men for religious guidance. When her story was retold to the next generation, Hutchinson was presented as an American Jezebel. This was the version John Winthrop told in his *A Short Story of the Rise, reign, and ruine of the Antinomians, Familists, and Libertines* (1644): Hutchinson, in asserting her autonomy as a female prophet, "seduced" men, body and soul, with her dangerous principles and her precedent of female public preaching.

The generations after Hutchinson continued to tell this story, regarding her as an Eve who generated a host of Eves, her women followers snaring their husbands in sin and delusion. As Amy Schrager Lang shows, by the time that Dickinson wrote, Hutchinson had been "fictionalized" into an untrustworthy figure of seduction and temptation, a woman who wooed her followers away from the path of truth and who corrupted the American Eden.[3] Thus, one tradition of American female prophecy that had continued into Dickinson's day saw women prophets as unlawful and even dangerous, powerful in their spiritual and sexual influence over men and thus a threat to society. This tradition also saw female public speakers as immodest, even unchaste or "unsexed," a view that continued into the nineteenth century the seventeenth-century rhetoric surrounding Anne Hutchinson.

Above all, according to these early American retellings of her story, Hutchinson's great error was her transgression of cultural boundaries, her stepping out of woman's accepted cultural role by teaching her contemporaries on her own authority and thereby defying the proper social organization.[4] Certainly, Dickinson would have known the Hutchinson legacy and would have been aware of the problems surrounding the female prophet who feels compelled to speak truth yet is denied both unmediated vision and access to a public forum because she is a woman. Dickinson relied on her craftiness—her choice of her own audience and her frequently veiled expressive strategies, such as missing referents or ambiguous metaphors—to maintain her prophetic voice within a patriarchal culture that denied it, borrowing and manipulating the defining features of Judeo-Christian prophecy to serve her purposes. Those strategies, even the ambiguity of her verse, suggest her to have been a poet who chose an audience that would be fit but few; she preferred to speak in veiled ways rather than not speak at all, to direct her verse to small audiences rather than the broader ones that ultimately contributed to Hutchinson's defeat.

As Wendy Martin observes, Dickinson "refused to be diminished by the constraints of feminine virtue and propriety that paralyzed so many Victorian women"; unlike most American women, Dickinson trusted "her antinomian impulses."[5] The word "antinomian" is well chosen. In the hands of Hutchinson, antinomianism, with its emphasis on total and direct submission to Christ alone, offered women new power as it rendered women the spiritual equals of men: according to Hutchinson's reading of Scripture, both men and women were relegated to the status of malleable inferiors in the hands of a higher being. All power emanated from God, respecting no sex, rather than from men who attempted to interpret God's Word.[6] As an antinomian, Hutchinson has represented herself as utterly subordinate to Christ—and thus autonomous of the Puritan patriarchy. "Claiming to be nothing in herself but all in Christ," Lang describes, "Hutchinson reduced herself to a medium through which God spoke and, in this way, empowered herself more fully than the men in whom the community invested power." The antinomian renunciation of self to Christ thus functions as an assertion of self; seeming passivity is power.[7] As we will explore later in greater detail, Dickinson would discover the same strategy of renunciation for her own empowerment as a female prophet-poet, drawing on the possibilities that Christian renunciation offered for the female speaker of religious truth.

Feminist scholars have noted the silencing effect on Dickinson of her religious inheritance and the ways in which she overcame it, focusing their studies on the patriarchal elements of that inheritance as it was expressed in a repressively rigid nineteenth-century American culture.[8] Yet, as American history has demonstrated increasingly since the seventeenth-century Quaker model of womanhood, Christianity need not silence: it can spiritually empower women to be speakers and preachers of the Word. The Quaker model of women's role in the church, contributing to a countertradition to Puritan silencing that gained momentum in the nineteenth century, pointed to a way in which Dickinson may have read the Scriptures, namely, as authorizing a feminine prophetic role. Indeed, many nineteenth-century women saw women as particularly suited to prophecy, as we saw earlier in the theologically diverse examples of Margaret Fuller and Sarah Josepha Hale.

Finding support in the Scriptures, even Quakers in colonial America allowed women in church to argue with men on an intellectual level, to speak declaratively, and to exercise dominion over their religious lives. They emphasized an informing, indwelling divine light and believed in the direct inspiration of individuals regardless of sex, like many radical sects of seventeenth-century England but unlike the New England Puritans after the Antinomian Controversy. The Quakers' relative lack of sex bias would have appealed to Dickinson; for them, there was nothing to hinder the work of the divine light in females. Hence, the Quakers saw women as capable of prophetic speech. George Fox, seventeenth-century leader of the Quakers, told his male and female audiences as he paraphrased Paul's message to the Galatians, "Ye are all one *man* in Christ Jesus" [italics mine].[9] Such an emphasis allowed women to assume a role as religious speakers.

Indeed, from seventeenth-century New England into Dickinson's time, Quakerism provided women the opportunity to assume a public prophetic role and one of the most prestigious positions in society: that of preacher. Fox had accentuated the fact that Christ was as strong in women as in men and had asserted that God preferred some women before thousands of men. He had argued that the biblical example of female preachers—women like Miriam, Huldah, and Philip's four daughters—could be repeated in contemporary times.[10] Significantly, this reading apparently was adopted by at least one Puritan church, John Fiske's church at Wenham, Massachusetts, which produced scriptural examples of female prophets to justify its practice of allowing women to read aloud their own statements of religious experiences when joining the church. Thus, before the antinomian crisis, even the Puritan tradition was in conflict over the extent to which a woman could assume the voices of religious testimony and prophecy.

Notably, by Dickinson's time Quaker women were drawn to the public platform, long accustomed to speaking and hearing other women speak publicly. Angelina Grimke, Lucretia Mott, and Abby

Kelley Foster, all Quakers, were among the first to assume the public platform, gathering around them audiences consisting of both men and women, much as Hutchinson did. But these women went even further than Hutchinson by speaking to audiences of all denominations. Most significant, they refused to accept the sectarian view that women could speak only to other women. Their example and their readings of the Scriptures indicate the openness of the Bible to women's functioning as prophets, an understanding important for its potential for Dickinson. Empowered to speak by their Quaker doctrine and church experience, these women forged the way in the 1830s for other women to speak publicly and even to assume roles as religious, prophetic leaders. Antoinette Brown, for instance, accepted an appointment as pastor of the Congregational church at South Butler, New York, in 1852. In the same vein, non-Quaker Lucy Stone in the 1840s relied on close readings of the Scripture to argue that the Bible allowed women a public speaking role, prophetically pointing out abuses of Scripture. These women were part of a gradual historical transformation from the complete silencing of such women as Anne Hutchinson to increasing challenges to cultural resistance by a few women in a Christian tradition.

By the time that Dickinson penned her first poem in 1850, more and more women orators were gaining access to the public platform. Cultural resistance remained strong, but the late 1850s and early 1860s saw some acceptance of women publicly speaking their religious and social visions in churches, schools, and other arenas. The women orators implicitly and explicitly challenged ideologies of gender and societal expectations of feminine reticence, reclaiming an oral wisdom-giving role for women. They undoubtedly contributed to Dickinson's understanding of the function of and possibilities for female rhetoric. In those women's speech, Dickinson could find the continuation of an oral tradition of women's prophecy affirmed in the Scriptures—a lineage that, along with the sermonic oratory of her time, could serve to shape her prophetic voice. Dickinson undoubtedly felt no need to justify to herself or to others the fact that women do prophesy; but the example of the contemporary female prophets and their parallel to biblical ones demonstrate that women historically have striven (and even agitated) to proclaim their religious perspectives.

As we saw earlier, instead of rejecting all male models, Dickinson worked the homiletic tradition of prophecy, which tended to exclude women, alongside the scriptural rhetorical patterns, which also emphasize male voices. Although her adoption of "male" patterns may disturb some feminists, the choice seems less surprising when we consider that subordinated groups (such as women, racial and ethnic minorities, or the poor) historically have appropriated, subconsciously or otherwise, the devices of the dominant, hegemonic group. A woman of her time, Dickinson followed the strategy of the female orators, who despite the radical nature of their decisions to ascend the public platform adopted the prooftexting and emphasis on logic that their male counterparts privileged. All of these women demonstrated their implicit acknowledgment that the dominant group shapes understandings of power. Creatively, they exploited those cultural patterns of power even as they sought to adjust cultural ideas.

Despite—and perhaps even because of—their methods, the women orators did experience sexist obstacles to the public platform and in their churches. They endured attacks on their own femininity—the popular nineteenth-century criticism was that they were "unsexed"—by the popular press and even, more subtly, by such (otherwise) progressive leaders as Ralph Waldo Emerson. In his lecture titled "Woman," given to the Women's Rights Convention at Boston in September 1855, Emerson spoke in admiration of women's "oracular" nature (and even defended women's right to hold property), but ultimately he called women "victims of the finer temperament." He saw as a liability what he perceived in most women to be a more "personal" style. Emerson thus called on women to avoid the public arena and instead to look to men as their "guardian[s]."[11] Thus, as Emerson's colleague Margaret Fuller discovered, even in transcendentalist circles (which tended to be socially progressive) women had to learn to take the word "manly" as praise when it was applied to them, so entrenched was the practice of deifying the style associated with men, one seen as factual, analytic, organized, and impersonal. An "effeminate" or "womanly" style was systematically devalued—and that meant any style not conforming to the "manly" one.

But the obstacles facing women who prophesied from the public platform were even more profound than the harassment and criticism articulated verbally and in print. Traditions of public discourse, after all, had been constructed to exclude women. The nomenclature of Aristotelian rhetoric—"the eloquence of the bar" (judicial contexts), "the eloquence of the assembly" (forensic speaking; legislative contexts), and "the eloquence of the pulpit"—used in the eighteenth and nineteenth centuries contributed to the hindrance of women's access to the public platform, for English common law, with its laws of "coverture," kept the bar and the assembly completely out of women's reach well into the nineteenth century.[12] A large part of the hindrance to women's oratory involved the wide acceptance of this mid-nineteenth-century Aristotelian ideal. It was found in the most popular rhetoric textbooks: Hugh Blair's *Lectures on Rhetoric and Belles Lettres* (1783), George Campbell's *Philosophy of Rhetoric* (1844), Richard Whately's *Elements of Rhetoric* (1834), and John Quincy Adams's *Lectures on Rhetoric and Oratory* (1810). And it was articulated and emphasized in rhetorical instruction for both children and adults. Blair's textbook, for one, was quoted, adapted, and referred to so much by other writers that it became a staple of instruction for half of the educated English-speaking world.

All in all, effective public speaking was understood to be rational, impersonal, and instrumental, working in the service of some specific ambition or business. It was supposed to persuade, not merely to please (which was seen as effeminate or womanly). Because of the widespread belief that men's minds, not their emotions, governed their discourse, men's speech was seen as inherently superior to women's. A bold, energetic style that appealed to reason presumably convinced audiences most effectively—and was a style understood as springing from man's (not woman's) fundamental nature.

According to Aristotle, the persuasive elements of a speech could be divided into the devices of rhetoric, on the one hand, and the persuasive value of the speaker's character, on the other. That character was necessarily reflected in the speech or piece of writing; as *ethos*, the speech expressed the image of the maker to the audience. For Aristotle, the image of a persuasive speaker or writer should be that of a person of intelligence, rectitude, and goodwill. But by their very natures, as nineteenth-century Americans understood gender, women could only be disqualified from public speaking and writing. Women who ascended the platform were criticized as not having high moral character and goodwill, two of Aristotle's three characteristics of the "ethical proof" that would inspire confidence in a speaker. Because the female sex was seen as naturally delicate, emotional, noncompetitive, and nurturing, women aspiring to deliver ideas instead of (or in addition to) babies were presumed to want to be men and therefore were presumed defective as women—hardly the qualities of someone with high moral character. By their very desire to speak publicly, then, women were disqualified as acceptable speakers.

Aristotle's third characteristic of *ethos* was intelligence—and whether women had that was a matter of public debate. The issue of whether women should or even could be educated had engaged public attention since the American Revolution; it was not until the late 1850s that there was any kind of consensus that woman was intelligent enough to be educated and that she was an intelligent being worthy of being educated.

Given the power and presence of the Aristotelian rhetorical ideal in nineteenth-century culture, it is no wonder that many women turned to conservative, sentimental verse as the vehicle through which to "preach" their visions of spirituality. And even those visions tended to be conformist, at least on the surface. To be published and read, one's best bet was to support the dominant gender ideology. As editor Caroline May [Kirkland] asserted in her preface to *The American Female Poets* (1848), warm domestic affections and pure religious feeling were what was wanted by audiences, and by and large, that was what the female poets gave.[13] Dickinson looked to these poets for examples of female religious voices, but not for their model of the woman speaker—piously orthodox, refined, and necessarily conformist.

Given these formidable obstacles to women's public speech, it is amazing that any woman successfully gained the platform in American civic and religious life. But the 1830s witnessed the beginnings of such gains, as women began speaking to groups of friends and female associations, then to mixed or "promiscuous" audiences in churches, schools, and elsewhere. Dickinson's own denomination, the Congregational church, was first to issue an official rebuke to women orators in 1837. Still, despite the lack of support from many church leaders, by the late 1850s and early 1860s women's names increasingly appeared in the list of professional lectures advertised in the newspapers, until eventually their speaking was common occurrence, "if not happily accepted, at least countenanced by public opinion," according to Doris Yoakum.[14] Women were learning that oratory, perceived by Americans to be powerful enough to engineer major social change, was one way that individuals could be roused to action in the causes of temperance and abolition, the two dominant reform movements among women in the early nineteenth century. Frances Wright, a Scotchwoman lecturing on free inquiry; Maria Stewart, a black female politician; Angelina Grimke, who spoke out against slavery; and Abby Kelley Foster, a schoolteacher turned abolitionist were persuasive pioneers in women's oratory, attracting not only female audiences but male ones as well. The 1840s especially proved to be a decade of increased activity of women on the public platform, as a number of women, overcoming their fear of Saint Paul's misinterpreted dictum that women should remain silent, assumed the platform at reform meetings and conventions. Many of these early orators, as well as many abolitionists of the 1850s—Amy Post and John Greenleaf Whittier among the antislavery activists—came from Quaker circles, congregations that apparently were not threatened by a more egalitarian distribution of power.

Indeed, the Quaker women and Margaret Fuller provided more apt models for Dickinson of the female voice of the visionary than did the female poets of her time. Although she made no mention of them in her letters, Dickinson certainly knew about the female orators. The newspapers she read listed lyceum and church speakers, and her contemporaries were increasingly preoccupied with "the woman question" and the role of women in public life. Why, then, did she make no reference to these issues in her letters? Given the attention that the controversies generated in some quarters, Dickinson's silence is eloquent. She made no mention of the female American poets either, but we do know that she read their verse in the publications to which her family subscribed.

Dickinson's silence on both counts suggests that she saw herself doing something pointedly different from both groups of women. She placed herself somewhere between them. Iconoclastic as the female orators often were in challenging established practice and tradition, Dickinson nonetheless kept her iconoclasm for her private fascicles, saving her prophecy for "those who have ears to hear." She did not throw her "pearl," her poetry, before swine. In one sense, her fascicles resemble the biblical prophets' form of publication, collection in "books" for future generations. Like those writings, as well as the messages of the female orators, her poems are oral in nature. They take the rhythm and meter of song and the style and form of the sermon. But Dickinson rejected the female orators' interest in social protest; she preferred instead the preachers' and female poets' emphasis on wisdom and spiritual truth. All in all, Dickinson expressed wisdom in a form more akin to that of the female prophets of the Scriptures, with their musical forms and spiritual emphasis, than to the "prophecy" of any other group. Certainly, Dickinson's poetry is notable for the ways it continues that tradition of female prophecy. She is silent on her contemporaneous models because, indeed, her wisdom giving is decidedly different, even if she was inspired and influenced by them.

Dickinson's voice of prophecy becomes more distinctive when we compare her poetry to the verse characteristic of her day. The poetry of both men and women tended to be conventional, overtly instructive, and unsurprising in its affirmation of broadly shared beliefs. Women, even more than men, were expected to express "the heart," not the intellect. Nineteenth-century American women writers were expected to write about their private lives, specifically, their emotional responses to their experiences. But there were many emotions and desires that "good" women were not supposed to feel and which were therefore off-limits as poetic material: anger, sexual passion, and ambition, to name a few.

Like her contemporaries, Dickinson often did express her personal emotional responses, and she frequently employed the same themes, topics, and images as they did. For example, she conformed to the practice of her contemporaries in exploring love, death, and nature in her art. But the difference in the voice of the poetry is striking, for Dickinson went beyond her female contemporaries by adopting a distinctive poetic voice. When we consider poems that include the popular image of a bird, for example, the contrast between the authority and challenge of Dickinson's voice and the tone of a poem characteristic of the day is significant. Here is a poem by Elizabeth Oakes Smith:

> A simple thing, yet chancing as it did
>   When life was bright with its illusive dreams,
> A pledge and promise seemed beneath it hid;
>   The ocean lay before me, tinged with beams
> That lingering draped the west, a wavering stir,
>   And at my feet down fell a worn, gray quill;
> An eagle, high above the darkling fir,
>
> . . . .
>
>   O noble bird! why didst thou loose for me
> Thy eagle plume? still unessayed, unknown
>   Must be that pathway fearless winged by thee;
> I ask it not, no lofty flight be mine,
>   I would not soar like thee, in loneliness to pine.[15]

In contrast, here is Dickinson's poem:

> It is a lonesome Glee—
> Yet sanctifies the Mind—
> With fair association—
> Afar upon the Wind
>
> A Bird to overhear
> Delight without a Cause—
> Arrestless as invisible—
> A matter of the Skies.   (#774)

Both poems center on the idea of flight—indeed, in Dickinson's, the speaker may even be suggesting herself as a bird in flight, "Afar upon the Wind"—but the speakers' evaluations of flight are vastly different. Smith's speaker tentatively examines the feather of the bird, looking for some immediate moral lesson, but the lesson is one she cannot accept. The bird is brave in assuming the "lofty" path of flight, but fear of loneliness keeps the speaker restricted to the ground. The "pledge" and "promise" come to nothing; she cannot ultimately identify with the bird, because, as Paula Bennett points out, she sees it as calling her to choose between irreconcilable opposites: flight and acceptance, freedom and love.[16]

Smith's language, lax in its reliance on pronouns and function words (half of the total), slow the poem's rhythm down. The effect is one of sluggishness that captures too well the speaker's weighty plight of being pinned to the ground. That, presumably, is the "proper" place for a nineteenth-century woman, and Smith's vague or clichéd phrases and words ("life" as "bright," "illusive dreams," "noble bird") make the poem properly conventional. The poem purports to instruct the reader (because we are invited to identify with the speaker), but it results in no real challenge, which is the pattern of a prophetic voice. On the contrary, although we have a glimpse of the bird from a fresh angle—its possibility to signify free flight—Smith backs away from that conclusion, constrained by the conventions of propriety for women of her day. Her poetic voice is uncertain and resigned, as we see in the central question of the poem, "Why didst thou loose for me / Thy eagle plume?" The speaker dares not defy but, instead, gives a lesson through example (in the last two lines) in circuitous syntax—"no lofty flight be mine"—that may even mask the real desires of the poet.

How different Dickinson's "moral" about flight is. Soaring "afar upon the Wind" may be "lonesome," but it is a "lonesome Glee"; Dickinson brings the opposites together in a memorable oxymoron that dominates the poem. Unlike Smith's speaker, Dickinson's can identify with a bird in flight. We cannot be certain what "it" is, in the opening line (solitude? inspiration?); the ambiguity seems a clever acquiescence to the expressive constraints on women, as Dickinson refuses an outright statement of what brings such rewards. Indeed, she seems to tease us by withholding the referent. We do know that "it" involves flight, not the confines of a well-run home. And it is something so powerfully satisfying that it can make the mind "sanctified" or holy, set apart (line 2). The association with the wind (*pneuma*?) suggests inspiration, the idea of divinity speaking to her. "It" is, after all, "a matter of the Skies," perhaps heavens, and the phenomenon seems to involve communication of some sort—a bird can "overhear" despite its inability to understand.

Whatever the case, the poem is striking for the crispness of the language and the certainty of the voice, even given the ambiguity. That which brings solitude may also bring loneliness, but the state is ultimately positive, "sanctifying" the mind. Dickinson's prophetic voice is recognizable in this poem not only for its authoritative quality, especially as we hear that forcefulness in the proverblike statements, but also for the poet's surprising (and insightful) reversal of expectations regarding solitude and flight. Even in this poem in which any overt prophetic application is withheld, the poet teaches us, helping us to see something in a new way.

Poets such as Elizabeth Oakes Smith could show Dickinson an expression of female spirituality (indeed, much of the nineteenth-century women's poetry is more religiously confessional than the example here), but Dickinson would find in the female orators voices that were more profoundly prophetic (in the scriptural sense) than the poets' expressions. The voices of the orators, more than those of the poets, captured biblical features: they were authoritative, spiritually intense, willing to challenge widely held beliefs and practices. They served as an important conduit between Dickinson and older female prophetic traditions—Hutchinson's and the Bible's.

I have suggested that Dickinson embraced wholly neither the practices of the female orators nor those of the female poets, but also that she was influenced by both. Before we leave the orators entirely to consider poetry, it is helpful to examine an important emphasis of the early orators, as well as to outline some of their methods—both of which have a bearing on Dickinson's practice. Dickinson may not have been alive or old enough to hear the early women speakers, but those orators' messages are significant for what they suggest about the assumptions and thinking that were possible (given the prevailing ideologies) for mid-nineteenth-century women such as Dickinson. If the women speaking in the 1830s and 1840s could see the liberating possibilities of the Bible for women's speech, surely Dickinson, who wrote her verse ten or twenty years later and who shared their interest in rhetoric, detected similar emphases; these women needed no twentieth-century women's movement to show them the openness of the Scriptures to female speech. Dickinson may not have valued scriptural authority to the extent that the orators did, but the history surrounding key biblical texts illuminated cultural assumptions—the certainties and uncertainties of Dickinson's contemporaries—about women's place.

As early as the 1830s, women publicly used the Bible against itself to refute what they saw as misinterpretations of biblical passages, such as the idea borrowed from Paul that public speaking was not part of women's "appropriate sphere" ("Let your women keep silent"). Lucretia Mott, Lucy Stone, and Sarah Grimke all evidently believed in the consistency of the Bible and sought to show, through close readings of Scripture, that the Bible did not contradict what it seemed to assert or assume in some places in its canon. For instance, Mott, Stone, and Grimke all argued that the "sphere" assigned to women was manmade, not God-made, and they attempted to persuade by relying on the practices of logic and close exegesis, which they knew were valued and privileged by the cultural (male) elite. Mott, studying the Hebrew and Greek texts and arguing from circumstance of time and place, pointed out that not only did Paul's admonition in 1 Cor. 14:34 apply to women being silent in the church, not in the public arena, but also that his advice was to bring greater propriety to the Corinthian church. Stone and Grimke pointed out that the Gen. 3:16 passage "thy husband . . . shall rule over thee" was a prophecy of what would happen, not a command. Both argued for woman's equality with man: she is made in God's image, Grimke maintained, referring to Gen. 1:26–27; the "new dispensation" in Christ, according to Stone's argument, was that "there is neither Jew nor Greek, . . . bond nor free, . . . male nor female," a refutation from Gal. 3:28.

All in all, these female orators pointed out, the Scriptures do not support patriarchy; woman is subject to God, not man. They derived their views from their own apprehension of the text, rejecting men as mediators and affirming the Protestant emphasis on the priesthood of all believers. Their assumption that women could directly apprehend and communicate spiritual truth was one that Dickinson continued in her art. As we saw earlier in poems such as #401, "What Soft—Cherubic Creatures—," or #241, "I like a look of Agony," Dickinson also sustained their practice of pointing out inconsistencies between Scripture and social life—which for Dickinson often meant exposing the hypocrisy of her contemporaries.

Dickinson would have known that the female public speakers of her day for the most part drew their oratorical arguments from their experience in the church and in the home, even as she herself looked to those institutions for her poetic images and metaphors. Indeed, the Bible was the most frequent source of material for women orators before the Civil War, Lillian O'Connor points out.[17] Although Dickinson revised much of nineteenth-century biblical interpretation, it is clear that she, too, looked to the Bible for material to challenge, adopt, or shape. The gradual acceptance of women as orator-prophets offered Dickinson an impetus for assuming a prophetic stance in her poetry; with the pulpit as their platform (women often spoke in churches, thanks to generous male ministers), they presented a powerful reminder to their audiences of prophetic possibilities for women. And their speeches indicate the liberating interpretations of the Scriptures possible to nineteenth-century Christians, interpretations that we generally associate with the twentieth century. Dickinson may not have cared as deeply as the orators about guarding the content of the Bible, but nonetheless, the early female orators demonstrate the empowerment that the Christian tradition could offer to women of their day.

Moreover, understanding the orators' sense of a moral imperative to speak contextualizes Dickinson's. Dickinson indicated that she, too, experienced a sense of obligation, even a compulsion, to write, as when she said to Thomas Wentworth Higginson, "When I try to organize—my little Force explodes."[18] That sense of a moral imperative is central to the Judeo-Christian prophetic stance. Dickinson continued these traditions of Hutchinson, the orators, and the religious poets when she wrote Poem #384:

> No Rack can torture me—
> My Soul—at Liberty —

Behind this mortal Bone
There knits a bolder One—

You Cannot prick with saw—
Nor pierce with Cimitar—
Two Bodies—therefore be—
Bind One—The Other fly—

The Eagle of his Nest
No easier divest—
And gain the Sky
Than mayest Thou—

Except Thyself may be
Thine Enemy—
Captivity is Consciousness—
So's Liberty.

The poem is characteristic of Dickinson in her presentation of an authoritative, assertive speaker. No outside force—no "Rack," "saw," or "Cimitar"—can limit her "Soul" (a word chosen from religious rhetoric, not surprisingly). In fact, the poem even suggests that the speaker claims two "Bodies" or identities, one that she presents to the public—the one associated with her "mortal Bone," or mortality—and one "bolder," a body that "flies" when the other is "bound," presumably, when constraints are put on her public persona. Not surprisingly, Dickinson represents that flight as heavenward, to the "Sky," possibly a figure for the domicile of her inspirer. But what is more important in this poem is the speaker's claim of a self "at liberty": nothing can stifle the soul, not even captivity; for, as the last two lines suggest, both captivity and liberty are "consciousness," that is, as long as she struggles against the constraints that would keep her "down to earth" (as opposed to claiming the vast limits of the "Sky"), the speaker is "conscious," alive, not dead or numb in passivity. As we will see in Chapter 8, for Dickinson's speakers, struggle can be positive. Only "Thyself"—not the public or external pressures—can be "Thine Enemy," she asserts; only the soul chastening itself can limit the free flight of the "bolder" self.

The idea of the free self recalls Thoreau's prophetic emphasis throughout *Walden*, but Dickinson's speaker is more defensive than Thoreau's regarding the constraints that bind the self—perhaps an indication of Dickinson's acute awareness of the limitations she experiences that are related to her gender. The shift in pronoun (from "me" to "Thou") toward the end of the poem, seen clearly by stanza 3, is important, too, for its indication that Dickinson the prophet moves away, like Thoreau, from a personal expression of her struggle to an attempt to universalize it. Her experience, she suggests, is one from which her audience can derive guidance. The application of her account stands in the last two lines, typical of Dickinson for the proverbial, memorable form and content: "Captivity is Consciousness— / So's Liberty."

Writing was one way that Dickinson and her female contemporaries could express their strong religious convictions, an avenue that perhaps offered more possibilities than oratory. After all, even nineteenth-century Quaker women, whose religious tradition seemed more open to their public speaking, met with cultural obstacles. The nineteenth-century changes in the dominant gender ideology after the Industrial Revolution, with its increased proscriptions on women's public role, may have worked counter to Quaker doctrine within the Quaker church, as gender ideology exerted its power to hinder expressions of female prophecy. Sarah Grimke, for example, was drawn to the Quaker church by the doctrine, only to discover sexism as a barrier to her plans of becoming a preacher. As Dickinson would also do as a daughter of prophecy, Grimke turned from her frustrated plans to secular forms of writing, including letters, as a way of prophesying the Word of God; directing their prophecies through letters allowed both women the opportunity to interpret Scripture while having greater control than the orators had in selecting (and rejecting) potential audiences. Speaking as a prophetic chastiser—a role that Dickinson would later adopt—Grimke in her *Letters on the Equality of the Sexes, and the Condition of Woman* (1838) emphasized the spiritual equality and value of women. Writing, not preaching, came to serve as her prophetic mode, as it did for Dickinson and other women.

Yet even women writers could not wholly escape the cultural prohibitions against them as speakers for divinity. Dickinson's contemporaries realized the implications of Hutchinson's strategy of renunciation to the godhead; they saw it as a means to dangerous female empowerment, as is pointedly demonstrated in a sketch written by Nathaniel Hawthorne for the Salem *Gazette*. Extending the implications of Hutchinson to literary women of the nineteenth century, Hawthorne in this 1830 sketch of "Mrs. Hutchinson" found a resemblance between the nineteenth-century "public women" and Hutchinson, the new breed of women being no less threatening and far more numerous than that "public woman" of the past. Hawthorne's sketch voices the mid-nineteenth-century anxiety over contemporary women writers, who were perceived as being as dangerous as earlier women who had seen themselves as prophets. Although the women authors did not directly and consistently urge "strange and dangerous opinions," as Hutchinson reputedly had done (instead emphasizing the virtues of the home), these women, according to Hawthorne, committed the same offense as Hutchinson: their "feminine ambition" led them to abandon their true art and calling—embroidery—for careers as "public speakers" and writers. Like Anne Hutchinson, who confused "carnal pride" with the gift of prophecy, the misguided author yielded to the "impulse of genius like a command of Heaven within," Hawthorne maintained. Each stepped out of her appointed place and indelicately displayed her "natal mind to the gaze of the world"; each was urged on by an apparently irresistible "inward voice," said Hawthorne—a female prophetic voice that, by implication, would threaten the societal order as it challenged the strictures on women's prescribed role. In Lang's words, "The story of 'The Woman,' as Hawthorne . . . calls Hutchinson, is offered as the quintessential story of female empowerment"—empowerment that had its origin in an "inward voice" deriving from the Christian prophetic tradition.[19]

In exploiting the possibilities of poetry, Dickinson obviously chose a different path from that of her antinomian predecessor Anne Hutchinson and from that of the nineteenth-century feminist orators. She continued Hutchinson's tradition of speaking her own inspired words when she expressed a radically new vision of religious devotion. But it was in the Bible itself, with its poetry of prophecy and wisdom literature, that she found the most compelling models of prophecy. The biblical examples and the tradition of the scriptural female prophets gave Dickinson a sense of justification as a prophet; and as we saw earlier, the rhetorical techniques of Judeo-Christian prophets gave her a rich store of materials to draw on and adapt, including the formal model of Hebrew poetry.

In one characteristic poem, Dickinson indicated the opportunities that she found in her chosen medium to pursue her religious calling:

> I dwell in Possibility—
> A fairer House than Prose—
> More numerous of Windows—
> Superior—for Doors—

Of Chambers as the Cedars—
Impregnable of Eye—
And for an Everlasting Roof
The Gambrels of the Sky—

Of Visiters—the fairest—
For Occupation—This—
The spreading wide my narrow Hands
To gather Paradise—   (#657)

Certainly, poetry *is* possibility for the speaker of this poem. Not limited by the expectations associated with the prose "prophecy" of her day—limitations that could include gender, form, or dogma—this speaker finds in poetry not only "Windows" through which, as a prophet, she can figuratively see but also "Doors" that give her the opportunity to interact with the world, if she chooses, yet retreat to the safety of her "fair house" to write. Significantly, the image of doors suggests movement, not limitation or imprisonment. And the "Roof" of her house of poetry is the steep slope or "gambrel" of the sky itself, an image that suggests her house's contact with the heavens. That contact seems especially important when we consider the religious terms in which she describes her poetic vocation: "The spreading wide my narrow Hands / To gather Paradise—." Poetry is a religious calling for this speaker. And it is not confining. To bring "Paradise" to herself through her "narrow" female hands—a reference, perhaps, to her culture's perception of her as limited, because of her gender—is possible despite cultural constraints, the speaker implies. Equally important, she "gathers paradise" not for herself but for her "visitors." Not only does she have an audience or community that participates in her spiritual calling as receivers of her religiously inspired poetry, but that audience consists of "the fairest" visitors. It is an image that suggests an audience specially attuned to her, an important prerequisite for a speaker who will defy expectations of dogma and genre.

Dickinson's art continued an important tradition in women's poetry. Indeed, other women artists established precedents for her strategy of drawing on biblical traditions to invest literary works with persuasive power and immortality. As I have argued elsewhere, Anne Bradstreet imitated the Psalms, adopting of the Davidic voice to give her Andover Manuscript poems sanctity, pedagogical importance, and immortality. Like Dickinson, she imitated the basic rhetorical structure of the biblical poetry—the Hebrew parallelism—as well as its colloquial style and vivid imagery. A contemporary of Hutchinson, she rejected Hutchinson's antinomian practice but established another strategy for empowerment deriving from the biblical traditions of prophecy and wisdom: that of a "prophetic mother" who gives birth both to children and to poems that speak wisdom to those children and to others, even frequently forming her verse around female figures of biblical wisdom.[20] As Dickinson would do after her, Bradstreet negotiated between her impatience with her Christian culture, which would oppress her or demand her silence, and the inspiration and models that the scriptural tradition afforded her poetry.

The audience for Bradstreet's understanding of spiritual truth was her children, an acceptable audience for Puritan women; but we should not minimize the importance of her poetic decisions. Although a woman's instruction of her children was approved in Bradstreet's day, poetry was still conceived of as a primarily masculine occupation.[21] Despite the surprising number of women writing poetry (as attested by Pattie Cowell's anthology of prerevolutionary women poets), Bradstreet and other women interested in a literary avocation were hampered by rigid role definitions and societal expectations and took a considerable risk—censure by fathers, husbands, and other men—when they stepped outside their carefully prescribed role by making public their poetic interests.[22] Bradstreet turned to the Scriptures to find a biblical model of verse to legitimize and even sanctify her Andover Manuscript poems—poetry through which she spoke her own version of spiritual truth. Her strategy prefigures Dickinson's practice, as both women looked to the Christian tradition to find a way to confront the patriarchy.

Bradstreet knew, of course, that women who were outspoken in proclaiming their views of religious truth faced verbal and even physical punishment, as was the case for Puritans Sarah Keayne and Katherine Finch. Both women imitated Hutchinson in their outspoken addresses on spiritual truth and served as examples of what could happen to prophetic women. Sarah Keayne was found guilty in 1646 of "irregular prophesying in mixed assemblies," and Katherine Finch was whipped in 1638 for "speaking against the magistrates, against the churches, and against the elders."[23] After the Hutchinson incident, other women—such as Mary Dyer, Hutchinson's friend—left the Puritan communities to join the Quakers, who permitted women a role in interpreting religious truth. Bradstreet's choice of children as the audience for her religious verse and the conventionality of her re-

ligious teachings seem more understandable in the context of the
strictures against female poets and would-be prophets. Understood in
this context, her drawing on the scriptural tradition to invest her
poetry with sanctity and persuasive power becomes a noteworthy assertive strategy. Her early position in the New England tradition of
women's prophecy is important for her suggestion of a maneuver that
later female religious speakers, Dickinson included, could draw on for
enablement.

In Bradstreet and Dickinson, we see the coherence of a tradition of
women's religious verse that operated in a less public arena than did
men's prophecy but whose message still was not kept private. Both
Bradstreet and Dickinson decided against commercial publication—at
least initially, in Bradstreet's case—choosing a relatively private way to
speak despite their claim of an authoritative voice. Bradstreet, impatient with the limitations placed on her as a poet, wrote poetry intended only for those closest to her and thereby avoided the risk of
censure; it was her relative who initiated the attempt at commercial
publication. Likewise, Dickinson sent her poems to friends and family
and adopted her own form of publication in the fascicles, refusing
commercial publication despite the urging of friends and publishers.
These women rejected the national audiences that the male prophets
seem to have claimed, and show us an alternative practice of limiting
one's audience.

Expressing Bradstreet's self-assertion and self-abnegation, the lines
of "The Prologue" are important for the way that they replicate the
stance of Hutchinson:

> Men can do best, and women know it well.
> Preeminence in all and each is yours;
> Yet grant some small acknowledgement of ours.[24]

Despite their differences in theology—Bradstreet was much more conservative than Hutchinson—both women renounced themselves (to
the patriarchy, in Bradstreet's case; to Christ, in Hutchinson's) in order
to assert their voices. Whether or not Dickinson knew her work,
Bradstreet's strategy, along with Hutchinson's, is significant for the
ways in which it looks forward to the poetry of Dickinson. Dickinson,
like Hutchinson and Bradstreet before her, saw in the renunciation
advocated by the Puritan tradition a strategy so powerful that it became one strong, important stance she struck as prophet-poet. Dickinson found power in social self-renunciation, writing within the relative

privacy of her home and giving up opportunities for public recognition. As we will see in greater detail in Chapter 8, Dickinson repeatedly expressed the importance of this strategy in her poetry, reiterating throughout her verse the value of abnegation as a way to achieve triumph.

Yet Bradstreet stands as a forerunner of Dickinson in a more powerful way than in her strategy of self-denial. As Dickinson also would do, Bradstreet, like Hutchinson, drew on the Bible for devices to shape an authoritative voice for her Andover Manuscript poems; she imitated the Psalms in technique, stance, and thematic patterns, because she, like her culture, saw the psalmic poetry as sanctified. Although she was not as daring as Dickinson, who would boldly revise scriptural and theological concepts, Bradstreet in the Andover Manuscript poems set an early precedent as a poet who attempted to gain legitimacy by continuing the devices and voices of sacred poetry in her art. Men historically have also adopted this strategy (the myriad Puritan ministers who adapted the Psalms for singing come to mind), but Bradstreet's practice is particularly significant because her gender totally disqualified her among her contemporaries from being a recognized poet. She, like Dickinson after her, looked not to the verse of her male contemporaries for a model to imitate but to a sacred text, one believed to have been truly written by God through the hands of his followers. Understood as blessed and sanctioned by God, the Psalms offered Bradstreet an approved poetics that, through her adoption of the devices, could give her an effective pedagogy to draw on for her children as well as a tradition of literary immortality—David's, because of God's presumed blessing of his verse. Dickinson may not have been seeking the blessing of a conventional God when she imitated the Bible, but undoubtedly, she also desired the cultural authority and even the lasting importance that the biblical poetry had attained in her day.

It is notable, too, that all three poets structured their content around the form of song: David drew on Hebrew song and has been recognized by generations after him as a singer (one of the few male singers mentioned in the Scriptures); Bradstreet patterned her Andover Manuscript poems on the rhythms of the *Bay Psalm Book*; and Dickinson, as we have noticed, adopted the meters of Isaac Watts's hymns.[25] Song was the genre chosen by several women prophets in the Bible and seems particularly appealing to women as a vehicle of prophetic truth.

The Anglo-American female tradition of religious poetry that began with Bradstreet remained unchanged in Dickinson's day in some significant respects. Although women's publication was more acceptable in the mid-nineteenth century than it was in colonial America— more acceptable as long as the poets seemed to express the proper emotions, piety, and themes—the poetry of American (and British) women continued to show female poet-prophets, including Dickinson, that women could assume a role as religious speakers in their vocations as poets. More important, the poetry demonstrated the Hutchinson-Bradstreet model of power and triumph through renunciation. Dickinson would take this tradition even further, but it is important to note here the literary and religious contexts out of which she emerged.

Dickinson undoubtedly knew the female poetic tradition well, especially as it included numerous poets, colonial and nineteenth-century. She owned Rufus Griswold's *The Sacred Poets of England and America* (1849), which included the poetry of Anne Steele (d. 1799), Anna Letitia Barbauld (d. 1835), and other early female poets who expounded their views of spirituality. Three other anthologies of her time, *Griswold's Female Poets of America* (1848), Thomas Buchanan Read's *The Female Poets of America* (1855), and Caroline May's *American Female Poets* (1848), brought to the American reading public the poetry of many more women, including Anne Bradstreet. Bathsheba Bowers (1672–1718), a Quaker preacher, earlier had articulated her vision in her spiritual autobiography, *An Alarm Sounded to Prepare . . . the World to Meet the Lord* (1709), which is notable for its inclusion of poetry (and therefore its continuation of this tradition), whether or not Dickinson knew it.[26] Judith Sargent Murray (1751–1820), whose devout Universalism occasionally led to controversy, even more directly in her poetry asserted herself as religious speaker, firmly holding to the legitimacy of her themes:

> Say, who is authoriz'd to probe my breast,
> Of whatsoever latent faith possess'd; . . .
> Religion is 'twixt God and my own soul,
> Nor saint, nor sage, can boundless thought control.[27]

Despite her Universalism, Murray voiced a precept dear to most Protestants: that her religion was between her and her God, not to be mediated by any priest except herself. It was a tenet that many women undoubtedly found particularly meaningful, including those, like

Dickinson, who would go so far as to cast off the constraints of the church and develop their own version of spirituality.

But American and English women more conventional than Bowers and Murray also found in poetry a vehicle by which to "preach" their beliefs about God. Hannah More (d. 1833) and Felicia Hemans (d. 1835) both wrote hymns that appeared in Griswold's *Sacred Poets of England and America.* According to Griswold, Anne Steele, a devotional lyricist, also wrote many hymns that eventually appeared in the collections of most of the churches of her time.[28] Her "Morning Hymn" and similar poems by other women share with Dickinson's verse the hymn meter—"common meter"—found in many of Bradstreet's Andover Manuscript poems. As we noted earlier, the genre of song seems particularly appealing to women as a vehicle to express spiritual vision. These nineteenth-century women continued the tradition presumably begun by women (Miriam, Deborah, possibly others) and carried on by David. Most American women poets versified dogma, but some, like Murray, began to challenge conventional Christianity as it had been established by patriarchal institutions.

In the anthologies, popular periodicals, and newspapers of her own time—including the publications her family subscribed to, such as the *Springfield Republican, Harper's New Monthly, Scribner's Monthly, The Atlantic Monthly,* and *The Amherst Record*[29]—Dickinson could find a wealth of sentimental, evangelical verse written by women and models of women poets preaching the word of Scripture through their poetic visions. The *Springfield Republican* consistently printed poems by women, often introduced by the admiring comments of editor Samuel Bowles. George Frisbie Whicher finds the *Republican* "next in importance to the Bible in determining the mental climate of [Dickinson's] formative years."[30] The poet herself once mentioned, in a letter to her friends the Hollands, "I read in it [the *Republican*] every night" (*L,* 1:264). And as Richard Sewall points out, Dickinson read women's sentimental fiction with enthusiasm; this fiction also continued the evangelical, didactic mode of the women's poetry.

Nineteenth-century poets such as Lydia H. Sigourney, Alice and Phoebe Carey, Caroline May, Sarah J. Hale, Elizabeth Oakes Smith, and Frances Sargent Osgood all focused on Christian themes and imagery with a highly intense emotionality that contributed to the production of a feminine, Christian poetic voice, which Dickinson arguably adopted, popular as these poets were in her own time and, indeed, with Dickinson herself, as evidenced by her steady reading of the poems in the periodicals. Poet Sarah Edgarton Mayo in her "The Supremacy of God" shows a pattern that Dickinson herself adopted, that of Christian renunciation leading to access of power. She calls for humble praise of the all-powerful godhead, describing in the poem's last line the intimacy with the divine that results from a meek stance before God: the "adoring hearts" that praise will "stand in God's own light, communers with God's soul." The line suggests the empower- ment as communicators that "adorers" of God gain in "communing" with the divine, their renunciation and humility leading to power as they assume the role of praising God.[31] Similarly, Lydia H. Sigour- ney—who was more popular than William Cullen Bryant in their day—in "Death of a Friend" figures her friend as "self-sacrificing, upright, pure," and gaining as a reward ascension to God's "courts" to "find a mansion there"—that is, accessing the power of God through self-denial.[32] These and other female poets spoke as authoritative teachers of spiritual truths, forming an important context for Dickin- son's poetic venture, despite the fact that they were more conven- tionally didactic than their experimental poetic sister. "Remember! let thy mercy flow, / And bless for heaven those pangs of wo [*sic*]," Sigourney writes in "Lord, Remember Us," suggesting the suffering implicit in her poetic stance. She calls on God to vindicate her "pangs of wo" as a religious speaker.[33] In expressing their religiousness, Si- gourney and others communicate an emotional intensity similar to that found in, for example, Dickinson's "Jesus—it's your little 'John'! / Don't you know—me?" as Dickinson's speaker, too, calls on divine recognition (#497, "He strained my faith—," lines 15–16).

Read's and Griswold's anthologies of American women poets in- clude the works of eighty-four and ninety-three poets, respectively, most of them contemporary with Dickinson and most addressing Christian themes and pronouncements. As Emily Stipes Watts has pointed out, "Most American women poets have been religious"—by which she means, most have communicated in their poetry their beliefs about God and spirituality.[34] In the nineteenth century, according to Ann Douglas, middle-class women and northeastern clergy both be- lieved they had "a genuine redemptive mission in their society" as they propagated their own view of religion—what Douglas calls "sentimen- talized" theology.[35] Whether or not that "sentimentalizing" should be attributed only to women and preachers, at least we can say that the female poets and novelists, with their authoritative, didactic voices, modeled for Dickinson the preacherly impulse of the Judeo-Christian prophet, a practice that the female orators of her time also adopted. And not only women poets but also women novelists, through their female characters, taught the stance of Christian submission or renunciation that empowers; as Jane Tompkins has argued, the female characters became "all-powerful" as they "mak[e] themselves into vehicles of God's will."[36]

Dickinson thus had not only her own Christian tradition to draw from—and its models of women prophets from the Bible and colonial history—but the practices of women in her own day: poets, fiction writers, and female orators, all of whom functioned as religious speakers. Perhaps most significantly, these women showed her that women could indeed participate, in some way, in the New England prophetic tradition.

Other critics have recognized this tradition of women writers who present themselves as religious truth tellers. In her work focusing on women's poetry, Cheryl Walker sums up one of the directions she notices in that art:

> Ultimately, it seems that these women poets have acted in a similar capacity to women prophets. They have constituted themselves as *'femmes sage,'* wise women, midwives of a sort, whose knowledge as it is passed on to others carries a female burden of dark and sometimes secret truths. . . . Women poets throughout this tradition share with Bradstreet the delight of assuming an authoritative stance of this kind. With the same sense of exuberance they compose female power fantasies.[37]

Dickinson goes further than most of these American poets by claiming the rhetorical structures of prophecy to communicate her authority. But in employing poetry to express her wisdom, she is not so unlike her female literary contemporaries. Neither is she unlike them in choosing renunciation as a vehicle to power, a theme Walker explores in more detail with respect to women's poetry. What separates Dickinson from her female literary contemporaries—and aligns her more closely with the female orators—is the deliberateness with which she seizes prophetic, visionary authority. She is more daring than almost any of the female poets preceding her.

One literary model of an assertive religious voice that Dickinson did have was novelist Harriet Beecher Stowe. More than any other

American woman novelist of Dickinson's time, Stowe functioned as a female literary "prophet." Though she seems to have been more theologically conservative than Dickinson, nonetheless she shared Dickinson's claim of religious authority. Stowe adopted the preacher's stance in composing *Uncle Tom's Cabin*, writing the novel as a kind of sermon, as Tompkins has shown, by drawing on typology and religious myth.[38] It is Stowe's skill at handling these sermonic elements that gives the novel its power. Like Bradstreet and others, she was able to defy the pejorative connotations of the woman prophet that followed from the Hutchinson incident, speaking prophetically while not seeming to transgress cultural boundaries. And she attained for herself lasting literary importance even as she worked within or drew on the Calvinist tradition. As one who shared Stowe's (and Bradstreet's) theological heritage, Dickinson, too, wrote within that tradition. Her relatively unorthodox vision and iconoclastic form have, until recently, obscured the similarities to her female contemporaries in voice and theme; critics have, for the most part, dismissed the popular female religious poets because of the conventionality of their verse. In reconsidering Stowe, as recent scholars have done, we can begin to understand the strategies and spirituality of American female writers, Dickinson included.

Certainly, for a woman writer to express a nonconformist religious vision required creativity, even subversiveness, if she wanted to see her literature in print. Direct social protest by women was, in general, not tolerated. The acceptable motives for women's publishing were limited: the desire to be "an instrument of good" and a pressing need for money. Indeed, female poets of Dickinson's day faced enormous obstacles to female self-assertion. Dickinson herself did not have financial need, and although she was motivated partly by didactic intent, her didacticism—if we can call it that—took a much different form from that of the female poets of her time. Dickinson was not moralistic, as many of her female poetic contemporaries were; rather, her attempt to improve the moral and spiritual fiber of humanity took the shape of an expansive spiritual vision expressed in the forms and genres of the prophet, including generalized insights into human nature and into the living of one's life. Thus, Dickinson did not meet either of the accepted criteria for women's publishing, and in fact, as a poet-prophet, she aligned herself with a tradition characteristically closed to American women, at least publicly. Publication would have brought public scrutiny and an identity that she apparently did not want: that of a celebrity taking her place among the other published female poets who wrote seemingly quaint, tame verse. Convincing evidence does exist that she could have published her poems but chose not to, despite pressure from friends and publishers.[39] It seems likely that Dickinson instead wrote her poems for an audience of anagogic inclinations, including posterity, seeing beyond the general audiences of her day who would undoubtedly have misread her and her art. Saving the poems for a future audience would, moreover, safeguard them from the tinkering of well-intentioned publishers, from the compromising of her poetic wisdom.

Dickinson knew well the conventions of female verse and the constraints on women who attempted to write. As Hutchinson had experienced earlier, women prophet-poets confronted cultural expectations of female reticence, which was considered a primary requirement for the respectable woman in nineteenth-century America. Expected socially to strike a pose of submission, literary women had to adopt, as Joanne Dobson puts it, "expressive restrictions so stringent and so ingrained that they amounted to a culturally endorsed and culturally monitored feminine community of expression. Dickinson would have learned these "strategies of reticence"—indirect expression, nonpublication, and reliance on feminine stereotypes—through her socialization and reading, as her feminine community of expression modeled devices designed to allay anxiety about nonconforming female articulation. She stands out as one woman who not only acquiesced to the expressive constraints but also brilliantly usurped them in achieving her poetics of prophecy.[40] Yet not only did she transform some of the conventional responses to those constraints through her "slant" expressive strategy, her refusal to publish through conventional means, and her manipulation of feminine images and stylistic devices, as Dobson demonstrates, but she found in her own Christian tradition an empowering stance and strategies for assuming a prophetic voice, which Dobson fails to identify. Like many of her female literary counterparts, Dickinson drew on the possibilities of the pose of renunciation, even rooting her religious vision in that stance. But she went further in transforming social reticence into a claim of religious power (and thereby, in overcoming contemporary societal strictures on female self-assertion and prophecy) by exploiting the prophetic tradition for a range of strategies and rhetorical techniques to gain an authoritative voice.

As Chapter 8 will show, Dickinson adopted renunciation as both a stance and a central theme in her poetry, not expressing it in a gesture of retreat, as her patriarchal society would have had her do, but finding in it a means to authenticate her poetic and prophetic voice, as Hutchinson, Bradstreet, and contemporary female writers did. Reinterpreted and emphasized with renewed vigor by Jonathan Edwards and his followers, the stance of renunciation shaped Dickinson's self-representation as a nineteenth-century woman poet living in her father's home, and as a theme, renunciation shaped her vision of spirituality. Perhaps most important, it gave her prophetic authority. Hutchinson had paved the way for empowerment through self-abnegation: denial of the self to Christ meant for Hutchinson a special relationship to God, in which he spoke through her, empowering her as religious speaker. Denial of the self thus could lead to assertion of the self and autonomy from the patriarchy. Dickinson, too, claimed this strategy for enablement. Figuring herself as a prophet inspired by a divine Other, she found in renunciation a stand that, in the tradition of the biblical prophets and Hutchinson, could legitimate the poetry of her religious vision as she subordinated herself to her inspirer. Perhaps more than any other idea, the theme and prophetic stance of renunciation align Dickinson with her female predecessors, distinguishing her prophecy as particularly female.

8. "And I Sneered—Softly—'Small'!": Renunciation and Power

"THE CENTRAL PARADOX of [Dickinson's] thought," according to Richard Wilbur, "is a discovery of something about the soul, . . . that privation is more plentiful than plenty; that to renounce is to possess the more."[1] Dickinson's discovery was born out of her experience of her religious milieu as much as her personal experiences. Certainly, critics have noted her pattern of renunciation—Wilbur, Karl Keller, and Cheryl Walker among them—but we need to understand this theme more squarely in connection with Dickinson's Protestant heritage and her claim of a female prophetic voice. The idea of self-denial propounded in the Bible and preached by Jonathan Edwards a century before Dickinson wrote her poems became so central to nineteenth-century evangelicalism—especially in defining Christian womanhood—that she could hardly have escaped its influence on her own sense of self. But unlike any writer of her day, Dickinson took evangelical Protestant dogma and recast it, with startling results. That she questioned the ideal of self-denial is apparent in her many poems expressing the pain of loss. Cultural expectations, at least for poets, constrained honest, unqualified expressions of loss in print. In contrast to many poets of her day, Dickinson offered her experiences of loss without apologizing, couching the pain in obscure diction, or offering a simplistic moral lesson. Even more noteworthy is that she exploited the evangelical ideal of renunciation to legitimate her own voice, and she reinterpreted it to furnish a key component of her wisdom.

Self-denial has been an important concept to Christians of various traditions, eras, and places, because the idea was clearly articulated, emphasized, and modeled by Christ (the best example being his crucifixion). In the early part of the nineteenth century in America, evangelicals continued the renewed focus on the idea begun by Jonathan Edwards, urging a strenuous, self-forgetful type of Christianity. This was the expression of Christianity that Dickinson knew; the movement was not so much a doctrinal system but a moral and spiritual force, preaching warm evangelical life and practical Christian living characterized by self-sacrifice.

Growing up in antebellum western Massachusetts, Dickinson knew the centrality of self-denial to New England Protestantism as the concept had been emphasized by Edwards's disciple Samuel Hopkins (1721–1803) and Hopkins's followers. For Hopkins and his students, the test of a true Christian was a complete, willing, and disinterested submission to the divine disposal—as Dickinson put it, to become "Last—Least—," as "the Cross" had "requested" of Christ, asking him to humble himself to the point of death (#573, "The Test of Love—is Death—"). Christ's renunciation had brought him exaltation and glory, as described in Phil. 2:5–11, to which Dickinson's poem alludes: Christ "thought it not robbery to be equal with God: But made himself of no reputation," the biblical text states (vv. 6–7). Christ "humbled himself, and became obedient unto death," with the result that God "hath highly exalted him" (vv. 8–9). As modeled by Christ, complete self-denial—or "disinterested benevolence," to use Hopkins's term—was key to Christian virtue and thus to Christian triumph. The Hopkinsian school of thought was so well known in Dickinson's day that her contemporary Harriet Beecher Stowe made a fictionalized Hopkins central to her *The Minister's Wooing* (1859). As a student at Mount Holyoke, Dickinson was taught that self-denial was one of the principal elements of Christian charity; its doctrine was preached to all who desired to become Christians. This religious tradition, as interpreted by Hopkins and his followers, would be the most important influence on Dickinson's spirituality—a tradition whose doctrines and emphases she learned at school and in the Congregational church she attended as a young girl.[2]

The emphasis on self-denial propounded by Hopkins and other evangelicals undergirded nineteenth-century understandings of conversion, as well as of the sanctification that was to emerge from conversion. In refusing to assert independence, the believer was promised to find the real self; in abandoning self-assertion and self-seeking for the sake of Christ, the believer would, paradoxically, find grace. The idea derived from Christ's admonitions in such passages as Matt. 16:24–25: "If any man will come after me, let him deny himself. . . . For whosoever will save his life shall lose it; and whosoever will lose his life for my sake shall find it." When Dickinson celebrates in her poetry the rewards of privation, she is adapting for her own vision the idea that surrender and submission to Christ result in the surest gain: the new self transformed by grace. What she does is shape that pattern of reward into a vehicle of power. In the tradition of Anne Hutchinson, Dickinson claims the renunciation of one who gives up all in order to find not only a new self but a self filled up with grace—not just transformed by grace—to speak divine words. Like the self-denial of Hutchinson and the biblical prophets, Dickinson's renunciation results in empowered speech as part of her divine gain. In drawing on the Edwardsian concept of self-denial, then, she "contributes to" and "refreshes" the Edwardsian system, to use Keller's words, as she adopts a role as prophet.[3]

"Simplicity, simplicity, simplicity!" Thoreau preached in *Walden*, advocating the renunciation of everything but food, shelter, clothing, and fuel as the way to front the essential facts of life.[4] He emerged from his experience at Walden Pond renewed from his encounters with the divine, compelled to speak about the virtues of living deliberately, of being spiritually alive. In Dickinson we find the convergence of this romantic emphasis with the evangelical Protestant tenet. But her idea of renunciation differs significantly from Thoreau's: while both advocate the stripping away of things that distract one from truly living, Thoreau urges only the giving up of (select) material items—food, shelter, clothing, fuel. Dickinson's renunciation is more complete. Most notably, she models the renunciation of public life, of social life, of the ego and self. She urges on her audience an experience of total loss. And the outcome? For Thoreau, it is the gain of the soul, an experience of "truth" and "living deliberately"—no small reward, indeed. Yet the consequences that Dickinson suggests take on even greater metaphysical proportions. The deeper she plunges into the well of self-denial, the higher she rises in a claim of victory and grace.

Dickinson often described her reward in the language of evangelical Protestantism, not romanticism, suggesting that she lacked nothing that her evangelical contemporaries had gained, only their conventional religious experience. Equally significant, her pattern captures one that we have seen was important to female prophetic speakers of the Christian tradition: the emptying of the mundane self in order to be filled up with God's grace and thus to be a source of divine light. As the Judeo-Christian tradition expressed it, prophetic authority came through a life and posture of renunciation. Jeremiah, Amos, and even Christ forfeited much in their service as divine agents. Dickinson transformed the renunciation expected of nineteenth-century women into this renunciation, the privation of the prophet.

For women of Dickinson's day and locale, sacrifice, including a withdrawal from public life, was held as a normative practice—a norm that Thoreau never had to confront, because of his gender. Although the Scriptures made no distinction of gender in their descriptions of self-denial—the death of the "natural" self to achieve subsequent spiritual rebirth—in antebellum American daily life, self-denial had different implications for women and men. Religious and larger cultural expectations did not converge as neatly around self-denial for men as for women. The "self" that the nineteenth-century woman was expected to deny extended to her self-interest, ego, personal ambitions, and any independence, financial or otherwise, that she might desire. Renunciation for women thus often took the form of emotional, personal, and spiritual retreat. Marriage, which called for self-denial to one's husband, meant to be "Bridalled," as Dickinson put it, the wife subjugating her desires and ambitions to her husband's (#1072, "Title divine—is mine!"), in contrast to the command and status of royalty that Dickinson's speaker claims as "Empress of Calvary." But the "self" of the nineteenth-century man included certain features of ego that were in conflict with Christian constructions of ideal selfhood— independence, material acquisitiveness, investment in competition, and economic self-sufficiency. Thus, it is not surprising that, in the nineteenth century, self-surrender and benevolent service were seen as the special virtues of women. Women were seen as, by nature, particularly fit for the service of others that serving the Lord in the denial of self came to mean. This self-denial meant for women the complete supression of ego.

Dickinson challenges this understanding of women's renunciation. For her, renunciation is an aggressive, confident, triumphant posture. She goes beyond her female contemporaries (literary and otherwise) in the strenuousness of her gesture, shaping a version of the prophet's renunciation that is appropriate to her gender. She emerges with a self-denial that acts as a vehicle of power and voice. Dickinson stands out for her success in transforming the cultural expectation of female renunciation—which could lead to powerlessness, voicelessness, and cultural invisibility—into the Judeo-Christian prophets' aggressive seizure of authority and, ultimately, reward.

Throughout her poetry—from poems dating as early as 1858 (#32, #35), to the verse of her later years—Emily Dickinson expresses such renunciation and the victory that results, adopting a stance not of defeat or withdrawal but of certainty and power. "Emergence through opposition becomes an aesthetic principle for her," Karl Keller points out; "peace must be sought through ordeal upon ordeal, the self through selflessness, power through pain, the highest through the lowest, heaven through humility."[5] It is an aesthetic grounded in Edwardsian ideas about survival, apocalypse, triumph. Expressing the importance of renunciation and the rewards it can bring throughout her canon, Dickinson makes self-denial a theme in her vision of spirituality, treating it directly in particular clusters of poems. The stance empowers her in her prophetic role as one who points the way toward holiness; and it forms the core of her religious vision, one that both draws on and revises biblical patterns of power.

The importance of the concept of renunciation to the Dickinson canon becomes apparent when we consider the clusters of poems that emphasize (1) the loss and pain of renunciation, (2) the access of power, and (3) the emotional return gained through it. According to Charles R. Anderson's count, the poems in the entire "despair cluster" total nearly two hundred; another cluster, including as many as three hundred poems, focuses exclusively on ecstasy, implicitly emerging from the renunciatory stance we discover in the other two clusters.[6] Seeing the poems in another light, Barbara J. Williams observes a cluster that focuses particularly on deprivation, giving us, as she puts it, "the greatest poetry of deprivation in our language"; but an even larger portion, according to Williams, expresses "the ecstasy of fulfillment." To any reader familiar with the Dickinson canon, her cluster on deprivation clearly is equaled by her poetry of reward. Indeed, Dickinson could "experience the heights of joy because she had first plummeted the depths of despair."[7] A third group of poems, celebrating the power gained through renunciation, links these two groups, indicating that Dickinson achieves her "ecstasy of fulfillment" precisely through her deprivation—a nonretreatist stance, ultimately, that derives from the Edwardsian tradition.

Given the sheer number of poems on these themes, we can see that the concepts of renunciation—loss and triumph and the relationship between them—remained central to Dickinson's religious vision. The emotional structure of renunciation visible in her apparently secular poems grew out of her early Congregationalist training and became a psychological construct that informed her poetry even after she apparently relinquished engagement with theological dogma. We see renunciation perhaps most frequently in the early verse, peaking in the 1862 poems; yet she employed it throughout her canon, abandoning it as a theme only in the last decade or so of her life when she adopted a consolatory voice, less frequently expressing extremes of loss and ecstasy. For Dickinson, renunciation was a stance that served her religious and emotional prophetic vision throughout most of her life—a stance she adopted even in her personal life in her father's home.

In recent years, feminist scholars have identified Dickinson's renunciation as expressed in her poems and letters, maintaining for the most part that she was forced into a renunciatory position by her patriarchal culture. Renunciation for many of these scholars can be only negative; they work from the assumption that Dickinson's identities as a woman and as a woman poet who was oppressed by her culture were primary for her, and that she must be distanced from her repressively conventional culture in order to write. For these critics, the cultural expectation of feminine renunciation could be only a liability for Dickinson as she expressed in her poetry her struggle to overcome the societal strictures.[8] These readings have been invaluable for increasing our awareness of Dickinson's struggle as an artist, but they have tended to focus either on her strategies for transcending her "anxiety of gender" or on the historical formation of such anxiety, as in John Cody's study, which argues that Dickinson the daughter was forced into renunciatory roles by her family.[9] All connect her stance of renunciation with the larger social formation of her identity as a woman, minimizing the influence of her religious tradition or, at worst, denigrating that influence.

Yet Dickinson's self-denial sprang not only from her culture's religiously authorized restrictions on womanhood but also from her Calvinist religious tradition, which, as she received it, contributed positively to her art. As part of her theological position, her stance of renunciation was not so much an expression of her frustration as a poet as it was an empowering part of her identity as a prophet and, subsequently, an element of her spirituality. As feminist scholars have argued, Dickinson indeed withdrew from public life, apparently in part because of her patriarchal culture. I argue, too, that she was able to put that gesture in the service of her own ends: she could reframe "withdrawal" to be an aggressive act of power. Significantly, her own evangelical Christian tradition taught her that self-abnegation could lead to triumph, the triumph emerging from deprivation. It was a pattern important to any believer from conservative circles, even more so to people who, like the preachers, saw themselves as prophets.

In the Edwardsian tradition, the authentic self—the "new person" in Christ—was gained through self-denial in the individual's struggle against sin; for the prophet, especially, the emptying of self—the disregard of self-interest—was a prerequisite for being filled with divine power as a speaker. For Emily Dickinson, surrender to her divine inspiration empowered her to speak, as it did for Anne Hutchinson. It enabled her to "[go] against the World" (#540, "I took my Power in my Hand—") rather than be another example of conformity to cultural expectations of females' passivity and silence. The philosophy of renunciation subsequently developed as a strategy for achieving ambition and power, key to her understanding of redemption.

Dickinson mentioned her special interest in the idea of self-denial as early as 1846, having observed two Chinese people who were working in a museum in Boston: "There is something peculiarly interesting to me in their self *denial*," she writes (*L*, 2:37); in China they had been "Opium Eaters," but here, she says, they have entirely overcome the practice, "lest it destroy their lives." She sees here that deprivation of pleasure can lead to greater life, even survival, and that, as Walker puts it, "value is achieved through deprivation."[10] For Dickinson, as for the opium eaters, self-denial was a way of life, not a step toward ultimate deprivation. More specifically for Dickinson, it was a stance that allowed her to speak out the influx of spiritual power which ensued from submission to the divine, as she had learned from figures in her Christian training—the models of preacher, prophet, Christ.

Dickinson's version of self-denial was probably threatening to her culture in its service as vehicle to power. As Lawrence Buell has accurately pointed out in comparing Dickinson's literary universe to Stowe's, Dickinson's poems, like Stowe's *The Minister's Wooing*, "set up on some level an equation between self-fulfillment and self-denial rather than self-assertion or self-reliance in the Emersonian sense."[11] This motif, Buell continues, relates to the concept of disinterested benevolence described by Samuel Hopkins.[12] Certainly, in Dickinson's poems on renunciation we often find a mood of exaltation, as she celebrates the enablement gained through self-denial. But Walker, placing Dickinson in the history of women poets, points out that "women have chosen renunciation, because often it represented the only form of power available to them. . . . One must always remember that the power claimed by . . . [Dickinson] is presented as a triumph of the powerless."[13] For Dickinson as a female prophet, this power had particular importance, given her culture's anxiety about women prophets. Emerson in "The Poet" underlined the need for renunciation of power in its usual forms—political, economic, social—for the poet to achieve visionary power, a point that highlights the cultural contrast between nineteenth- and twentieth-century understandings of power. Yet Dickinson as a female poet-prophet in the Christian tradition went even further, renouncing the self more totally to access divine power. In one characteristic poem, her speaker asserts, "Joy to have perished every step— / To Compass Paradise" (#788, "Joy to have merited the Pain—," lines 3–4). Dickinson's deprivation is willing, and it is total; and so are the spiritual rewards—in this case, "Paradise"—resulting from material loss.

Dickinson does, at times, show some ambivalence about the posture of self-denial, as we know from the poems figuring images of explosiveness—bonfires, guns, volcanic eruptions. In poems such as #601, "A Still—Volcano—Life—"; #754, "My Life had stood—a Loaded Gun—"; #1132, "The smouldering embers blush—"; #1677, "On my volcano grows the Grass"; and #1748, "The reticent volcano keeps," we see the anger and frustration that can accompany potential moments of renunciation. Poem #754, "My Life had stood—a Loaded Gun—," stands out for its intensity of emotion and violent images. Such poems are noteworthy not only for their rejection of a self-denying stance, showing Dickinson's periodic ambivalence, but, perhaps even more important for Dickinson as a prophet-poet, for the way they point to what Joanne Dobson has called "expressive anxiety."[14] Poem #754, difficult to penetrate with its missing referents and elusive metaphors, lends itself to a variety of interpretations, as the multitude of readings given in the past years attests.[15] Yet we do know that the poem seems to be one about utterance: the gun "speaks" as it fires, and the "Vesuvian" qualities we know from other poems are often associated with speech. As Dobson explains, in this poem and in others, "pressure to speak vies with the need to 'veil' the subject to the point of unintelligibility," the resistance of the verse embodying the nineteenth-century cultural expectation about women's reluctance to speak.[16]

In her use of obscuring devices such as irony, ambivalence, and the omission of referential markers, alongside the incendiary imagery that suggests a deep desire to speak, Dickinson indicates her struggle with the strictures on women's expression, which mandated reticence as a primary requirement for "respectable" females. Such reticence was important not only for literary women but also for female prophets. As the example of religious verse by her female contemporaries attests, women were expected to be, for the most part, conventionally orthodox, not challenging the religious status quo. When Dickinson shrouds aggression in metaphors, irony, and even ambivalence, she adopts strategies protective of herself as an unorthodox poet-prophet. The imagery of destructive explosiveness further relates to the belief, common into her time, that a woman prophet's expression was dangerous, as was seen in the case of Anne Hutchinson. Yet, ultimately, Dickinson's poetic strategies serve her stance of renunciation as it enables her prophetic-poetic role, rather than being a retreatist capitulation to the expectations of her patriarchal culture, as we see in her manipulation of the "strategies of reticence," the focus of Dobson's work.

Dickinson's stance is not, as Buell describes it, an "almost voluptuous celebration of self-denial in the role of New England nun."[17] Such description feminizes and diminishes the power of her renunciation, which is closer to the self-denial of Christ and the biblical prophets than to that of a nun. In calling herself "Empress of Calvary," for instance (#1072, "Title divine—is mine!"), Dickinson's speaker feminizes her spiritual stance but, in doing so, presents access to more spiritual power and status than the figure of the nun represents. Her speaker is "Royal," an "Acute Degree" conferred on her, and she claims such great distinction as "Queen of Calvary" in another poem that all creatures bow "in gentle deference" to her (#348, "I dreaded that first Robin, so," line 24). Continuing stereotypes of femininity, even in Buell's fine work, obscure Dickinson's adoption of the Protestant Christian tradition, as well as the power of her work. Her renunciation is not the passive stance expected of women of her time or the subordinate role of service to patriarchal ecclesiastical structures that Buell's figure suggests. Her acceptance of loss and deprivation is not merely stoic or existential or a form of sensual masochism. Rather, as Keller describes, it is rigorous, creative, aggressive: Dickinson turns "tragedy into hope, . . . the dark into an opportunity," boasting that "anguish, pain, death, despair, disappointment, anxiety are productive."[18] Paradoxically, aggressive self-denial leads to freedom, excitement, fulfillment, and inspiration to write rather than to accept silence.

We have briefly considered how the women's fiction of her time showed Dickinson examples of this pattern of power, the female characters demonstrating that self-abnegation could bring women spiritual power. By subjecting themselves to God, Jane Tompkins explains, "[the] female characters become nothing in themselves, but all-powerful in relation to the world," bypassing "worldly (male) authority and . . . cancel[ing] it out."[19] Through her Christian education and reading of the biblical prophetic writings, Dickinson learned the same concept of power: that the renunciation of the self could lead to status and the power of divine inspiration. Isaiah, Jeremiah, Miriam, and the other scriptural prophets all emptied themselves to the divine and thereby gained a prophetic voice, denying their own ambitions and egos for access to prophetic power. Dickinson would have seen that this understanding of power had special relevance for both women and prophets.

Renunciation, of course, characterized Dickinson's life as a woman poet, as feminist scholars have pointed out; what is important is that it was not a passive capitulation for Dickinson but her way of self-preservation, a conscious effort to retain power. "Not to marry was not to lose self," Charlotte Louise Nekola explains:

> Retreating to a room in a house instead of joining a community which praised self-lessness as highest virtue for a woman perhaps was a way of creating a world in which a voice could learn to speak for itself. To denounce publication when denied it, or when publication for women meant ornament . . . may have also been an act of self preservation.[20]

For Dickinson's personal life as well as for her moments of inspiration, her transformation of cultural understandings and practices was strategic. Her success as a poet was not simply a monolithic art of compensation.[21] Renouncing the conventional roles of nineteenth-century woman, wife, and mother, which were obstacles to her calling, she aggressively pursued her vocation as a poet and a prophet, shrewdly becoming a recluse to focus on her art, as Thoreau had done at Walden Pond. Her creativity was undoubtedly encouraged and sustained by her audience of female friends, and she relied on her sense of a calling to speak to fuel her art. As Wendy Martin explains, "It is . . . accurate to view Dickinson's isolation as self-imposed, a measure of her freedom rather than her fear," a gesture that places her "in the tradition of protest and reform that is a basic dimension of American culture." Dickinson arranged her domestic routines around her creative task, Martin points out, and even enlisted the support of her family, especially her sister, Lavinia, to enable her to pursue that task.[22] She refused to be constrained by the nineteenth-century ideology of womanhood— the limits of the public roles denied to women, the constructions of feminine spirituality and morality, the silence imposed on women's voices in the church in the Pauline tradition as it was then interpreted. Dickinson transformed renunciation, defining what she had renounced—her "womanly" or "social" self—in her own terms rather than society's.[23] Certainly, such a transformation was necessary for the woman prophet in America, who had to alter a conventional social role of renunciation into renunciation as prophetic stance. Dickinson's decision to be reclusive in order to write and her decision to publish in her own way, the fascicles, were measures of her determination and sense of selection as a prophet; they were not an exercise in self-effacement.

Thus, Dickinson's social stance is not the defensive one of a woman faced with no better alternatives. In fact, as exemplified by the biblical prophets—Isaiah, Jeremiah, Christ, and others—it is the strategy of one refusing to be compromised in a religious calling. These prophets, Dickinson included, renounced their "social selves" in order to remain true to their calling as wisdom givers, paradoxically adopting a strategy of isolation in their role as speakers to their communities. Yet, although the (male) biblical prophets were compelled to renounce even the home in their identity as social recluses, for Dickinson as a female prophet in nineteenth-century America, the home provided a place to pursue her calling as she renounced conventional female roles to adopt a preaching stance, a decision that was not without its personal pain and loneliness. Christ had called his disciples—individuals who would become apostles, or New Testament prophets—to give up their families and homes, but Dickinson revised this aspect of prophecy and claimed the home as a haven that could protect her.[24] It was a place where she seemed to find pure religion: she keeps the Sabbath by "staying at home," she indicates in #324, "Some keep the Sabbath going to Church—."

Dickinson thus adopts a conventional nineteenth-century view of the home, describing home as true and bright while the world loomed as unreliable, lonely, alienating. Yet she does not accept the prevalent construction of the home as a private, personal place, isolated from the public sphere; rather, it is the place that can equip her to speak to that public sphere, at least as posterity. This complex view of the home and of her position as prophet-poet within it—the home as a place of poetic inspiration—explains her identification of the home with self, love of home as selfishness, rejection as homelessness, desolation as homesickness. She sees the home as a place that combines the awe and warmth of family affection, important to her survival as a prophetic poet, and thus it is the place in which her "letter to the World" originates (#441, "This is my letter to the World").

Renouncing socially prescribed roles for women in order to pursue her poetry, Dickinson figures herself as dwelling in the "House" of "Possibility— / A fairer House than Prose—" (#657, "I dwell in Possibility—"). She describes her domestic "occupation" as "the spreading wide my narrow Hands / To gather Paradise—," a metaphor indicating her conceptualization of poetry as religious calling (lines 10–12). Her "Hands" extend beyond a "narrow" domestic role to embrace a religious role of "gathering Paradise," of bringing paradise to herself through her own power. As a prophet, she herself explains the terms of redemption—terms of "Possibility"—not accepting the "prosaic," constrained existence of women who live in less "fair" houses. Dickinson proclaims her vision of paradise and religious "Possibility" through her prophetic voice.

Dickinson on occasion showed her contempt for conventional femininity and domesticity, at least for the aspects that would deprive her of a voice. She had to renounce the limits of a conventional domestic role in order to pursue her calling: she commanded God to "keep me from what they call *households*, except that bright one of 'faith'" (*L*, 1:99), and she leveled her criticism at the institution of marriage and conventional domestic life: the notice "she is to be sacrificed in October" was her way of announcing a friend's wedding.[25] Dickinson's interpretation of domesticity was not the domestic pietism typical of nineteenth-century New England. Like many theologians and other women writers, she located religious virtue in life at home; but whereas they saw that virtue in family life, she redefined it in terms of solitude—the solitude associated with the renunciation of a social self, necessary for the female prophet—as the many poems on the solitary soul attest (#789, "On a Columnar Self"; #303, "The Soul selects her own Society"; #383, "Exhilaration—is within—"; and #306, "The Soul's Superior instants," to name a few. It was within this circumference of renunciatory solitude that she, as a prophet, "endured the agonies of Calvary and encountered the royalty of God; she suffered the tortures of the damned and tasted the tenderness of love."[26] The solitude of social renunciation, not the conventional roles of wife and mother, enabled her to pursue her poetic prophecy.

Social renunciation not only paradoxically preserved the poet's self in her nineteenth-century world; it also invigorated her art. She drew domestic life into the circumference of her soul, her renunciation intensifying the ordinary experiences of her life and expanding her imagination. The solitude resulting from her renunciation transformed domesticity, taking her into the reaches of the circumference that she mentions in several of her poems. It also gave her figures for her poetry and letters, as when she drew on the home to depict her household "occupation" as "gathering paradise" (#657, "I dwell in Possibility—"). "Home is a holy thing," Dickinson wrote in a letter; "home is the definition of God" (*L*, 1:59, 483). Her renunciation went beyond a defensive posture against the social constraints placed on her; the pattern informed her poetry as a preface to accessing vision and spiritual power. She transformed social renunciation into religious terms, adopting renunciation as a prophetic stance, after the model of the evangelical preachers, and prophesying deprivation and loss as a way to spiritual ecstasy.

As feminist critics argue, self-denial for women could be under-stood to entail silence, the denial of the roles of poet and spiritual leader; yet Dickinson found empowerment in the larger Christian tradition as she looked to the model of the preacher, who extended the prophetic tradition. The figure of the preacher as one specially called to a life of renunciation provided Dickinson a model of self-denial more conducive to her art than the models of the lives of most other nineteenth-century Christian women, for the preacher offered an au-thoritative voice.[27] In the example of the preachers, Dickinson could see that a stance of self-denial authorized the expression of religious vision. The reluctant but increasing acceptance of female preachers—who had begun accepting pastoral appointments in the 1840s—may have also suggested the appropriateness of the stance to female speak-ers of religious truth.

The renunciation expected of women in nineteenth-century Amer-ica meant, for the most part, submission, reticence, and self-denial in favor of the husband and family, but the renunciation expected of the preacher was seen as directly imitating that of Christ—including Christ's ultimate victory. Like any astute observer of New England religious practice attuned to the Edwardsian themes, Dickinson would have noticed the tensions between the practices and theology of self-denial as applied to the preacher and those identified with women. The most apparent variable was that of gender. Although the doctrines sounded similar, they were worked out in some distinctly different ways.

For the prophet-preacher of Dickinson's Connecticut Valley Chris-tian tradition, self-denial ideally meant the renunciation of self-interest, material rewards, social status, pleasure, even friendships with peers, as the preacher followed the example of Christ. Dickinson saw such self-denial modeled by some of the pastors she knew in Amherst. As Edwards had described, the preacher should have a "spirit of humility and lowliness of heart"; "contempt of the glory, wealth, and pleasures of this world"; a "spirit of submission"; and, in summary, "the same zeal, diligence, and self-denial that Christ had," even "retiring from the world" on occasion, as Christ had done. Christ's virtue, said Edwards, "and therefore ministers'," was in his abasement, humility, meekness, and self-denial—an interpretation that also applied to women as individuals well suited by their nature (so the argument went) to a life of self-sacrifice.[28]

Yet, as it was worked out in practical life, such self-denial did not mean the public silence of the preacher, as it did for the nineteenth-century woman; it did not mean even his total renunciation of ego, ambition, and social status, which was expected of women. The emptying of the self meant for the preacher to be full of divine spiritual power as God's speaker. As an inheritor of the Calvinist understanding of the minister as it had been mediated through Edwards, Dickinson would have known that the minister served one of the same offices that Christ did, the prophetic office, and that the minister was to imitate Christ in that office. Thus, Christ offered the preacher a spiritual model of a voice, authority, and power grounded in renunication, a model generally denied to women of Dickinson's time. For Dickinson and other women, having identified with Christ's model of renunciation, it was not hard to imagine or appropriate also the prophetic power that flowed from it. As Edwards put it, the minister was to imitate Christ "in the manner of his preaching, who taught . . . with authority, boldly, zealously, fervently, insisting chiefly on the most important things in religion . . . insisting not only on the outward, but also on the inward and spiritual duties of religion."[29]

As one particularly called to imitate Christ as minister and prophetic speaker, the preacher was to live a life of self-denial, renouncing the self so as to be a greater receiver of God's inspired messages and spiritual power. Yet, as prophet, the preacher had the task of instructing an audience about spirituality and thus had the power of influencing how others thought and acted. Thus, the renunciation of the preacher meant empowerment of the prophetic voice in two ways: (1) in the emptying of self to God's divine inspiration, and (2) in the model of true spirituality that the preacher offered to his audience. Indeed, self-denial meant divine empowerment for the (usually male) preacher instead of the loss of ego it meant for Christian women. It meant a triumph greater than that experienced by Christian women. While the triumph of the self-denying Christian woman was solely otherworldly, the triumph of the male preachers was, in part, of the here and now, as evidenced by their reception as speakers to their communities and their assurance of redemption as people who embraced and explained the very terms of that redemption. For Dickinson, the figure of the preacher offered an appealing model of renunciation, one that produced a self capable of speaking divine messages, modeling authoritative spirituality, and experiencing redemption.

Thus, significantly, for the Edwardsian prophet-preacher—and for Emily Dickinson—renunciation did not mean ultimate self-abasement but rather triumph, the glorification awaiting them for their prophetic service to God. As Edwards described, in the ministers' "abasement, labour, and suffering" as they carried out their prophetic role, ministers would gain "full title to the crown of exceeding glory." "Crown," of course, is one of Dickinson's repeated images, signifying her glory or special title, as we see in poems such as #195, "For this—accepted Breath"; #336, "The face I carry with me—last—"; #356, "The Day that I was crowned"; #508, "I'm ceded—I've stopped being Their's—"; and #608, "Afraid! Of who am I afraid?" In #1735, "One crown that no one seeks," she mentions Christ's crown of thorns as a crown of abasement and of glory. The crown she describes for herself resembles the crown of spiritual exaltation that Edwards described for ministers, who, following Christ the Great Prophet's example, would be "exalted," would "shine with him."[30] Dickinson's crown, with its "one small Diadem," brings her "supremest name" and rank (#508), as she is chosen ("Baptized") as spiritual "Bride" (#473). Like the ministers, Dickinson hopes to gain spiritual glorification in her adoption of renunciation and the prophetic role.

Dickinson may adopt some of the ideas of Edwardsian spirituality, but ultimately, she reworks them, translating spiritual themes into emotional ones. For her, life is less a spiritual warfare, as her Congregational tradition would have described it, than a psychological one; she explores the emotional states associated with the life of faith. As a prophet, she gives generalized psychological and philosophical insights into human nature and the living of one's faith: "To wait Eternity—is short— / If Love reward the end—," she declares in #781 ("To wait an Hour—is long—"), drawing on religious rhetoric to describe human longing (lines 3–4). Focusing not on social issues— poverty, hunger, social injustice—as Aaron Kramer has shown was common in the "prophecy" of many of her female contemporaries, Dickinson instead explains the dynamics of emotional or spiritual hunger, poverty, and the injustice suffered at God's hand, as in #579, "I had been hungry, all the Years—," or #597, "It always felt to me—a wrong / To that Old Moses—done—."³¹ According to her vision, these and other experiences of renunciation and loss—whether in the form of pain, loss at death, or loneliness—can lead to ecstasy, which is her translation of a spiritual concept, salvation, into an emotional one. Renunciation is a more trustworthy term of faith than God, who often "cannot be found" (#1551, "Those—dying then," line 5).

Prophesying her version of renunciation, Dickinson indicates in her poems an awareness that those who know a way to spiritual life should proclaim it. "The Province of the Saved," she says, "should be the Art—To save—." Part of that "art" involves distinguishing defeat from absolute death, helping individuals understand the despair associated with defeat:

> The Province of the Saved
> Should be the Art—To save—
> Through Skill obtained in Themselves—
> The Science of the Grave
>
> No Man can understand
> But He that hath endured
> The Dissolution—in Himself—
> That Man—be qualified
>
> To qualify Despair
> To Those who failing new—
> Mistaking Defeat for Death—Each time—
> Till acclimated—to—   (#539)

As a prophet, one who has made the spiritual journey and endured, Dickinson is "qualified" to explain despair, to help those starting down the path of spiritual life understand that their renunciation—what seems like defeat—is not death. And she must continue "to qualify Despair" until those individuals are "acclimated" to the renunciatory way of life. This is her task as prophet and poet: the art of "saving," proclaiming the way of "salvation," as she uncovers the emotional states associated with religious life, and indeed, as she uncovers both the pain and the merits associated with renunciation.

Dickinson returns to the renunciation theme throughout her poetry, expressing it often in terms of her own experience of it. Drawing on an Edwardsian concept, she sees trial or "woe" as generative of aesthetic vision. In his "Treatise on Religious Affections," Edwards had written that "trials are of further benefit to true religion. They make its genuine beauty . . . remarkably to appear."[32] For him, trial had value, even aesthetic value, as it brought out the "genuine beauty" of Christianity. Likewise, for Dickinson, the woe of renunciation quickens her perception, her vision being anchored in at least an emotional if not a theological structure of Christian renunciation:

> Must be a Wo—
> A loss or so—
> To bend the eye
> Best Beauty's way—   (#571, lines 1–4)

Indeed, the poem suggests the necessity of loss, pain, and renunciation to aesthetic vision. Renunciation awakens the speaker's aesthetic sense, crucial to her vocation as poet. For her, as for Edwards, beauty is closely related to truth—"Themself are One—," she says in #449, "I died for Beauty—but was scarce" (line 7). And as a prophet, her task is to articulate the truth, to speak of beauty. Truth and beauty are even worth dying for, she says in #449, the speaker undergoing death, the ultimate trial, in pursuit of her expression of those elements. Edwards's tradition of renunciation thus serves Dickinson as both poet and prophet.

Dickinson's nineteenth-century religious culture expressed this view of suffering in much the same way that Edwards had. We find one such example in a volume by F. D. Huntington, which Dickinson's father gave her:

> "Ye shall have tribulation"; for it is through much tribulation that any soul entereth into the kingdom of heaven. . . . Christ means to show us the ultimate joy to be gained by the suffering. He treats it as a necessity of our spiritual education; and so bids our fortitude face it, our submission accept it, our faith endure it, our Christian principle draw strength from it.[33]

Likewise, Dickinson maintained that fulfillment would be achieved by patient struggle and pursuit, Christian "strength" through "suffering," even agony, as in her poem "I like a look of Agony" (#241), in which she figured sweat-bead jewels "strung" around the forehead like a crown of triumph. The "Agony" can also express the "truth" (line 2) that lies at the heart of the prophet's task.

Dickinson undoubtedly saw in nineteenth-century women's poetry the pattern of fulfillment emerging from suffering and submission. But for her, the struggle associated with pursuit ultimately gave her "Bliss" of an immediacy and magnitude far beyond that described by her contemporaries. Struggle, for Dickinson's speakers, is at times associated with an apprehension of bliss that is grounded in seeing; bliss is almost palpable, not a mere ethereal hope:

> I gained it so—
> By Climbing slow—
> By catching at the Twigs that grow
> Between the Bliss—and me—   (#359, lines 1–4)

> I had a daily Bliss
> I half indifferent viewed
> Till sudden I perceived it stir—
> It grew as I pursued   (#1057, lines 1–4)

Her pursuit leads to a beatific vision that visibly "stirs," growing in magnitude as she pursues it. Her statements in these poems seem less an exercise in self-consolation than assured declarations of truth: pursuit and struggle do have value. For Dickinson, the struggle often means defeat, even pain, but those experiences are not final. When she asserts, "Success is counted sweetest / By those who ne'er succeed. / To comprehend a nectar / Requires sorest need" (#67, lines 1–4), she points out that the agony and defeat of the dying soldier precede the triumph and "comprehension" of victory, even causing that comprehension. Here, she sees suffering as enabling "telling": the soldier is the one most able to "tell the definition" of victory because he has suffered (line 7). Indeed, in this poem she seems to argue even the superiority of defeat over victory, since the former results in spiritual gain.

Dickinson often speaks of self-denial in terms of suffering, proclaiming that spiritual awareness comes from the suffering associated with self-denial. Spiritual awareness, of course, is crucial for the prophet. She does not value suffering in and of itself; in no poem does she appear to approve of senseless suffering, like that of the Civil War.[34] An individual's experience of pain is not inherently meritorious, only inasmuch as it provides opportunity for the growth of spirituality. Thus, Dickinson's poems on renunciation, suffering, and pain are rarely theocentric. She does not associate growth of spirituality with achieving a state of grace in God's eyes, the Puritan goal (iterated in Dickinson's day by Huntington and others). Spirituality, as Dickinson seems to define it, has to do with the survival and growth of the soul itself.[35] She seems interested in the soul not to offer it up to God for divine mercy but to celebrate it. Not surprising, the reward she envisions is not the tenderness of divine grace but triumph and power.

A poem such as #365, "Dare you see a Soul *at the White Heat?*" shows Dickinson's continuities with and contrasts to her Puritan tradition:

> Dare you see a Soul *at the White Heat?*
> Then crouch within the door—
> Red—is the Fire's common tint—
> But when the vivid Ore
> Has vanquished Flame's conditions,
> It quivers from the Forge
> Without a color, but the light
> Of unannointed Blaze.
> Least Village has it's Blacksmith
> Whose Anvil's even ring
> Stands symbol for the finer Forge
> That soundless tugs—within—
> Refining these impatient Ores
> With Hammer, and with Blaze
> Until the Designated Light
> Repudiate the Forge—

While a Puritan (Anne Bradstreet, for example) would have seen an episode of suffering as a type for the working out of the soul's redemption—that is, as a "testing" procedure by God—and thus would have centered the poem on God, Dickinson omits God from that center. Indeed, her "finer Forge," perhaps even the "Blacksmith," is "within." God stands outside the poem; the forge within, not God, is what refines the ores. Even the blaze is "unannointed." Yet, in repudiating the Puritan idea of preparing the soul for God, Dickinson nevertheless adopts the Edwardsian emphasis on the benefit of suffering. The "White Heat" of pain and suffering can and should result in "refinement." As Paula Bennett has pointed out (though with a different emphasis), in this poem "the soul is empowered through its capacity to survive and transcend pain."[36] The result is a kind of triumph, the light of the blaze becoming so brilliant that it "repudiates" the forge itself. As we saw in other women's poems, including Bradstreet's, suffering can result in victory. For Dickinson, that victory more often than not involves the power of the soul itself.

Indeed, the soul transformed through renunciation, not directly by God, is central to Dickinson's spirituality. For her, the path of redemption goes out to the circumference of the imagination, where the divine resides. Dickinson's God is consistently displaced from the center of the world. In Elisa New's words, "God encounters man on a 'limit' which is of a character necessarily veiled or unknown. . . . It is this very limit, traced round in her poetics by circumference, that Dickinson comes to situate her encounter with God."[37] Dickinson's spirituality brings her to the limit traced by circumference. The godhead may serve as an inspirer, but the divine does not have ultimate power over her; she is no puppet. Neither is the attainment of divine mercy a stated goal. Dickinson suggests that she does not live passively in service to the godhead but ultimately she pursues the development of her own soul. Renunciation is not an end in itself.

Renunciation and self-denial can be difficult, requiring, if not agony, at least personal strength or "Energy":

> To put this World down, like a Bundle—
> And walk steady, away,
> Requires Energy—possibly Agony—
> 'Tis the Scarlet way
>
> Trodden with straight renunciation
> By the Son of God—
> Later, his faint Confederates
> Justify the Road— (#527, lines 1–8)

The scarlet "Road" of renunciation is "justified," but Christ's "confederates" grow "faint" or weak with the agony of following in his way of renunciation and agony. Unlike #791, "God gave a Loaf to every Bird," the focus here in stanza 1 is on the pain of the renunciation, not the reward. To "justify" the way of Christ—a Miltonic word—is the role of the prophet; indeed, Christ's "confederates" or disciples are, first, the biblical apostles, who were commissioned like the Old Testament prophets to speak and write the words of God, and then, by extension, others who "later" serve in that role.

Yet, Dickinson does not end Poem #527 with a focus on deprivation;

rather, she speaks of the sacrament that is the triumph emerging from the Crucifixion:

> Flavors of that old Crucifixion—
> Filaments of Bloom, Pontius Pilate sowed—
> Strong Clusters, from Barabbas' Tomb—
>
> Sacrament, Saints partook before us—
> Patent, every drop,
> With the Brand of the Gentile Drinker
> Who indorsed [*sic*] the Cup—   (lines 9–15)

To renounce the world as Christ did may require "Energy—possibly Agony—," but in the long run, it leads to new life, to "Bloom." His renunciation led to the affirmation of life signified in the "Sacrament" of the Last Supper, which he victoriously opened up to "Gentile drinkers." This renunciation empowers the "faint Confederates" (including Dickinson), whose role in the prophetic tradition includes "justifying" Christ and his way through prophesying, preaching, and, for Dickinson, poetry. They can "justify" him because they see the merit of his way. The poem itself stands as a prophecy in the sense that it is a means of justification, the poet exploring and defending the costs and rewards of renunciation.

Anguish itself can even lead to a vision of ecstasy. In fact, it seems to make ecstasy possible:

> For each extatic instant
> We must an anguish pay
> In keen and quivering ratio
> To the extacy   (#125, lines 1–4)
>
> To learn the Transport by the Pain—
> As Blind Men learn the sun!   (#167, lines 1–2)

Just as the blind may see the brightness of the sun only after experiencing the emotional pain of sightlessness, so the speaker sees the brightness of the blissful vision after enduring pain. Indeed, pain makes the vision even more rapturous: "Delight—becomes pictorial— / When viewed through Pain—" (#572, line 1). In Edwards's tradition, power was gained through pain and suffering; as Dickinson puts it, "Power is only Pain—" (#252, line 10). For her, as a woman prophet in a culture reluctant to admit such speakers, the statement is particularly incisive: she knows firsthand the pain of nonrecognition.

Poem #745, her longest and most famous treatment of renunciation, shows the reward and the suffering associated with renunciation:

> Renunciation—is a piercing Virtue—
> The letting go
> A Presence—for an Expectation—
> Not now—
> The putting out of Eyes—
> Just Sunrise—
> Lest Day—
> Day's Great Progenitor—
> Outvie
> Renunciation—is the Choosing
> Against itself—
> Itself to justify
> Unto itself—
> When larger function—
> Make that appear—
> Smaller—that Covered Vision—Here—

Consistent with her other poems, here renunciation is not negative; it is a "Virtue," albeit "piercing." Fulfillment again is the reward for spiritual self-denial. As Dickinson puts it, we "let go" of the "Presence," the here and now, for an expectation not fulfillable now. Renunciation is not easy; it involves cost. It is like putting out one's eyes just at sunrise, lest day "outvie" "Day's Great Progenitor," God: day is so attractive, as is the expectation of it given by sunrise, that one must "put out" her eyes so as not to be wooed by the day away from greater reward given by "Day's Great Progenitor," the giver of light, God.[38] Thus, renunciation is like forsaking the experience of day as one waits for greater light, important for greater, "uncovered" or spiritual vision (line 16). Renunciation involves choosing against what is present now so that, as David Porter paraphrases, the choice "will be justified later when a greater reward will make what filled one's vision here appear smaller by comparison."[39] The pain of renunciation lies in letting go of the present, the worldly, the concrete, in favor of an expectation, the "not now." Justification, or virtue, occurs in the choosing of the expectation, the more spiritual, less corporeal. When the reward comes, it makes the renunciation or the expectation—the "Covered Vision"— appear "smaller." The "vision" will presumably be "uncovered." Dickinson's choice of the theological term "justify"—meaning, "to make or be made acceptable before God"—is not surprising. Renunciation will justify her in heaven, bringing her reward, just as she prophetically "justifies" the Christ of her experience and his renunciatory way, as we saw in #527 ("To put this World down, like a Bundle—"). Her reward is not only spiritual vision but also, presumably, heavenly beatitude as her reward for faithfulness in her task.

To Dickinson and her contemporaries, Christ exemplified renunciatory suffering for an unearthly reward. As Dickinson points out, "Our lord—thought no / Extravagance / To pay—a Cross—" for his bliss (#571, "Must be a Wo—," lines 13–15). His bliss was no "common bliss," because the price he paid was so great (line 9). "The price—is," as she indicates, "even as the Grace—" (lines 11–12). But what "Joy to have merited the Pain," she says in another poem (#788, line 1). Although the "Gain" may be "perceiveless," it does come:

> I made slow Riches but my Gain
> Was steady as the Sun
> And every Night, it numbered more
> Than the preceding One
>
> All Days, I did not earn the same
> But my perceiveless Gain
> Inferred the less by Growing than
> The Sum that it had grown.   (#843)

Significantly, Dickinson's position is not merely that gain or fulfillment exists in the face of pain but that the pain and deprivation are generative of, able to lead to, future exaltation. The structure of renunciation makes sense in terms of her early Christian training. Hers is the position of Edwards, who in his "Treatise on Religious Affections" described the benefits of trials and loss to "true religion": "The divine excellency of real Christianity is never exhibited with such advantage, as when under the greatest trials."[40] For both Edwards and Dickinson, excellency and trial do not merely coexist; trial has generative value.

Dickinson's speaker may go through the "education" of trials, but prophetic "ecstasy" awaits her. In #392, "Through the Dark Sod—as Education—," Dickinson propounds her spirituality of renunciation. She follows not only Edwards's theology but also his method, reading spiritual meanings into events of nature, the poem's religious discourse—the "faith" of line 4—suggesting the Christian reading. Just as the lily must pass through "Dark Sod" before experiencing "ecstacy," so must one experience deprivation before gaining victory. The poem recalls Psalm 23: the lily walks through the darkness, but she fears no evil, her faith giving her fearlessness:

> Through the Dark Sod—as Education—
> The Lily passes sure—
> Feels her white foot—no trepidation
> Her faith—no fear—
>
> Afterward—in the Meadow—
> Swinging her Beryl Bell—
> The Mold-life—all forgotten—now—
> In Extasy—and Dell—

Dickinson reads into this event not just the safety and protection promised to believers in Psalm 23 but even greater reward: "ecstasy" awaits her who has endured deprivation. Soon forgetting the "Mold-life," such a one will gain even the bliss of the New Jerusalem, signified by beryl, which is one of the stones described in Rev. 21:20 as forming the foundation of the New Jerusalem.

Generative of ecstasy, the renunciation that Dickinson expresses is not a passive stance. Here we see her revision of evangelical Protestant spirituality and virtue. She does not see herself forced into renunciation by her culture or even by conventional Christian doctrines. Rather, she consciously and assertively adopts the stance, like the biblical prophets who underwent deprivation for the sake of their calling.[41] Dickinson over and over celebrates self-denial, solitude, submission. "All—is the price of All—," she asserts, noting that "the hallowing of Pain / Like hallowing of Heaven, / Obtains at a corporeal cost—" (#772, "The hallowing of Pain"). Yet such a cost seems worthwhile to her, as poems such as #442, "God made a little Gentian—"; #1099, "My Cocoon tightens—Colors tease—"; and #365, "Dare you see a Soul *at the White Heat*?" suggest. Her stance "is not," as Keller points out, "the same as Emersonian compensationism," in which "everything is righted in one's hopes."[42] Her renunciation is the triumphant, confident stance of the preacher-prophet, not the merely hopeful, passive attitude that her culture expected of women.

We see the joy of Dickinson's renunciation in #791:

> God gave a Loaf to every Bird—
> But just a crumb—to Me—

I dare not eat it—tho' I starve—
My poignant luxury—

. . . .

It might be Famine—all around—
I could not miss an Ear—
Such Plenty smiles upon my Board—
My Garner shows so fair—

I wonder how the Rich—may feel—
An Indiaman—An Earl—
I deem that I—with but a Crumb—
Am Sovreign of them all—   (lines 1–4, 9–16)

Although she possesses "but a Crumb—," she regards herself as privileged over "the Rich," "An Indiaman," and "An Earl," whose "garners" presumably are much fuller than hers. But she experiences "Plenty" in her little crumb. Her crumb is small, but it is from God. We suspect that those other figures' garners do not keep such crumbs. When we read the persona as a poet, we see renunciation associated with not only fulfillment but even power, the persona deeming herself "sovereign" with her divine "crumb" of poetic power. The idea of eating the crumb (line 3) recalls John's eating the scroll in Rev. 10:9–11, an image that captures his empowerment to speak divine words: "You must prophesy again," the angel told John when he had eaten the "little scroll." In Dickinson's poem, the speaker, of course, "dares not eat" her little crumb for food; it signifies something greater than mere food. In a pun associating "ears" of corn with "ears" that hear, she suggests that she remains aware of all ears (line 6) amid which she celebrates her crumb of power and privilege.

In other poems, however, Dickinson expresses the idea that surrender may be more difficult. Paradoxically submitting to power to gain power in the role of the prophet, she usually shows in her poetry her acceptance and often her enjoyment of self-denial, but that surrender could be frightening. As one critic explains in a study of female spirituality, "Submission to the power that terrorized her soul gave her an intimacy with power that activated the explosive dance within her soul and inspired her poetry."[43] Aware of the extremes of experience that inspiration can include, Dickinson in #512, "The Soul has Bandaged moments—," expresses both horror and ecstasy in her encounter with an inspiring power. At one limit of her consciousness, the intimacy gives her "Bandaged moments" when she is "too appalled to stir" (lines 1–2). Her soul is bound, damaged, accosted in her fright of the power that inspires. She figures the submission to the power as her being "shackled" as she is "led along" in her "song" (stanza 5). But the other extreme of renunciation to the power is prophetic dance and ecstasy:

> The soul has moments of Escape—
> When bursting all the doors—
> She dances like a Bomb, abroad,
> And swings upon the Hours   (lines 11–14)

It is notable that she captures both extremes in a single poem, an indication that she does not see the opposites of fear and ecstasy as irreconcilable.

In another poem, Dickinson expresses acceptance of "inundation" by the inspiration that wells up within the soul and overpowers it, the soul submitting to its "enlarging" power:

> The inundation of the Spring
> Enlarges every soul—
> It sweeps the tenement away
> But leaves the Water whole—
>
> In which the soul at first estranged—
> Seeks faintly for it's shore
> But acclimated—pines no more
> For that Peninsula—   (#1425)

In this poem, Dickinson uses imagery of water in the same way that she uses "sea" in other poems: to signify the imagination.[44] Whether the "inundator" is outside the soul or located within, the soul adding to itself through natural cycles, the flood of inspiring power requires the soul's submission. Such power overflows, adversely affecting the "tenement" or body, the place where the soul has its residence. But the imagination is left intact, "whole." At first, the soul is overwhelmed by the influx of thought—it feels "estranged" and seeks security, the "shore" (lines 6–7)—but eventually it "acclimates" to the surge of the imagination. The soul needs a power to activate the imagination and thereby empower her speech. The speaker submits to it, leaving the "shore" of safety in a poem that ultimately affirms the value of submission as a way to empowerment.

Dickinson often portrays this submission in sexual terms, using the imagery of sexual passion to celebrate religious ecstasy and her own high calling as wisdom giver. She again draws on water imagery in #506 to represent the surge of the imaginative, inspiring power—"the awful sea":

> He touched me, so I live to know
> That such a day, permitted so,
> I groped upon his breast—
> It was a boundless place to me
> And silenced, as the awful sea
> Puts minor streams to rest.
>
> And now, I'm different from before,
> As if I breathed superior air—
> Or brushed a Royal Gown—
> My feet, too, that had wandered so—
> My Gipsy face—transfigured now—
> To tenderer Renown—
>
> Into this Port, if I might come,
> Rebecca, to Jerusalem,
> Would not so ravished turn—
> Nor Persian, baffled at her shrine
> Lift such a Crucifixial sign
> To her imperial Sun.

Here, religious and sexual imagery are intertwined, and both involve submission. The poem may disturb some in its seemingly conventional portrayal of a woman's sexual submission to a male lover; indeed, in submitting to the lover, the woman is stilled by his touch and "ravished" (line 15). In his touch she finds peace, Sabbath "rest." But the outcome of the encounter is anything but conventional. Dickinson displaces the male from the center of the poem. The speaker has no trouble submitting to him, perhaps because she knows that she can transcend him; surrender to him does not mean defeat or acquiescence. "Different from before," she is spiritually reborn, and in his air she finds "breath," inspiration. She is "transfigured now— / To tenderer Renown," called to the high task of bard.

The experience described here has as its background the Old Testament story of Rebecca (Genesis 24), which, in explaining how she was chosen for the wife of Isaac, emphasizes the guidance and overruling providence of God. Rebecca eventually gave birth to Jacob and thus became part of the lineage of Christ—she "came into the port" of "Jerusalem." As a foremother of Christ, Rebecca stands as one elected by God, submitting to the divine, and, consequently, called to play a glorious role, as the biblical text Rom. 9:4–13 also describes.

Similarly, the speaker here tentatively suggests her calling and entrance into a great lineage, one of royalty and renown, gained through her self-renunciation to the inspiring lover of stanza 1. The "Crucifixal sign" denotes not only the sacrifice of the Son of God but triumph. It also denotes the significance of the renunciation of flesh for a greater glory—the payment by death of Christ's fleshly body for "the glory" of the children of God, represented by the chosen offspring of Rebecca, according to the Romans passage. The "imperial Sun" is, for Rebeccca in the poem, God, her source of light and life; it is also the "morning sun," that is, Christ the Son, Rebecca's own future "son." Like nineteenth-century women, Dickinson's Rebecca is deified by her motherhood, her submission bringing her honor. But Dickinson here predicts even greater delight and triumph for herself: the metaphor of motherhood suggests, as Amanda Porterfield points out, "her poetic fertility," and "the labors of her imagination recall the ecstatic moment of her religious surrender" and of her calling.[45] The speaker suggests that the renunciation of the opportunity for motherhood "in the flesh" is a prerequisite for poetic motherhood, both practically and in terms of a calling to the spirit over the flesh, signified by the spiritual transfiguration of her face (line 11).

In #616, the speaker describes a religious and sexual event that again features submission as a way to gain power. But this time, the power that the speaker attains through her encounter she willingly puts to service for the lover:

> I rose—because He sank—
> I thought it would be opposite—
> But when his power dropped—
> My Soul grew straight.
>
> I cheered my fainting Prince—
> I sang firm—even—Chants—
> I helped his Film—with Hymn—
>
> . . . .
>
> And so with Thews of Hymn—
> And Sinew from within—

> And ways I knew not that I knew—till then—
> I lifted Him—   (lines 1–7, 20–23)

The speaker had thought that her submission to her lover would bring his elevation: "I thought it would be opposite," she says, having anticipated the reverse of her "rising" at his "sinking." She willingly surrendered her power to him, cheering him on, even singing to him. But she finds herself holding and lifting him in her embrace. She discovers power and strength in her poetic song—"Thews of Hymn" and "Sinew from within." Her evalution of the event is that "I rose—because He sank." Her access of power depends on "Him" as a source. The surrender to him activates the power located in her poetry, as she "lifts" him with "Thews of Hymn."

Another poem distressing to some readers for its seeming conventionality, "I rose" nonetheless continues a tradition of power found in other women's art. Dickinson, like other women poets of her day, does not openly value personal mastery over acquiescence. And as we see in this poem, even her conception of the singer-poet is not, as one scholar has pointed out, a heroic one;[46] her speakers are not motivated by expectations of recognition but by service and its rewards. This speaker finds, through her submission, power to "lift." And the poem suggests a doctrinal paradox of power through submission: it is God's "sinking" into flesh that enables her resurrection, her "rising." The "dropping" of his "power" is what makes her soul "grow straight," that is, upright or righteous (as in Pss. 11:7; 7:10). Thus, she suggests her own justification and redemption—her ultimate glorification. Her surrender to him brings her power and status as he "sinks" into flesh, a concept of power she would have learned in her Christian training. But Dickinson's power, as we have seen in other poems, does not bring merely grace but "sovereignty," as she puts it in #791, "God gave a Loaf to every Bird—."

In expounding her prophetic message, Dickinson underscores that renunciation is a virtue having special significance to the prophet. As one of the terms of faith as she sees it, renunciation—even pain and deprivation—not only brings power and reward but enables some to speak poetic prophecy. The reward for her steadfastness as a self-denying prophet will be the "bliss" that will "swell—like Horizons—in my vest—":

> A solemn thing—it was—I said—
> A Woman—white—to be—
> And wear—if God should count me fit—
> Her blameless mystery—

A hallowed thing—to drop a life
Into the purple well—
Too plummetless—that it return—
Eternity—until—

I pondered how the bliss would look—
And would it feel as big—
When I could take it in my hand—
As hovering—seen—through fog—

And then—the size of this "small" life—
The Sages—call it small—
Swelled—like Horizons—in my vest—
And I sneered—softly—"small"!   (#271)[47]

History would affirm the special status Dickinson realized within
herself. In the end, she would no longer be depreciated, "small"; she
would wear blameless mystery as the dress of her divine calling as poet-
prophet. The color of the dress is white, the color of sheer brightness
and extraordinary glory. In later life, Dickinson had a habit of wearing
white, perhaps signifying her holiness as one "set apart" and ritualizing
the religious mysteries of her femininity. Her vocation demanded of
her "a hallowed thing," the highest act of renunciation: "dropping" a
life "into the purple well—," that is, giving herself up totally, risking
earthly life for life in the divine and purple well, on the chance that a
royal immortal would return. The speaker's ultimate bliss will be to
wear the purple of royalty and resurrection; her pure white will take the
purple dye. Contemplating the reward awaiting her, she swells in her
vest as no man can. She, as a bard, has a godlike role, no "small" task
indeed.

Dickinson describes part of her vision of paradise—her reward—in
#756:

One Blessing had I than the rest
So larger to my Eyes
That I stopped gauging—satisfied—
For this enchanted size—

It was the limit of my Dream—
The focus of my Prayer—
A perfect—paralyzing Bliss—
Contented as Despair—

> I knew no more of Want—or Cold—
> Phantasms both become
> For this new Value in the Soul—
> Supremest Earthly Sum—
>
> The Heaven below the Heaven above—
> Obscured with ruddier Blue—
> Life's Latitudes leant over—full—
> The Judgment—perished—too—   (lines 1–16)

The bliss is "perfect—paralyzing"; it annihilates "Judgment." And after gaining such ecstasy, she will "speculate no more" on "why Bliss so scantily disburse— / Why Paradise defer— / Why Floods be served to Us—in Bowls—" (lines 17–19). Submitting oneself to "Want" and "Cold" and the "Floods" of despair that are served in the daily "Bowls" of experience eventually leads to "new Value in the Soul—." Her renunciation has brought her power—not only paradise and fulfillment but the ability to see and understand, as she has no more need of "speculation." It has brought her the power of aesthetic vision, as we saw in #571, "Must be a Wo—." The power she has gained from her spiritual encounter she describes in #361:

> What I can do—I will—
> Though it be little as a Daffodil—
> That I cannot—must be
> Unknown to possibility—

A single act of creation—a daffodil—is as easy for her as any grand event. What she cannot do, no one can do, she says.

Discovering that spiritual power could lie within renunciation, Dickinson sought as a prophetic poet to impart her knowledge to others, to those "who have ears to hear." She adopted the stance of the preacher, whose renunciation would bring prophetic power and heavenly reward. It offered her more than the self-denial practiced by other nineteenth-century women, promising a spiritual transformation that would access power. For Dickinson, this transformation seems to have involved, in Porterfield's words,

> moments when the bottom falls out or the lid flies off, moments in which some sudden infusion of energy enables ideas and images to be radically rearranged. In the paradigm of conversion . . . the infusion of volatile energy is identified as

grace. Grace has been reported by American christians and understood by their theologians as an experience of beauty and, often, as an ecstatic experience. Ecstatic experiences . . . can involve—for women at least as commonly as for men— such dramatic physical and emotional expression as weeping, singing, and dancing.[48]

Ecstatic experience has also traditionally taken the form of inspired prophecy or poetry. Dickinson's ecstasy and her prophecy involved singing, with Isaac Watts' hymn meter providing for her the best medium for dramatic expression of spirituality. Weeping, dancing, and singing throughout her poetry, Dickinson offered a spirituality that acknowledged both the heights of ecstasy and the depths of despond, a vision that reconciled the extremes of experiences more satisfactorily for her than did the pronouncements of her religious contemporaries. Those individuals perhaps were too constrained by dogma to see the possibilities of grace—a cultural pattern conducive to and even demanding the rise of an American prophet. And prophets did emerge. Rejecting dogma, narrow moralisms, and earthly constraints, Emerson preached the spirit, Thoreau urged simplicity, Whitman celebrated the body and the soul—and Dickinson, as female prophet, sang the self-denial that leads to power, possibility, and bliss.

9. "'Tis so appalling—it exhilarates": Dickinson's Wisdom of Wonder

WITH THE EXCEPTION of Harriet Beecher Stowe, Emily Dickinson is the only well-known nineteenth-century American writer who had personal roots in New England evangelicalism and who reflected that heritage in her art. Conservative religious circles in this country simply have not had much of a track record in producing memorable literature. Nathaniel Hawthorne, who often wrote about the Puritans, did so from a theologically liberal position, rejecting wholesale the legacy of his forebears. Herman Melville as well, although he knew Calvinism from his mother and other sources, rarely, if ever, expressed the evangelicalism we associate with points lying outside of his native eastern New York. Emily Dickinson alone provided a critique of New England orthodoxy from within the very circles she protested.

Although Dickinson certainly was influenced by Unitarian, transcendentalist, and other liberal strains—even to the point that her poetry sometimes sounds straightforwardly agnostic—the poet demonstrated over and over a genuine (albeit complex) relationship to New England evangelicalism. It was that dynamic relationship with her theological heritage—a position of protest, acceptance, revision, resignation—that fueled her prophecy. Like so many wisdom figures before her, she prophesied not simply as an exercise in rebellion against her religious heritage (she sometimes did that, but too many critics today read her as "needing" Calvinism against which to write) but to revitalize faith and spirit. The first generation of readers to explore her work, the audience of the 1890s, read her poetry in this light; they valued and admired it for the spiritual insight, the wise words, and the poet's apprehension of truth.

Dickinson's prophecies do touch on a range of subjects: God, faith, nature, art, daily living, and more. In this chapter, I summarize some aspects of her wisdom, with two qualifying remarks. First, Dickinson's poetic voices are often inconsistent, even contradictory, and a full description of her wisdom emphases is probably impossible. She obviously does not attempt to be creedal, and a single poem can be ripe for multiple, even conflicting, interpretations. Second, Dickinson takes up ostensibly secular subjects as often as purely "religious" ones. Indeed, her prophetic vision is grounded in the wonder of daily living, with the poet often focusing on the drama (and even cosmic importance) of seemingly ordinary events and phenomena. The line between "secular" and "religious" in her art can be very blurry—understandably so, when we recall that Dickinson was profoundly influenced by the old Calvinist idea that all of life is religion.

As I have maintained throughout this study, Dickinson gives much evidence that she regards her poetry as a religious calling. For her, as for the Puritans before her, nothing in life falls outside the purview of religion. For purposes of study, however, I focus on three traditionally theological themes in her art: revelation (its sources and means), soteriology, and cosmology. These can help us understand a few broad but separable clusters of poems that capture some of the emphases of her wisdom.

Dickinson, we may guess, chafed against traditional conceptions of revelation, soteriology, and cosmology, as she so often did regarding other points of conventional theology. But she did not entirely abandon mainstream theology. We should not underestimate the extent to which the orthodoxy of her locale had a positive shaping effect on her art. When we consider some of the religious history of New England and Dickinson's place within that line, we can begin to see that her practice of prophecy derived powerfully from not only the women before her (as we saw in Chapter 6) but also her own heritage of Protestant ministers—those individuals who wanted to purify practices of faith. Dickinson, when understood as a daughter of prophecy, joins an important body of individuals concerned with refreshing New England orthodoxy. Her emphases are often curiously similar to theirs. Although we have considered throughout this study aspects of the orthodoxy that Dickinson knew and the ways in which she played her poetry off of those, in this chapter I draw those pieces together as I summarize and expand on the wisdom themes that emerge in Dickinson's poetry.

To begin, we need to acknowledge that the Calvinism that Dickinson knew was a more warmhearted Christianity than earlier Puritans had expressed, the result of attempts to revitalize the faith made first by Jonathan Edwards and others of the Great Awakening, later by leaders of the Second Great Awakening in Dickinson's own century. All of these individuals tried to breathe life into worn-out forms and infuse the faith with their own contagious passion. The Second Great Awakening, led early in the nineteenth century by Edwards's grandson Timothy Dwight and then, in its later phases, by Nathaniel W. Taylor, Lyman Beecher, Albert Barnes, and Charles Grandison Finney, continued Edwards's efforts to adjust Calvinism to meet the exigencies of the times, including Unitarian departures from orthodoxy. Dickinson's own adjustments of the faith followed the alterations that Christianity had first undergone at the hands of the leaders of the Great Awakenings; they, too, wanted to shape a Christianity relevant for the times. Dickinson, perhaps unwittingly, continued some of their innovations.

Specifically wanting to organize a revival among Congregational churches, Lyman Beecher teamed with Nathaniel Taylor, one of the finest theologians in New England, to restate or reinterpret Calvinism and thereby bring religious vitality to New England churches, including those in Dickinson's locale. Despite Edwards's earlier attacks on Arminian tendencies that vitiated Puritan orthodoxy, in an ironic reversal, Beecher and others expressed an "Arminianized" Calvinism that proliferated in New England, powerfully affecting both the doctrine and the milieu of the Connecticut Valley. Eschewing Calvinist notions about predestination, the revivalists emphasized the role of human volition in the salvation process, apparently in an attempt to overcome criticisms that God in Calvinist theology was a cruel, merciless tyrant—a criticism with which Dickinson is often identified. Indeed, in Dickinson's poetry we see her softening divinity in the figure of Christ to be an accessible, warm personality who could mediate between her and a more distant God (recall the ways in which she represented her inspirer). Beecher, in combating criticism about an authoritarian God, took a similar tack, shifting attention away from the role of God the Father. He focused instead on the role of the individual believer.

But focusing on the individual's role—specifically, the individual's response to the claims of the gospel—necessarily affected the role of the preacher. Beecher and others modified Edwardsian theology to emphasize the role of the preacher, in order to press the Word of God and the kingdom of God so forcefully on their audiences that the sinner would clearly understand that superior happiness could be obtained only by "choosing God" and repenting of sins. The individual's apprehension of faith thus lay at the center of the Congregational revivals—an emphasis we also find in Dickinson's art, as opposed to a focus on the community's response or even a purely intellectual experience of faith, as some other groups of Calvinists emphasized. The power of God's word, Beecher and others believed, when applied energetically to the human heart, would make the individual see and feel a sense of divine reality. Moral suasion became a key focus of these leaders of the Second Great Awakening; the heartfelt response of the sinner to the power of a text—God's text and the preacher's text, delivered with fervor and irrefutable reasoning—remained central. Upon that ability to persuade depended an audience's spiritual destiny.

As we saw in Chapter 3, Dickinson continued in her art the twofold emphasis on textual power, as is demonstrated by the rhetorical structures and the style she adopted. Like the revivalists, she expressed her own belief in the power of the prophetic word—*her* word—to affect an audience both intellectually and emotionally. She, too, wanted a heartfelt response to faith. We will return to some of these themes when we consider directly her positions on revelation, but first we need to reflect briefly on some of the salient features of evangelical dogma as a context for Dickinson's prophecy.

Along with the patterns that the revivalists focused on in their practice of the faith, the New England doctrinal emphases powerfully affected the content of Dickinson's prophecy. Despite the shift away from predestination, the Congregational orthodoxy that Dickinson knew retained other Calvinist ideas. In distinction from Unitarianism, Beecher and others defined Christian orthodoxy in terms of the Reformation themes of total depravity, human accountability to God for one's actions, the doctrines of the Trinity and Atonement and a historical Incarnation and Resurrection.[1] Dickinson was influenced by several religious cultures, including her editor T. W. Higginson's Unitarianism (shared with some friends and even family members), but the effect on her of the Protestant evangelical doctrines was one of the most powerful. She heard it expressed from the pulpit, at school (Mount Holyoke), and among her peers. More or less Calvinist in its dogma, evangelicalism also emphasized, in distinction from Unitarianism and other liberal movements, the centrality of personal conversion, the quest for an affective piety, and, in many circles, a suspicion of wealth, worldliness, and ecclesiastical pretension.

As a prophet, Dickinson would likewise come to protest the cultural phenomena that distract one from pure and heartfelt faith. In her case, however, she also attacked many of the evangelical dogmas, emphases, and practices, including the hypocrisy she saw, as barriers to the simplicity and truth she urged on her audience. At the same time, she retained and emphasized some of the doctrines of the evangelical movement, working them to fit her own sense of truth. Renunciation, we saw in the last chapter, was a key idea she developed in her wisdom literature, and the other truths she expressed tended to have a similarly personal and even individualistic focus—a notable phenomenon when we consider that Calvinism historically, except for some of its American expressions, emphasized the communal dimensions of faith. All of the truths Dickinson expressed, in fact, seem to have been rooted in her personal apprehension; one thing that distinguishes her verse from other American poetry (with the exception of other nineteenth-century women's poetry)—and what has so far misled critics as to lead them to call the poetry "private"—is her apparent emphasis on the heart or emotions as the measure of truth. Surely she derived this idea from New England, romantic evangelicalism. It lies at the crux of her beliefs about revelation, a topic that strongly associates Dickinson with the religious heritage we have been considering.

As I suggested earlier, evangelicalism—a sentimentalized version of the older American expressions of Christianity—emphasized "the intuitive perception of truth through the feelings or emotions of the heart," as one scholar put it; evangelicalism of the nineteenth century was "a Christocentric theology in which the 'personality of Jesus' became more important than the moral order of God." With that focus came "a concomitant sentimentalized idealization of women, children, and parenthood as the most perfect embodiments if not the most efficient means of grace."[2] This version of Christianity retained dominance in America at least until the Civil War, surviving denominational battles and onslaughts from liberals. Although Dickinson protested the idealization of women that antebellum Christianity suggested, she did not reject the perspective on revelation and aesthetics that arose from this New England *ethos*.

In distinction to the positions on revelation expressed by Emerson and Thoreau, who both suggested the importance of nature and right seeing as guides to truth, Dickinson presents the heart as central to determining truth and falsehood. We touched on this idea earlier in regard to the kind of rhetoric she employs to move the hearts of her readers; here, we want to consider the issue from a theological perspective. For Dickinson, dogma itself can never be truth, but only that which moves the heart. Her poems constantly appeal to experience or the heart to justify their truth; truth involves more than simply correct vision (as we find implied in, for example, Emerson's image of the transparent eyeball) or understanding. And in contrast to Puritan conceptions of revelation, for Dickinson, the soul is ultimate authority, not a document (the Bible), God, or even an inspirer. None of these has ultimate authority over her; rather, any truth from these sources or from nature must be subjectified. Dickinson's prophetic truth emerges (and pushes against the limits of evangelical orthodoxy) when she translates the theological into the psychological, the religious into the emotional. Revelation, then, is not confined to a document or even to an inspirer, as in the conventional forms of prophecy, but for Dickinson is mediated by subjective experience and the soul's apprehension of that experience. And for the poet as prophet, revelation gives way to art when the soul expresses its experience of revelation.

Dickinson's seizure of authority to reinterpret (and add to) the truths in traditional religious sources can sound much like the Puritan emphasis on the priesthood of the individual—the ability and moral responsibility of the individual to the community to express his or her spiritual consciousness and, through that expression, contribute to the larger social and moral order. Such was the mark of a true citizen of the spiritual community. As Sacvan Bercovitch, Lawrence Buell, and other critics have observed, the Puritan legacy of the Connecticut Valley made New England a locale especially conducive to the rise of the romantic *ethos*, since both movements emphasized the corporate dimension of the celebration of the self. New Englanders' views on spiritual revelation, as well as on aesthetics—Dickinson's positions included—understandably reflected an emphasis on individual responsibility. Dickinson's personal burden for truth as apprehended by the individual, who feels constrained to express it in some way to the community, reflected the concerns of both the Protestant evangelical and the romantic movements. "Truth is so rare a thing," she stated in her letters, "it is delightful to tell it." To Higginson she said about some poems she was sending, "Excuse them, if they are untrue."[3]

The speaking of truth through the structures and forms of Judeo-Christian prophecy distinguishes Dickinson as a prophet. She aligned herself with the romantic expositors of poetry as prophecy, who retained "a keen sense of social and moral responsibility" for art. As Buell describes it, the romantic aesthetic "during the era of Hawthorne and Dickinson . . . [was] an aesthetic that presupposed an interdependence of art and morality in which the latter legitimated the former."[4] Indeed, Dickinson's poetry is prophetic in part because she shared this aesthetic. As we can see throughout her poetry, she wanted not merely accurate "doctrine," an intellectual experience of truth, but an active truth, one concerned with right action and purity of soul. This emphasis connects her to the Judeo-Christian prophets who went before her, as well as to the secular prophets (Ralph Waldo Emerson, Margaret Fuller, Henry David Thoreau) of her own era. Ironically, however, the nineteenth-century Protestant *ethos* tended to retain suspicion of art and literature as a vehicle for the revelation of truth, especially when the "truth" transcended dogma or easy sentimentality. At least theoretically, New England evangelicals esteemed prophecy (as one of the sacred "offices") very highly, but they restricted it to particular groups of people (male, ordained ones) and to particular rhetorical modes (oratorical expressions). Romantic writers went much further than the evangelicals in seeing the visionary possibilities of poetry and prose, throwing off the constraints of established understandings of orthodoxy. Dickinson stands as one figure who generated art from the evangelical milieu, but the romantic influence seems to have been crucial to her poetic-prophetic enterprise.

The romantic writers, and Dickinson along with them, tended to see their poetic texts as "Scriptures" themselves, capable of speaking sacred truths apart from any established authority. Experiencing a revelatory moment, the poetic prophets themselves would turn to offer revelation through their art. The visionary strain of the romantics, like that of the evangelicals, still emphasized the importance of right action and thinking; Emerson was the most extreme expositor of this aesthetic, calling for the emergence of a new teacher who would speak supreme beauty and thereby instruct the masses about virtue. Dickinson, rather than rebelling against this conception as a patriarchal myth, drew on that *ethos* to shape her own figure of the poet-prophet—but one gendered female.[5] In doing so, she retained her links to other women poets who saw art as a vehicle to express a moral vision, while going beyond them in exploiting the possibilities of the aesthetic. She could do this because she, unlike many of her poetic contemporaries, rejected "the eighteenth-century notion of poetry as a repository of communal wisdom"—specifically, the New England community's understanding of its religious heritage—in favor of the visionary romanticism that saw the artist as "keeper of the collective conscience and prophet of a better society." With those figures, Dickinson participated in the Anglo-American romantic practice of "form breaking" that Buell describes so well, a "ground-clearing impulse" that began with protest against traditional forms.[6] The beauty of Dickinson's prophecy in part lies in her ability to participate in form breaking—defying traditional eighteenth- and nineteenth-century understandings of what a poem should do, for example—even as she continues some Judeo-Christian genres—the sermon, biblical poetry, and the hymn. Thus, even in the handling of form, Dickinson is prophetic, seeing the possibilities of older genres and revitalizing them almost beyond the point of recognition. Rhetorically, she operates in that space between outright conformity and outright dismissal or rebellion.

Dickinson occupies a similar intermediate space with respect to the content of her wisdom. As we saw in Chapter 7, she transforms the Judeo-Christian concept of renunciation (and nineteenth-century practices of it) into a principle that can empower the female as well as the male. It lies at the heart of her spirituality. Her manipulations of the idea of self-denial exemplify her acute awareness of the dark side of human existence—what her Calvinist contemporaries might have called "total depravity" or "original sin." Dickinson shows the aesthetic and prophetic uses of darkness, suggesting that the dark is necessary for fulfillment and makes imagination possible. Aware of the world of suffering and death, she does not respond with the pious platitudes of many people in her evangelical milieu but offers consolation and comfort in her role as prophet. Darkness, death, and loss, even more than God, can be depended on. As a significant aspect of her spirituality and thus of her prophecy (as we considered in Chapter 7), Dickinson's awareness of the dark and its possibilities contributes to a wisdom far-ranging in the subjects it touches.

Other dogmas and emphases of Connecticut Valley Christianity appear in a variety of ways throughout Dickinson's poetry, and her visionary innovations upon them lead her beyond the strictly doctrinal poetry of many of her popular contemporaries. Adopting the Reformation emphasis on the value of the vocation of the ordinary person, Dickinson affirms the idea that grace can be found in the commonplace. Sweeping out a house as holy activity becomes a powerful metaphor for her, as it was for Martin Luther, who declared that there was more holiness in the work of a housewife than in that of a monk. Dickinson's sense of grace leads her to envision a larger spirituality that includes reflections on nature, domesticity, love, and other ostensibly "secular" topics. She challenges readers to move beyond a narrow, doctrinal view of spirituality to realize a wider experience of grace.

Poems that begin with a focus on the commonplace often unfold to include metaphors of the faith: Poem #722, "Sweet Mountains—Ye tell Me no lie—," for example, begins as a poem about nature, but in her characteristic way, Dickinson turns in stanza 2 to see spiritual import in those mountains. The mountains become "Strong Madonnas" (line 7) that the speaker calls to "Cherish still— / The Wayward Nun— beneath the Hill— / Whose service—is to You—" (lines 8–9). The speaker in #249, "Wild Nights—Wild Nights!" envisions an erotic experience as "Rowing in Eden—" (line 9), a mixed metaphor that works here because it suggests not only paradisiacal pleasure but also, perhaps, the spiritual dimensions of her experience: she once again chooses a word from religious rhetoric, "Eden," to describe what others typically see as purely secular. With "Sea" (line 10) understood as the imagination, as is often the case for Dickinson, the poem even suggests that the erotic experience of this speaker leads to poetic inspiration, which further explains her ecstasy. As we see in these two poems and in others, grace, which often takes the form of spiritual vision, can be found in seemingly commonplace experiences such as those of nature and love. It is not the domain of a privileged (ecclesiastical, male) few but is ordinary in its accessibility. Yet, it is rich in what it offers.

But part of Dickinson's prophecy—her soteriology—is that an individual can do nothing to merit grace. She captures the old Reformation theme *sola fide* but pushes it to its limits: even faith, though it may be "a first necessity" for "vascillating feet," cannot guarantee grace (#915, "Faith—is the Pierless Bridge"). Faith, after all, "slips—and laughs, and rallies— / Blushes, if any see— / Plucks as a twig of Evidence— / And asks a Vane, the way—." Even if one could hold onto faith, "the Tooth / That nibbles at the soul—" cannot be "stilled" (#501, "This World is not Conclusion"). Rather, Dickinson advocates throughout her poetry that, to experience grace, the most one can do is simply to make oneself ready for its onset. Shunning hypocrisy, avoiding distractions, keeping oneself from presumption—indeed, renouncing all—are the ways in which one can prepare for an experience of grace.

The simple in heart and the pure in spirit are the people whom grace visits, Dickinson's poems suggest. Thus, many of her poems indict people for their hypocrisy, superficiality, presumption. "I like a look of Agony," she bitingly remarks in #241, "because I know it's true—." In #1207, "He preached upon 'Breadth' till it argued him narrow—," she exposes the "counterfeit presence" (line 8) of the liberal preacher whose sophistication would dazzle simple, pure, innocent

Jesus. The models she holds out to emulate are the simple creatures of nature, like the "little Stone" of #1510 ("How happy is the little Stone") "that rambles in the Road alone, / And does'nt [*sic*] care about Careers / And Exigencies never fears—" (lines 2–4). She admires it for its simplicity in lifestyle (lines 3–4) and appearance (lines 5–6), as well as its nonconformist spirit (lines 7–8). The important trait of the stone as a model is explicit in the last two lines: The stone "fulfill[s] absolute Decree / In casual simplicity—." The application of her wisdom is obvious: she would have her audience imitate the stone and thus gain the happiness (line 1) reserved for those who "fulfill absolute decree."

But even to the pure and simple, "the Heaven—unexpected come[s]," Dickinson's speaker iterates in #513, "Like Flowers, that heard the news of Dews" (line 13). This, we have seen, is her own experience with divinity, the surprising visit of the inspirer. Poem #513 presents a series of analogies to drive home the point that "heaven" visits, without warning, those "Lives that thought the Worshipping / A too presumptuous Psalm—" (lines 14–15). Heaven comes to the humble, to those who regard even worship as presuming too much upon divinity; they have no expectation that worship merits some good from the godhead. The flowers "that heard the news of the Dews, / But never deemed the dripping prize" as something that they would receive, along with the bees and "Arctic Creatures, dimly stirred," stand as examples of those who anticipate without counting on reward (lines 1–2, 7). They presume nothing about the future. Heaven, after all, may choose to visit with a "marauding Hand," she says in #1205, "Immortal is an ample word" (line 7). It remains wholly other, mysterious, and unpredictable.

The encounter with the divine can happen at any time, and individuals have no guarantee that divinity will know them. Dickinson's speaker describes her experience with Jesus in #497:

> He strained my faith—
> Did he find it supple?
> Shook my strong trust—
> Did it then—yield?
>
> Hurled my belief—
> But—did he shatter—it?
> Racked—with suspense—
> Not a nerve failed!

> Wrung me—with Anguish—
> But I never doubted him—
> 'Tho' for what wrong
> He did never say—
>
> Stabbed—while I sued
> His sweet forgiveness—
> Jesus—it's your little 'John'!
> Don't you know—me?

The speaker obviously knows "Jesus," even hinting at their intimate, affectionate relationship in the penultimate line. But that perspective is hers only, not necessarily Jesus'. He, after all, still chooses to "strain" her faith. Grace is no respecter of persons, even those who claim they have never doubted, as the speaker asserts about herself in the third stanza. Despite her suing his "sweet forgiveness" and even her triumph in sustaining his assault on her, Jesus in this poem nonetheless apparently fails to acknowledge his "little 'John.'"

The encounter with the divine can be terrifying to the person unprepared for it, as Dickinson's many poems on death attest. Even some of nature poems suggest this. Poem #986, "A narrow Fellow in the Grass," proceeds playfully enough, until the speaker realizes abruptly that the snake is not merely one of "Nature's people" for whom the speaker has "a transport / Of cordiality—" (lines 17, 19–20); he is a creature different from all the others in his ability to inspire terror, a "Zero at the Bone—" that seems otherworldly in the totality of the void that the image suggests. The snake, of course, is central to the Genesis account of the temptation and fall of humanity into godlessness and darkness. It seems to be more than coincidence that in #986 the snake is the creature that instills "a tighter breathing . . . at the Bone—" (lines 23–24); the strong emotion behind the reversal in the final stanza suggests that the poem is about more than a simple human fear of snakes. Rather, the suggestion is that even in the "cordial" world of nature's creatures, the supernatural is not far off, and one must be ready to meet it.

This leads us to consider Dickinson's cosmology. For her, the proximity of the afterworld to the world of the living can be startling. In her poetry, the two realms appear to be separate—Dickinson is no pantheist—but the spiritual can invade the natural without warning. Her cosmology is a curious mix of evangelical and more liberal understandings, the latter including a romantic view that expresses Platonic and pantheistic leanings. Over and over in her poetry, the natural order seems sacramental, the infinite comes to earth, the mundane transforms into the spiritual, which can be more essential than the material. Dying brings us in touch with eternity, a greater universe. But the world of spirit can be accessed in ways other than death, according to Dickinson. In #258, the speaker describes "a certain Slant of light" that seems to be not of this world:

> There's a certain Slant of light,
> Winter Afternoons—
> That oppresses, like the Heft
> Of Cathedral Tunes—
>
> Heavenly Hurt, it gives us—
> We can find no scar,
> But internal difference,
> Where the Meanings, are—
>
> None may teach it—Any—
> 'Tis the Seal Despair—
> An imperial affliction
> Sent us of the Air—
>
> When it comes, the Landscape listens—
> Shadows—hold their breath—
> When it goes, 'tis like the Distance
> On the look of Death—

Although it is akin to the light of "Winter Afternoons," the images used to describe this extraordinary slant of light emerge from the rhetoric of Christianity—"Cathedral," "Heavenly," even "Seal." Yet the images are not comforting; the light is eerie in its unearthly, divine invasion. It brings "Heavenly Hurt," an "imperial affliction" for which no one can prepare another (by "teach[ing]"), but it also brings no scar, only "internal difference," transforming the individual in the midst of its oppressing "Heft." It is a light that is weighty, solid, in its divine importance because it is "sent us of the Air." And it operates not only on the Soul but in nature as well: even "the Landscape listens—," and "Shadows—hold their breath—" when it comes. Certainly, this strange light is evidence of the proximity of the afterworld and demonstration that the divine can invade not only the individual soul but also nature.

Dickinson's sense of this nearness of the afterworld leads her to focus on the moment. She emphasizes the importance of such reflection, referring in #1125 to the moment as "Sumptuous" (line 1). And she characteristically dramatizes individual moments, finding profound meaning even in ones that might, to unreflective readers, seem minute, insignificant occasions. In #258, we saw her highlighting the importance of "a certain Slant of light." In #130, "These are the days when Birds come back," she images the end of summer as a sacred moment, referring to the fullness of being she experiences in summer as "Sacrament of summer days," "Last Communion in the Haze" (lines 13, 14). She longs for the permanence of that moment. But her delight is partially defined by the stance of retrospect her speaker assumes, a position that precludes the idea of luxuriating too long. Her wisdom here suggests that we find in the moment the wonder that she does, "partak[ing]" of nature's "sacred emblems" even as we avoid childish self-indulgence. Nature's divinity is of such a high order that children are not permitted to participate ("Permit a child to join," her speaker asks in line 15, implying that children's participation must be granted, not assumed). The sacred moment that comes at the end of the summer will not last long; Dickinson wants us to behold the wonder of it.

In fact, Dickinson consistently draws her readers' attention to the wonder of the moment: "Forever—is composed of Nows—," she reminds us in #624. Implicitly, she asks us to slow down, strip away what distracts us, and pay attention to the moment, for there we may discover the divine. Encountering the divine, for her, is always an emotional experience. Her Christology is neither purely Emersonian nor purely Edwardsian. On the one hand, she has a sense of the harmony of nature that the presence of divinity in it brings; nature is a place to discover God, as we know from poems such as #130, "These are the days when Birds come back," and #324 "Some keep the Sabbath going to Church." In poems such as these, she is assured, affirmative. On the other hand, Dickinson's Edwardsianism also gives her an existential view of the world, a sense of apocalypse and contingency: "'Tis so appalling—it exhilarates— / So over Horror, it half Captivates— / The Soul stares after it, secure—" (#281, "'Tis so appalling—it exhilarates—," lines 1–3). If the moment can reveal God, the measure of that appearance of God is the effect on the emotions. The encounter with God can be terrifying, but the experience of terror, as a heartfelt emotion, validates the encounter: "Wonder—," she says in #1331, "is not precisely knowing / And not precisely Knowing not— / A beautiful but bleak condition / He has not lived who has not felt—" (lines 1–4). Ultimately, the effect on the soul is the measure of the experience of the divine—or of the universe itself. "Feeling" wonder or terror in an existential kind of experience is a "Life blow," as she puts it in #816 ("A Death blow is a Life blow to Some"). Some people need a "Death blow" to attain vitality; others need a "Luxury to apprehend" (#815, "The Luxury to apprehend"). Grace comes in alternate ways, but ultimately, the measure of vitality is the receptivity of the soul itself.

Thus, the soul has ultimate authority, according to her view of revelation. She would have us live primarily in service to the soul, not to Christ or to any other conception of the divine. With visionary and revisionary authority, she raises questions about the Bible's authority, as in #1545, "The Bible is an antique Volume—," acknowledging instead the emotional force of the Scriptures and its expositors. For her, the Bible is meaningful only when subjectified. And this is part of the prophetic task she undertakes: to subject the Bible to her experience, to measure its truth by a consultation with the soul. The Bible is a dead document as long as it is not felt. Spiritual truth must be relevant, not merely syllogistic. In one poem she remarks, "Too much of Proof affronts Belief" (#1228, "So much of Heaven has gone from Earth"). She believes what she has felt. Thus, she can say in #1354:

> The Heart is the Capital of the Mind—
> The Mind is a single State—
> The Heart and Mind together make
> A single Continent   (lines 1–4)

It is only as the mind is convinced by the heart that belief can occur.

But if experience is the measure of truth, of what can we be sure? Such a universe sounds relativistic. And for Dickinson, perhaps it is. The focus of her spirituality is not rationality. Although her soteriology and cosmology remain fairly constant, ultimately, her concern is to bring us the "simple news that nature told" (#441, "This is my letter to the World," line 3), the wonder of the moment, and the wisdom we can glean through her observations of the moment. She gives us truths about living, death, and the spirit. Focusing on the moment, she suggests that she is not concerned so much with the past or the future but with the momentary apprehension of truth.

Dickinson's speakers console, visit the afterworld, report to us experiences of the divine. These subjects constitute her prophecy. More than anything else, she reminds us of the wonder of living, whether we experience that in daily domestic life (#443, "I tie my Hat—I crease my Shawl—"), experiences with nature (#219, "She sweeps with many-colored Brooms—"), or encounters with death (#465, "I heard a Fly buzz—when I died—"). Truth itself is wonder. Not surprisingly, sometimes her prophecy seems like a wondrous riddle, geared to only those readers attuned to hear her wisdom. After all,

> The Riddle we can guess
> We speedily despise—
> Not anything is stale so long
> As Yesterday's surprise—   (#1222)

The very experience of reading poetry should elicit marvel, she suggests by her practice throughout her oeuvre. Over and over, her poetry puzzles, disarms, and astonishes readers. Even when her wisdom seems fairly ordinary or her subjects small—as in "Opinion is a flitting thing, / But Truth, outlasts the Sun—" (#1455, lines 1–2)—the implications are weighty: "If then we cannot possess them both—," she concludes #1455, we should "possess the oldest one—," namely, truth itself. The application is not simplistic, though it is disarming in its simplicity: one cannot live under the good opinion of others and at the same time live true to oneself. Ultimately, in Poem #1455 as throughout her corpus, Dickinson exhorts her audience to choose truth. The wisdom undoubtedly arises from her own experience—she knows what it is like to be judged for being unconventional, whether in her verse, her lifestyle, or her womanhood, yet she dismisses that "flitting" opinion in favor of truth. Her poem stands as a challenge to her readers to take that harder road.

Much of Dickinson's poetry focuses on the importance of truth—of simplicity, of renouncing all to gain truth and thus to triumph in the end. She modeled this in her poetry, figuring herself as one who gives up the self in order to be filled with the truth of the divine. And she followed this path in her life, choosing solitude and privacy over convention and fame. Daring to face pain and tragedy in her quest for truth, daring to express anger and protest alongside humor and quiet reflection, Dickinson emerges the queen of poverty, both in art and in life, who ultimately gains a pearl of great price: a poetry of prophecy whose truth "outlasts the Sun" (#1455, line 2).

As Virginia Woolf commented many years ago, it is a rare woman artist who can write without compromising her vision in a patriarchal culture. Dickinson showed that she could take the materials and traditions available to her and shape a distinctive poetic, prophetic voice, refusing to serve public opinion regarding poetry, prophecy, or womanhood. She rejected the version of election handed down to her by male expositors of the Bible. Thus, in many ways, she is not prophetic in a traditional sense. Her prophecy may be far more ambiguous, far less a proclamation, and far more necessarily private than in the biblical and later traditions, yet it nonetheless is wisdom to those who have ears to hear.

In #326, Dickinson seems to indicate her awareness that she is not "doing it right" according to male standards—after all, "no Man instructed" her in her poetry of prophecy, which she often figures as dance or song:

> I cannot dance upon my Toes—
> No Man instructed me—
> But oftentimes, among my mind,
> A Glee possesseth me,
>
> That had I Ballet knowledge—
> Would put itself abroad
> In Pirouette to blanch a Troupe—
> Or lay a Prima, mad,
>
> And though I had no Gown of Gauze—
> No Ringlet, to my Hair,
> Nor hopped for Audiences—like Birds,
> One Claw upon the Air,
>
> Nor tossed my shape in Eider Balls,
> Nor rolled on wheels of snow
> Till I was out of sight, in sound,
> The House encore me so—
>
> Nor any know I know the Art
> I mention—easy—Here—
> Nor any Placard boast me—
> It's full as Opera—

She suggests here that she has to hide her art, at least from those who would be jealous or otherwise unaccepting—a "mad" prima, a troupe that would "blanch" at her "Ballet knowledge." But though she may not appear to be a conventional dancer—one who wears a "Gown of Gauze" and ringlet in her hair and politely dances, birdlike, until "out of sight, in sound"—she nonetheless is "possessed," as the speaker asserts in line 4. The verb is suggestive of a prophetic inspiration that overtakes her: when the "Glee" possesses her, she dances. And despite the fact that no one apparently knows she knows "the Art" of dancing "nor any Placard boast me—," nonetheless her poetry is "full as Opera—." The association, obviously, is with singing, the full, confident voice of the opera singer.

Both metaphors, dancing and singing, align Dickinson with those earlier female poet-prophet-singer-dancers Miriam and Deborah. As it did for them, the poetry of prophecy takes the form of song for her. And the metaphor here, as elsewhere in her poetry, connotes celebration, the speaker delighting in the powerful voice she expresses. As clearly demonstrated by Dickinson, song is a form ideally suited to the woman poet who would speak wisdom and who would have us, her poetic children, retain that wisdom in easily remembered lines. Louise Bogan many years ago described Dickinson aptly, as having "the power to say the unsayable—to hint of the knowable . . . the power of the seer."[7] Dickinson's prophecy, while drawing on the structures and emphases of traditional sources, takes a distinctly female form. It is the work of a singing, dancing "daughter of prophecy," who mothers wisdom for generations to come.

Appendix. A Sample of Dickinson Poems Showing the Sermonic Structure and Variations

BASIC STRUCTURE

Proposition	(Doctrine)
Elaboration	(Reasons)
Application/Concluding Comment	(Application)

##1, 2, 5, 8, 13, 22, 24, 35, 45, 62, 67, 68, 92, 116, 153, 159, 199, 401, 410, 413, 414, 419, 420, 429, 432, 443, 444, 445, 470, 501, 531, 573, 597, 624, 679, 711, 712, 715, 721, 965, 1058, 1129, 1263, 1331, 1340, 1424, 1545, 1732

I. VARIATIONS, WITH THE BASIC PATTERN RETAINED

A. Variations on the form of the proposition
  1. Proposition and elaboration given in a story:
     ##11, 51, 83, 178, 203, 442, 593

  2. Proposition given in form of a definition:
     ##254, 668, 705, 709, 744, 745, 790, 976, 983, 988, 997, 1070, 1118, 1475, 1512, 1660

B. Internal variations
  1. Parallelism used (can also be used in II below):
     ##29, 33, 60, 63, 84, 88, 89, 104, 107, 119, 120, 122, 130, 135, 171, 205, 221, 324, 409, 453, 510, 1260

II. VARIATIONS ON THE BASIC STRUCTURE

A. Inductive structure: proposition missing
  ##12, 70, 99, 106, 112, 138, 140, 165, 167, 194, 216, 758, 1031, 1075, 1102, 1568

B. Deductive: concluding comment missing
  ##80, 98, 126, 161, 230, 389, 437, 475, 477, 809, 830, 835, 1056, 1498

C. Poem as a single statement, usually consisting of only the proposition
  ##16, 21, 32, 38, 55, 57, 87, 105, 108, 170, 183, 206, 210, 226, 447, 707, 720, 883, 1141, 1179, 1688

Notes

EMILY DICKINSON'S POEMS are reprinted in accordance with Thomas H. Johnson's three-volume variorum *The Poems of Emily Dickinson* (Cambridge, Mass.: Harvard University Press, 1963). References to this edition in the text include Johnson's number of the cited poem. Unless otherwise noted, quotations from Dickinson's letters are taken from *The Letters of Emily Dickinson*, ed. Thomas H. Johnson and Theodora Ward, 3 vols. (Cambridge, Mass.: Harvard University Press, 1965). References to this edition appear in the text with the abbreviation *L*, followed by the volume and page numbers. All scriptural quotations are from the Authorized (King James) Version of the Bible, the version that Dickinson knew.

INTRODUCTION

1. Sandra M. Gilbert and Susan Gubar (*Madwoman in the Attic: The Woman Writer and the Nineteenth-Century Literary Imagination* [New Haven: Yale University Press, 1979]) have analyzed Dickinson as madwoman; Margaret Homans (*Woman Writers and Poetic Identity: Dorothy Wordsworth, Emily Bronte, and Emily Dickinson* [Princeton: Princeton University Press, 1980]) has seen linguistic disruption as an element of her power as a woman writer; Suzanne Juhasz (*The Undiscovered Continent: Emily Dickinson and the Space of the Mind* [Bloomington: Indiana University Press, 1983]) has argued that Dickinson lived in the mind to escape a male world; Vivian R. Pollack (*Dickinson: The Anxiety of Gender* [Ithaca, N.Y.: Cornell University Press, 1984]) has discussed Dickinson's "anxiety of gender"; and Joanne Feit Diehl, Barbara J. Williams, Sharon Cameron, and Jane Donahue Eberwein have discussed aspects of Dickinson's frustration or, as James L. Machor has described it, Dickinson's affectation of feminine timidity within patriarchal structures (see Joanne Feit Diehl, *Dickinson and the Romantic Imagination* [Princeton: Princeton University Press, 1981]; Barbara J. Williams, "A Room of Her Own: Emily Dickinson as Woman Artist," in *Feminist Criticism: Essays on Theory, Poetry, and Prose*, ed. Cheryl L. Brown and Karen Olson [Metuchen, N.J.: Scarecrow, 1978], pp. 69–91; Sharon Cameron, "'A Loaded Gun': Dickinson and the Dialectic of Rage," *PMLA* 93 [1978]: 423–37; Jane Donahue Eberwein, *Dickinson: Strategies of Limitation* [Amherst: University of Massachusetts Press, 1985]; and James L. Machor, "Emily Dickinson and the Feminine Rhetoric," *Arizona Quarterly* 36 [1980]: 131–46).

2. Richard Chase (*Emily Dickinson* [New York: William Sloane, 1951; reprint, Westport, Conn.: Greenwood, 1971]) has acknowledged the presence of Puritanism in Dickinson's poetry. One of the best treatments of Calvinism in the poetry is Ronald Lanyi, "'My Faith That Dark Adores—': Calvinist Theology in the Poetry of Emily Dickinson," *Arizona Quarterly* 32 (Autumn 1976): 264–78. Robert Weisbuch (*Emily Dickinson's Poetry* [Chicago: University of Chicago Press, 1975]) has argued that Dickinson's bridal role was a means of overcoming the guilt impressed on her by the Calvinist system, which she could not accept, through a strategy of asserting her innocence in emblems reserved for the elect. More recently, in a study of Dickinson's cultural contexts, Barton Levi St. Armand (*Emily Dickinson and*

Her Culture: The Soul's Society [New York: Cambridge University Press, 1984]) has similarly seen Dickinson's theological past as mainly negative in its influence, citing Calvinism as "ultimate limitation" for Dickinson with its tyrannical, "wrathful" "Father-God" (pp. 193, 93, 94). St. Armand, however, does suggest that nineteenth-century sentimentalism may have contributed to Dickinson's tension with the faith. Karl Keller (*The Only Kangaroo among the Beauty: Emily Dickinson and America* [Baltimore: Johns Hopkins University Press, 1979]), meanwhile, has simply pointed out that the Puritan affinities in her aesthetics need to be traced in greater detail than they have been, as he tries to do by placing Dickinson in the context of Jonathan Edwards (pp. 67–96). He does not consider Dickinson's gender, however, with respect to that religious heritage. In the most thorough treatment of its kind to date, Benjamin Lease's *Emily Dickinson's Readings of Men and Books: Sacred Soundings* (New York: St. Martin's, 1990), pp. 1–34, 107–13, examines Dickinson's adaptations of Charles Wadsworth's theology, but he does not weigh Dickinson's gender, and he does not consider an interaction between Dickinson and Wadsworth, with Dickinson possibly influencing Wadsworth's thought.

3. Suzanne Juhasz, ed., *Feminist Critics Read Emily Dickinson* (Bloomington: Indiana University Press, 1983), p. 17.

4. William H. Shurr, ed., *New Poems of Emily Dickinson* (Chapel Hill: University of North Carolina Press, 1993), presents nearly five hundred new "poems" that Shurr has found embedded in Dickinson's letters, lines that Dickinson formatted as prose but which, reformatted as poetry, sound and look remarkably like the forms we recognize as Dickinson's poetry. Significantly, a large—perhaps even major—portion of these are proverbs, often given in the fourteener form. Shurr's findings suggest that Dickinson's wisdom-giving or prophetic impulse drove her even more profoundly and completely than an exploration of her collected poems alone indicates; and given the letters as Dickinson's own version of publication, Shurr implicitly challenges us to reconsider our views of privacy, publication, and poetry.

1. PROPHECY, POETRY, AND DICKINSON'S AMERICAN CONTENTS

1. Henry David Thoreau, *Walden* (1854), ed. F. B. Sanborn, vol. 2 of *The Writings of Henry David Thoreau*, ed. F. B. Sanborn and Bradford Torrey (Boston: Houghton Mifflin, 1906), 364.

2. Shira Wolosky, "Emily Dickinson's War Poetry: The Problems of Theodicy," *Massachusetts Review* 25 (1984): 31. For alternative views, see David Porter, *Dickinson: The Modern Idiom* (Cambridge, Mass.: Harvard University Press, 1981), p. 115; and Karl Keller, *The Only Kangaroo among the Beauty: Emily Dickinson and America* (Baltimore: Johns Hopkins University Press, 1979), pp. 104, 110; both see Dickinson as standing apart from the Civil War. Shira Wolosky (*Emily Dickinson: A Voice of War* [New Haven: Yale University Press, 1984], p. xviii), finds in Dickinson "a metaphysical conflict . . . accompanied by historical trauma" in her work, not an open engagement of political and social issues.

3. Ralph Waldo Emerson, "The Poet," in *The Complete Writings of Ralph Waldo Emerson*, 12 vols., ed. Edward W. Emerson (Boston: Houghton Mifflin, 1903–1904), 3:28. At the same time, as Lawrence Buell indicates, Emerson's stance does not necessarily imply "a high estimate of art as such: Emerson wants only the 'poetic gift . . . not rhymes and sonneteering, not bookmaking and bookselling'" (Emerson, "Poetry and Imagination," *Complete Writings*, 8:63–64) quoted in Lawrence Buell, *New England Literary Culture from Revolution through Renais-*

sance [New York: Cambridge University Press, 1986], p. 72). The romantic tension about poetry as marketable art may provide some of the explanation for Dickinson's reluctance to publish, as she, according to one theory, consciously withheld her poetry from the public and the marketplace. On Dickinson's reading "The Poet" in Emerson's *Essays: Second Series,* see Jay Leyda, *The Years and Hours of Emily Dickinson,* 2 vols. (New Haven: Yale University Press, 1960; reprint, New York: Archon, 1970), 2:20–21; she also owned *Poems,* as Leyda indicates (1:164). In a letter to Mrs. Mary Elizabeth Higginson, she called Emerson's *Representative Men* "a little Granite book you can lean on" (Leyda, *Years and Hours,* 2:262).

4. Ralph Waldo Emerson, "An Address Delivered before the Senior Class in Divinity College," in *Complete Writings,* 1:151.

5. Emerson discusses his view of women in print in his essay "Woman," in *Complete Writings,* 11:405–26. See Amy Schrager Lang, *Prophetic Woman: Anne Hutchinson and the Problem of Dissent in the Literature of New England* (Berkeley and Los Angeles: University of California Press, 1987), pp. 137–45, for an analysis of this essay and of Emerson's views on the nature of female power. As Lang points out, despite Emerson's focus on the literal empowerment of women through the franchise, he ends up limiting women's power (perhaps unwittingly).

6. Margaret Fuller, *Woman in the Nineteenth Century* (1845), reprinted in *Margaret Fuller: Essays on American Life and Letters,* ed. Joel Myerson (New Haven: College and University Press, 1978), pp. 161–62.

7. Ibid., pp. 162, 160.

8. Lydia Maria Child, *History of the Condition of Women in Various Ages and Nations,* 2 vols. (London: Simpkin, Marshall, 1835), 1:9–10.

9. Nina Baym, "Onward Christian Women: Sarah J. Hale's History of the World," *New England Quarterly* 63, 2 (June 1990): 249–70.

10. Sarah Josepha Hale, *Woman's Record* (1853; reprint, New York: Harper & Brothers, 1855), p. 563; quoted in Baym, "Onward Christian Women," p. 257.

11. George Faber, *A Dissertation on the Prophecies* (Boston: William Andrews, 1808), p. 382. Faber's book was one of several that were removed from the Dickinson collection at the Houghton Library in the interest of space, because they seemed irrelevant to George Frisbie Whicher and Thomas H. Johnson, who were asked to advise the library on its choices. Other family books that may have taught Dickinson about biblical prophecy and poetry are Simon Greenleaf, *An Examination of the Testimony of the Four Evangelists* (1846); Rosewell Hitchcock, *Analysis of the Holy Bible* (1870); and *The Paraphrased Psalm Book* (1810). The books removed suggest the possibility of a stronger influence of the scriptural tradition on Dickinson than has hitherto been acknowledged.

12. F. D. Huntington, *Christian Believing and Living: Sermons* (Boston: Crosby, 1860), p. 19.

13. Ibid., p. 20.

14. Edward T. Channing, *Lectures Read to the Juniors in Harvard College,* ed. Dorothy I. Anderson and Waldo W. Braden (1856; reprint, Carbondale and Edwardsville: Southern Illinois University Press, 1968), pp. 121, 120, 126.

15. Leyda, *Years and Hours,* documents the following dates on which Emerson spoke in Amherst: February 1849 (1:155); August 8, 1855 (1:334); December 16, 1857 (1:351); October 17, 1865 (2:102); and March 29, 1879 (2:310). He spoke March 21, 1855, in nearby Springfield (1:331).

16. Buell, *New England Literary Culture,* p. 137.

17. John Calvin, *Calvin: Institutes of the Christian Religion,* 2 vols., trans. Ford Lewis Battles, ed. John T. McNeill (Philadelphia: Westminster, 1960), 2:1155–57; and *Homilies on I Samuel,* quoted in *Institutes,* 2:1018 n.11.

18. Jonathan Edwards, "The True Excellency of a Gospel Minister," in *The Works of President Edwards*, 10 vols. (Edinburgh, 1847; reprint, New York: Burt Franklin, 1968), 10:498, 501.

19. Edwards Amasa Park, "The Influence of the Preacher," in *Pulpit Eloquence of the Nineteenth Century*, ed. Henry Fish (New York: Dodd, Mead, 1871), pp. 25, 20–21; Huntington, *Christian Believing*, pp. 322–34.

20. Brita Lindberg-Seyersted, *The Voice of the Poet: Aspects of Style in the Poetry of Emily Dickinson* (Cambridge, Mass.: Harvard University Press, 1968), pp. 57, 31.

21. Porter, *Dickinson*, p. 223.

22. Buell, *New England Literary Culture*, p. 72.

23. Murray Roston, *Prophet and Poet* (Evanston, Ill.: Northwestern University Press, 1965), p.313.

24. Buell, *New England Literary Culture*, pp. 177–84.

25. Quoted in ibid., p. 169.

26. As Buell (ibid., pp. 168–72) describes, Dwight subsequently advocated the literary representation of scriptural episodes and even tried to follow his own advice by attempting poetic reworkings of biblical narratives. Here he was following Puritan precedent, such as the paraphrases of psalms and Michael Wigglesworth's *Day of Doom*, but these Puritan texts were not embellished retellings of biblical passages for the sake of literary effect, as Dwight's work was. In Buell's words, "Dwight may be credited with ushering in a new era for New England authors in the literary appropriation of Scripture in the freedom with which he uses his sources and the degree of conscious stylization he gave to his materials," as in his *The Conquest of Canaan* (1785), based on the Book of Joshua. See Buell, *New England Literary Culture*, pp. 166–90, for a discussion of the use of Scripture by New England writers before the Civil War; on the visionary and moral dimensions of romantic art, see pp. 64–73.

27. See Jack L. Capps, *Emily Dickinson's Reading: 1836–1886* (Cambridge, Mass.: Harvard University Press, 1966), pp. 12, 22, 78–81, 111–18, 133, for details of her reading of British and American poets as she refers to these in her letters and poems.

28. Albert Barnes, *Notes, Critical, Explanatory, and Practical, on the Book of the Prophet Isaiah* (1844; reprint, New York: Leavitt and Allen, 1954), p. xxxix.

29. Roston, *Prophet and Poet*, p. 192.

30. Ibid., p. 193.

31. Capps, *Emily Dickinson's Reading*, p. 30. Calvin and others regarded the Psalms as prophecy since, as Calvin explains, "what we attribute to the prophecies is common to them" (*Institutes*, 2:1154).

32. The two prominent examples are Miriam's short reiteration of Moses' song, which appears in Exod. 15:20–21, and Deborah's very long song, given in Judges 5.

2. "A WORD THAT BREATHES DISTINCTLY"

1. Quoted in Millicent Todd Bingham, ed., *Ancestors' Brocades: The Literary Debut of Emily Dickinson* (New York: Harper & Brothers, 1945), pp. 76, 77.

2. Rosamond Rosenmeier, *Anne Bradstreet Revisited* (Schenectady, N.Y.: Twayne, 1991), esp. pp. 6–9, 44–47.

3. Wendy Martin, *An American Triptych: Anne Bradstreet, Emily Dickinson, Adrienne Rich* (Chapel Hill: University of North Carolina Press, 1984), p. 8.

4. Jonathan Edwards, "The True Excellency of a Gospel Minister," in *The Works of President Edwards*, 10 vols. (Edinburgh, 1847; reprint, New York: Burt Franklin, 1968), 10: 499.

5. Helen Hunt Jackson, "Renunciation," in *American Women Poets of the Nineteenth Century: An Anthology*, ed. Cheryl Walker (New Brunswick, N.J.: Rutgers University Press, 1992), pp. 283–84.

6. For a recent consideration of Dickinson's poems published in her lifetime, see Karen A. Dandurand, "Another Dickinson Poem Published in Her Lifetime," *American Literature* 54, 3 (October 1982): 434–37; "New Dickinson Civil War Publications," *American Literature* 56, 1 (March 1984): 17–27; "Publication of Dickinson's Poems in Her Lifetime," *Legacy* 1, 1 (Spring 1984): 7.

7. The reviews can be found in Willis J. Buckingham, *Emily Dickinson's Reception in the 1890s: A Documentary History* (Pittsburgh: University of Pittsburgh Press, 1989).

8. William Michael Rossetti, ed., *The Family Letters of Christina Rossetti* (1908; reprint, New York: Haskell House, 1968), p. 177. I am indebted to Joel Westerholm for pointing out this letter to me.

9. Paul Lauter, *Canons and Contexts* (New York: Oxford University Press, 1991), p. 125.

10. Ralph Waldo Emerson, "The Poet," in *The Complete Writings of Ralph Waldo Emerson*, 12 vols., ed. Edward W. Emerson (Boston: Houghton Mifflin, 1903–1904), 3:41.

11. "Ear" and "arguments" seem to be the words that Dickinson preferred; her original choices were "head" and "threnodies."

12. Thomas H. Johnson, *Emily Dickinson: An Interpretive Biography* (Cambridge, Mass.: Harvard University Press, Belknap Press, 1955), p. 52; Brita Lindberg-Seyersted, *The Voice of the Poet: Aspects of Style in the Poetry of Emily Dickinson* (Cambridge, Mass.: Harvard University Press, 1968), p. 29.

13. Cynthia Griffin Wolff, "The Reality of Emily Dickinson: An Anniversary Celebration," *Harvard Magazine* (November–December 1980): 51, 53.

14. Nancy Chodorow, *The Reproduction of Mothering: Psychoanalysis and the Sociology of Gender* (Berkeley: University of California Press, 1978); Jean Baker Miller, *Toward a New Psychology of Women*, 2d. ed. (Boston: Beacon, 1986).

15. Allen Tate, "Emily Dickinson," in *Collected Essays* (Denver: A. Swallow, 1959), p. 197; R. P. Blackmur, "Emily Dickinson's Notation," *Kenyon Review* 18 (Spring 1956): 227.

16. Elizabeth K. Helsinger, Robin Lauterbach Sheets, and William Veeder, *The Woman Question: Society and Literature in Britain and America, 1837–1883*, vol. 3: *Literary Issues* (Chicago: University of Chicago Press, 1983), pp. 40, 41, 42. The authors discussed Browning's poems in much more detail than I do here.

3. "CAPTIVATING SERMONS"

1. Richard Sewall, *Life of Emily Dickinson*, 2 vols. (New York: Farrar, Strauss & Giroux, 1974), 1:461.

2. Harry S. Stout, *The New England Soul: Preaching and Religious Culture in Colonial New England* (New York: Oxford University Press, 1986), p. 228.

3. Williston Walker, *History of the Congregational Churches in the United States* (New York: Christian Literature, 1894), p. 305.

4. Thomas Le Duc, *Piety and Intellect at Amherst College, 1865–1912* (New York: Columbia University Press, 1946), p. 5.

5. The number is a conservative one. I include only fifteen years of church attendance, starting when Dickinson was ten years old and continuing until her twenty-fifth year—some sources (e.g., Sewall, *Life*) maintain she attended church until she was thirty—and I do not count Mount Holyoke headmistress Mary

Lyon's "sermons." My number takes into consideration the Dickinson family practice of attending church twice on Sundays, which George Frisbie Whicher (*This Was a Poet: A Critical Biography of Emily Dickinson* [New York: Scribner's, 1938; reprint, Ann Arbor: University of Michigan Press, 1957], p. 6) points out.

6. Sewall, *Life*, 2:359.

7. Park's "Judas" sermon was almost certainly the one described by Dickinson and later recalled as "the loveliest" she ever heard. See *The Letters of Emily Dickinson*, ed. Mabel Loomis Todd (New York: Harper & Brothers, 1931), pp. 99, 251. Other Amherst preachers (or faculty members who occasionally preached) whom Dickinson admired were Aaron Colton (who delivered "enlivening" sermons [*L*, 1:120]), Professor William S. Tyler, and Edward S. Dwight, who, according to Sewall (*Life*, 1:359 n. 17), "seems to have been a favorite." As Dickinson wrote to Austin about Dwight on May 16, 1853, "I never heard a preacher I loved half so well" (*L*, 1:250).

8. She made her famous comment "sermons on unbelief ever did attract me" in response to Dwight's sermon on that topic (*L*, 1:311).

9. For a discussion of the probable details of Dickinson's meeting with Wadsworth, see Whicher, *This Was a Poet*, p.3103; and Richard Chase, *Emily Dickinson* (New York: William Sloane, 1951; reprint, Westport, Conn.: Greenwood, 1971), p. 74. See Sewall, *Life*, 1:453, for details of her first reading of a Wadsworth sermon. Benjamin Lease (*Emily Dickinson's Readings of Men and Books: Sacred Soundings* [New York: St. Martin's, 1990], pp. 1–34) explores in depth Wadsworth's hold on Dickinson. A volume of Charles Wadsworth's work, *Sermons* (New York and San Francisco: Presbyterian, 1869), was published during his lifetime. After his death, three more volumes appeared: vols. 1 and 2 in 1882 and vol. 3 in 1884.

10. Sandra M. Gilbert and Susan Gubar, *Madwoman in the Attic: The Woman Writer and the Nineteenth-Century Literary Imagination* (New Haven: Yale University Press, 1979), p. 583.

11. Edwards Amasa Park, "The Influence of the Preacher," in *Pulpit Eloquence of the Nineteenth Century*, ed. Henry Fish (New York: Dodd, Mead, 1871), pp. 14, 20.

12. Quoted in Richard Sewall, "The Lyman Letters: New Light on Emily Dickinson and Her Family," *Massachusetts Review* 6 (Autumn 1965): 774.

13. See Floyd Wesley Lambertson, "A Survey and Analysis of American Homiletics prior to 1860" (Ph.D. diss., State University of Iowa, 1930), 1:203–14. To date, Lambertson's is the only systematic and comprehensive study of the rhetorical structures of traditional preaching in America. The dearth of studies such as his no doubt impedes scholarly work on poetry and fiction which might draw on the sermons as context. Lewis Brastow, *The Modern Pulpit: A Study of Homiletic Sources and Characteristics* (New York: Macmillan, 1906); DeWitte Holland, ed., *Preaching in American History: Selected Issues in the American Pulpit, 1630–1969* (Nashville: Abingdon, 1969); and Stout, *New England Soul*, all provide some helpful material but tend to concentrate on subject matter rather than method. Fortunately for Dickinson scholars, enough sermons by preachers she knew are still extant to draw some informed conclusions.

14. Jack L. Capps, *Emily Dickinson's Reading: 1836–1886* (Cambridge, Mass.: Harvard University Press, 1966), p. 88. Edyth Wylder (*The Last Face: Emily Dickinson's Manuscripts* [Albuquerque: University of New Mexico Press, 1971]) explores Dickinson's dashes as elocutionary markings. Other scholars have also noted the orality of Dickinson's verse: Thomas H. Johnson (introduction to *The Poems of Emily Dickinson* [Cambridge, Mass.: Harvard University Press, 1963],

vol. 1:lxiii) interprets the dashes as "visual representations of a musical beat," while Charles Anderson (*Emily Dickinson's Poetry: Stairway of Surprise* [1960; reprint, Garden City, N.Y.: Doubleday, 1966], pp. 39–40) makes the point that Dickinson's poems often need to be read aloud to understand fully the sense: "the sound is sometimes key to sense" in her emphasis on intellect, logic, and oral persuasion.

15. W. S. Tyler, *The Great Commission*, sermon preached in the Amherst College chapel, 23 November 1856 (Amherst, Mass.: John H. Brewster, 1857), pp. 20–21.

16. Helen Hunt Jackson, "Acquainted with Grief," in *American Women Poets of the Nineteenth Century: An Anthology*, ed. Cheryl Walker (New Brunswick, N.J.: Rutgers University Press, 1992), p. 290.

17. The sermons of the Unitarian preachers, in contrast to those of Tyler and others of the Puritan legacy, focused less on structure and rhetorical craft and more on metaphor and colloquial simplicity. The Unitarians tended to value the sermon as an imaginative work of art, not merely as a transmitter of truth. See Lawrence Buell, "The Unitarian Movement and the Art of Unitarian Preaching in Nineteenth-Century America," *American Quarterly* 24 (1972): 166–90.

18. Claudia Yukman, "Speaking to Strangers: Dickinson's and Whitman's Poetics of Historical Presence" (Ph.D. diss., Brandeis University, 1986), p. 108.

19. David T. Porter, *Dickinson: The Modern Idiom* (Cambridge, Mass.: Harvard University Press, 1981), p. 8.

20. Stout, *New England Soul*, pp. 228–29.

21. Ebenezer Porter, *Lectures on Homiletics and Preaching* (Andover, Mass.: Flagg, Gould, Newman, 1834), p. 118.

22. For a discussion of William Ellery Channing's sermon style as representative, in many ways, of Unitarian preaching, see Teresa Toulouse, *The Art of Prophesying: New England Sermons and the Shaping of Belief* (Athens: University of Georgia Press, 1987), pp. 75–117. Toulouse demonstrates that Channing followed the structure advocated by rhetorician Hugh Blair—a model having three to six parts: introduction, proposition, narration, reason, the "pathetic" part, and the peroration. Significantly, Blair wrote as a rhetorician of demonstrative oration, not homiletics.

23. Chase, *Emily Dickinson*, p. 79. Mary Elizabeth Barbot ("Emily Dickinson Parallels," *New England Quarterly* 14 [1941]: 689–96) has also seen instances of Dickinson's imitation of Wadsworth's imagery as well as his figurative language, fidning seven specific parallels between the figurative language in certain poems of Dickinson and Wadsworth's poems. She points out that certain images recur in the work of both writers, such as Dickinson's metaphor of heaven as a schoolroom (cf. Wadsworth's *Sermons*, p. 13) and that of remorse as a "superior spectre" haunting the "corridors" and "cellars" of the soul (cf. *Sermons*, pp. 64–65). David Higgins (*Portrait of Emily Dickinson: The Poet and Her Prose* [New Brunswick, N.J.: Rutgers University Press, 1967], p. 82) has found another parallel. Richard Sewall (*Life*, 2:455–62) develops some of these parallels as well as some suggested by Jay Leyda, showing similarities in figurative language, theme, and poetic conception. Lease (*Emily Dickinson's Readings*, pp. 107–13), in a discussion of the nineteenth-century spiritualist movement and its appeal to Wadsworth, explores the ways in which Dickinson drew on and transformed Wadsworth's visions of heaven, which were influenced by the movement.

24. George Burrows, *Impressions of Dr. Wadsworth as a Preacher* (San Francisco: Towne and Bacon, 1863), p. 15.

25. Higgins, *Portrait*, p. 82; Jay Leyda, *The Years and Hours of Emily Dickinson* (New Haven: Yale University Press, 1960; reprint, New York: Archon, 1970), 1:77.

26. W. S. Tyler, *Integrity the Safeguard of Public and Private Life*, sermon preached in the Amherst College chapel, 17 October 1857 (Springfield, Mass.: Samuel Bowles, 1857), pp. 7, 24, 25–26.

27. Brastow, *Modern Pulpit*, p. 348.

28. Brita Lindberg-Seyersted (*The Voice of the Poet: Aspects of Style in the Poetry of Emily Dickinson* [Cambridge, Mass.: Harvard University Press, 1968], p. 92) has connected this use of concrete nouns (and Dickinson's use of paradox) to "the Puritan sermon tradition of Hooker, Shepard, and Cotton," homiletic forefathers of Edwards.

29. See Thomas Olbricht, "The Rise of Unitarianism in America," in *Preaching in American History*, ed. Holland, pp. 125–29; Toulouse, *Art of Prophesying*, pp. 75–117; and Buell, "Unitarian Movement," for discussions of Unitarian preaching. David S. Reynolds (*Beneath the American Renaissance: The Subversive Imagination in the Age of Emerson and Melville* [New York: Knopf, 1988], pp. 30–37, 428–29) compares Dickinson's poems to Unitarian preaching.

30. Jonathan Edwards, "The Excellency of Christ," in *Selected Writings of Jonathan Edwards*, ed. Harold P. Simonson (New York: Frederick Ungar, 1970), p. 120.

31. Tyler, *Great Commission*, pp. 31, 34.

32. Quoted in Leyda, *Years and Hours*, 2:236. See Sewall, *Life*, 2:450–52, 459–60 n. 16, for other reports of Wadsworth's deliveries.

33. Charles Wadsworth, "Self-Knowledge," in *Sermons*, p. 129. Lease (*Emily Dickinson's Readings*, pp. 8–9) discusses this text as it relates to Dickinson's art.

34. Burrows, *Impressions of Dr. Wadsworth*, pp. 10–11.

35. I am indebted to Carroll D. Laverty, "Structural Patterns in Emily Dickinson's Poetry," *Emerson Society Quarterly* 44 (1966): 12–17; and Suzanne M. Wilson, "Structural Patterns in the Poetry of Emily Dickinson," *American Literature* 35 (1963): 53–59, for the main points of the following discussion. Although they might seem to disagree regarding Dickinson's structural patterns, an understanding of the Edwardsian sermon shows their analyses to be more alike than dissimilar, as each critic unwittingly shows ways in which Dickinson imitates the Edwardsian sermon. Laverty's rhetorical analysis of Dickinson's poetry is more complete than Wilson's, yet Laverty does not identify Dickinson's method as deriving from the Edwardsian sermonic-prophetic tradition. Consequently, he does not consider Dickinson's purposes in using the structures to gain prophetic authority as a woman poet.

36. Barbara A. C. Mossberg, *Emily Dickinson: When a Writer Is a Daughter* (Bloomington: University of Indiana Press, 1982), p. 104.

37. Park, for example, adopted this approach in "Peter's Denials of the Lord" and in his famous "Judas" sermon. In each case, almost the entire sermon is his retelling of the narrative. See Edwards Amasa Park, *A Memorial Collection of Sermons* (Boston: Pilgrim, 1902), pp. 29–42, 43–72. Wadsworth used the technique frequently, as in "The Bright Side" (on Job 37:21), "The Treasures of Wisdom" (on Prov. 3:14), and "The Great Question" (on Matt. 16:26), all in his *Sermons*.

38. The terms *deductive* and *inductive* are Laverty's. They capture the traditional sermon's appeal to reason.

39. Other poems illustrating her use of such parallelism as an elaboration of the sermonic structure are #29, "If those I loved were lost"; #60, "Like her the Saints retire"; #66, "So from the mould"; #513, "Like Flowers, that heard the news of Dew"; #1032, "Who is the East?"; #1079, "The Sun went down—no Man looked on—"; #1084, "At Half past Three, a single Bird"; and #1418, "How lonesome the Wind must feel Nights—."

40. I derive my list from Laverty, who lists two additional poems (#695, "As if the Sea should part," and #1474, "Estranged from Beauty—none can be") that I would not include as true definition poems because, in each case, the definition is not the focus of the poem. Laverty also discusses analogy as a structural pattern, but I would not include it as a major pattern. Almost all of the poems he lists are those in which Dickinson uses metaphor in her first or final statement or bases her elaboration on an extended metaphor: #214, "I taste a liquor never brewed—"; #20, "Distrustful of the Gentian—"; #39, "It did not surprise me—"; #213, "Did the Harebell loose her girdle"; #228, "Blazing in Gold and quenching in Purple"; #240, "Ah, Moon—and Star!"; #722, "Sweet Mountains—Ye tell Me no lie—"; #1052, "I never saw a Moor—"; #1142, "The Props assist the House"; #1433, "How brittle are the Piers." Only #20 and #1142 of his list actually use analogy; in these it occurs as the final statement (the standard of comparison given in the initial proposition and elaboration, as in #1142), and in #20, the analogy could be called parallelism, the elaboration merely a repeat of the initial situation and offering an amplification of that situation. Dickinson uses analogy, but not as frequently as Laverty implies.

For a larger sample of Dickinson's poems categorized according to the ways in which they show the sermonic structure, see the Appendix.

41. Capps, *Emily Dickinson's Reading*, p. 44. Capps (pp. 38–59, 148–66) notes several other poems that are redactions of Old Testament stories: e.g., #702 (Genesis 19, Lot's demonstration of faith in entertaining strangers) and #540 (1 Sam. 17:50; she uses the story of David and Goliath as ministers do, offering it as a warning against ill-considered aspirations). Other poems capturing biblical stories are #662 (Gen. 3:10), #48 (Gen. 8:8–12), and #403 (Genesis 7–8, the story of Noah). Also, several poems are concerned with Eden (#1069, #1657) and the Fall (#1119, #1195). Dickinson includes many more allusions in her letters. According to Capps (pp. 38–59, 148–66), poems in which Dickinson took passages from the New Testament include #690 and #164 (Matt. 10:29–31); #70 (Matt. 19:14); #1574 (Matt. 11:28); #143 (Matt. 8:20); #1720 (Matt. 20:16; also Mark 10:31); #964 (Matt. 25:40); #234 (Matt. 7:13–14); #132 (Matt. 25:40); #313 (Matt. 26; 27); #193, #203, #1735 (John 18:18–27); #1180 (Luke 23:42–43); #1274 (John 3); #127 and #61 (John 14:2); #160 and #1241 (1 Cor. 2:9); #460 (Rev. 7:16–17); #1357 (Rev. 2:10); #1598 (Rev. 21:8). Poem #461 seems to be a commentary on Matthew 25, Dickinson's dramatization of the parable of the ten virgins.

42. Anderson, *Emily Dickinson's Poetry*, p. 12.

43. Aaron Colton, *In Memoriam. Discourse Delivered . . . at the Funeral of Mrs. Emeline G. Wright*, sermon preached in Easthampton, Massachusetts, 8 March 1863 (Northampton, Mass.: Trumbull and Gere, 1863), p. 10.

4. SPEAKING FOR "INFINITUDE"

1. Charlotte Louise Nekola, "Emily Dickinson and the Poetry of Silence" (Ph.D. diss., University of Michigan, 1984), p. 185.

2. Suzanne Juhasz, *Naked and Fiery Forms: Modern American Poetry of Women, a New Tradition* (New York: Octagon Books, 1976), p. 10.

3. Sandra M. Gilbert and Susan Gubar, *Madwoman in the Attic: The Woman Writer and the Nineteenth-Century Literary Imagination* (New Haven: Yale University Press, 1979), p. 607.

4. For a sample of these readings of Dickinson's inspirer, see Adrienne Rich ("'Vesuvius at Home': The Power of Emily Dickinson," *Parnassus* 5, 1 [1976]: 49–74), who identifies Dickinson's inspiring "muse" as her "daemon," her own active

creative power, whose gender is, significantly, male; he cherishes and tortures her, Rich indicates, exploring Dickinson's use of the "language of heterosexual love or patriarchal theology" as the poet speaks about her muse—or, as I argue, the male inspirer of her "prophecy." Joan Feit Diehl (" 'Come Slowly—Eden': An Exploration of Women Poets and Their Muse," *Signs* 3 [1981]: 572–87) suggests that the "muse" might have a female persona, although she also discusses at some length the male persona of the "muse," focusing more on suffering than on fulfillment because of the stress her thesis puts on Dickinson's "dilemma of [literary] influence." She argues that Dickinson conflates creative power with the restriction of rule by the Precursor/Father, given the long succession of literary fathers. Diehl's argument has its roots in Gilbert and Gubar's discussion of a woman writer's "anxiety of authorship," which considers the female artist as alienated from male predecessors and therefore experiencing her gender as painful, even debilitating, as she urgently senses a need for a female audience and female precursors. See Gilbert and Gubar, *Madwoman in the Attic*, pp. 46–53.

5. An alternative approach to the poem is the Jungian reading of Adrienne Rich, " 'Vesuvius at Home' "; Albert Gelpi, "Emily Dickinson and the Deerslayer: The Dilemma of the Woman Poet in America," in *Shakespeare's Sisters: Feminist Essays on Women Poets*, ed. Sandra M. Gilbert and Susan Gubar (Bloomington: Indiana University Press, 1979), pp. 122–24; and Joanne A. Dobson, *Dickinson and the Strategies of Reticence: The Woman Writer in Nineteenth-Century America* (Bloomington: Indiana University Press, 1989), p. 85. The "Owner," in Dobson's words, is Dickinson's "animus"—her own "dimly perceived 'masculine' self, the aspect of her psyche that had long been deprived in the 'real' world of recognition and expression." As Gelpi ("Emily Dickinson and the Deerslayer," p. 123) puts it, the image is "symbolic of certain aspects of her personality, qualities and needs and potentialities which have been defined culturally and psychologically with the masculine." One of the problems with this reading is that, in its assertion that the female poet cannot write without the aid of her male "self," it implies a compromised view of female creativity. Even aside from that, we must remember that Jungian ideas were not "in the air" during Dickinson's time and in her locale; they are a twentieth-century phenomenon.

6. Sandra M. Gilbert, "The Wayward Nun beneath the Hill," in *Feminist Critics Read Emily Dickinson*, ed. Suzanne Juhasz (Bloomington: Indiana University Press, 1983), p. 27.

7. See Dan. 2:19; 7:2; 9:21; Zech. 1:7–6:8; Acts 16:9; 18:9. Other individuals spoken to by God in nocturnal visions or dreams include Joseph (Gen. 37:4–6), Solomon (1 Sam. 15:16; 1 Kings 3:5; and 2 Chron. 7:12), and Job (Job 33:15).

8. Examples of these texts include Gen. 20:3–7; 1 Kings 3:5–15; Matt. 1:20–24; and Acts 18:9–10.

9. The text supports Deut. 13:1–5, in which the prophet is mentioned alongside the dreamer without any incongruity. The close connection between dreaming and prophesying is again revealed in Jer. 23:25, 32: "I have heard what the prophets said, that prophesy [*sic*] lies in my name, saying, I have dreamed, I have dreamed."

10. Poems that portray God the Father in this way include #49, "I never lost as much but twice"; #65, "I can't tell you—but you feel it—"; #116, "I had some things that I called mine—"; #475, "Doom is the House without the Door—"; #476, "I meant to have but modest needs—"; #597, "It always felt to me—a wrong"; #1317, "Abraham to kill him"; #1551, "Those—dying then"; #1584, "Expanse cannot be lost—"; and #1719, "God is indeed a jealous God—," to name a few.

11. On the religious symbolism of white, see, for example, Rev. 3:4, 18; 6:11; 7:9 and 13; cf. 4:4; 19:14. The wedding of the Messiah to the church, his bride, is

mentioned specifically in Rev. 19:7–10; 21:2–8 and is a theme informing the entire book.

12. Abraham J. Heschel, *The Prophets* (New York: Harper & Row, 1962), 1:48.

13. The principle is affirmed in Prov. 1:5–6; Isa. 6:9–10; Ezek. 2:5; Jer. 5:21; Matt. 11:15; John 8:42–47; and Rev. 1:3. Christ even tells a parable illustrating the principle, the parable of the sower (Matt. 13:1–23; also in Mark 4:1–20), explaining that he speaks in parables because his messages are for those who "hear with their ears" and "understand with their heart" (Matt. 13:15), an allusion to Isa. 6:9–10. The apostle Paul also reiterates the principle, quoting the Isaiah and Matthew passages in Acts 28:26–27 as he explains why the gospel has been sent to the Gentiles—they, unlike the Jews, whose "ears are dull of hearing" and whose "eyes have they closed" (v. 27), will listen. Dickinson's poem #945, "This is a Blossom of the Brain—," is similar in both theme and image to the parable of the sower.

5. CONSTRUCTIONS OF GENRE AND SELF

1. Victor Turner, *The Ritual Process: Structure and Anti-Structure* (Ithaca, N.Y.: Cornell University Press, 1969), p. 85.

2. Cynthia Griffin Wolff (*Emily Dickinson* [New York: Knopf, 1986], p. 235) agrees with this analysis, pointing out that in poems such as #445, "Just this time, last year, I died," and #712, "Because I could not stop for Death—," the "temporal continuum of each poem exists independently of the clock time in which both author and reader exist." She sees Dickinson employing "this deliberately unrealistic Voice precisely in order to force each reader to re-examine the premises about life and death that he or she has taken for granted." Such motivation is shared by the biblical prophets (although their premises differ from Dickinson's). Sharon Cameron (*Lyric Time: Dickinson and the Limits of Genre* [Baltimore: Johns Hopkins University Press, 1979]), in calling this conflation of time "lyric time"— meaning the kind of time expressed by lyric poets—also supports this reading of Dickinson.

3. David T. Porter, *Dickinson: The Modern Idiom* (Cambridge, Mass.: Harvard University Press, 1981), p. 12. The list is Porter's.

4. Wolff, *Emily Dickinson*, p. 238.

5. Cameron, *Lyric Time*, p. 92.

6. Abraham J. Heschel, *The Prophets*, 2 vols. (New York: Harper & Row, 1962), 1:10.

7. Ibid., 1:12.

8. Other such poems include #76, "Exultation is the going"; #623, "It was too late for Man—"; #624, "Forever—is composed of Nows—"; #761, "From Blank to Blank—"; #800, "Two—were immortal twice—"; #946, "It is an honorable Thought"; #963, "A nearness to Tremendousness—"; #976, "Death is a Dialogue between"; #1179, "Of so divine a Loss"; #1234, "If my Bark sink"; #1296, "Death's Waylaying not the sharpest"; #1499, "How firm Eternity must look"; #1599, "Though the great Waters sleep"; and #1684, "The Blunder is in estimate."

9. Porter, *Dickinson*, p. 175.

10. Douglas Anderson, "Presence and Place in Emily Dickinson's Poetry," *New England Quarterly* 57 (1984): 207.

11. Joan Burbick, "'One Unbroken Company': Religion and Emily Dickinson," *New England Quarterly* 53 (1980): 62–75.

12. Ralph Waldo Emerson, "An Address Delivered before the Senior Class in Divinity College," in *The Complete Writings of Ralph Waldo Emerson*, 12 vols., ed. Edward W. Emerson (Boston: Houghton Mifflin, 1903–1904), 1:151.

6. SCRIPTURAL RHETORIC AND POETRY

1. Stephen F. Winward, *A Guide to the Prophets* (Atlanta: John Knox, 1968), p. 24.

2. See Carlton Lowenberg, *Emily Dickinson's Textbooks* (Lafayette, Calif.: West Coast Print Center, 1986).

3. Benjamin Lease, *Emily Dickinson's Readings of Men and Books: Sacred Soundings* (New York: St. Martin's, 1990), p. 47.

4. Robert Lowth, *Lectures on the Sacred Poetry of the Hebrews*, trans. G. Gregory (1815; reprint, London: S. Chadwick, 1847), p. 58.

5. Hugh Blair, *Lectures on Rhetoric and Belles Lettres* (London: T. Allman, 1841), p. 500.

6. James L. Kugel, *The Idea of Biblical Poetry: Parallelism and Its History* (New Haven: Yale University Press, 1981), p. 51. Kugel explores the history of attempts to systematize the poetry, beginning with medieval and Renaissance scholars and culminating in Lowth's *Lectures*.

7. Murray Roston, *Prophet and Poet* (Evanston, Ill.: Northwestern University Press, 1965), p. 24.

8. David T. Porter, *Dickinson: The Modern Idiom* (Cambridge, Mass.: Harvard University Press, 1981), pp. 85–86.

9. I use Lowth's terminology, since, in Dickinson's day, he was the scholar credited with "discovering" the patterns of Hebrew poetry (and his classification system has proven extraordinarily tenacious). As Kugel (*Idea of Biblical Poetry*, pp. 1–58) points out, however, the terms do not precisely capture the different relationships of the first half-verse to the second, as we can see when we study the variety of nuances in the biblical poetry. For example, Lowth's category of "antithetical parallelism" would include a verse such as Ps. 34:22, wherein the negation, though present, actually creates agreement, not contrast: "The Lord redeemeth the soul of his servants: / and none of them that trust in him shall be desolate."

10. More examples occur in #335, "'Tis not that Dying hurts us so—"; #823, "Not what We did, shall be the test"; #1246, "The Butterfly in honored Dust"; #1270, "Is Heaven a Physician?"; #1309, "The Infinite a sudden Guest"; #1378, "His Heart was darker than the starless night"; #1455, "Opinion is a flitting thing"; #1462, "We knew not that we were to live—." Brita Lindberg-Seyersted (*The Voice of the Poet: Aspects of Style in the Poetry of Emily Dickinson* [Cambridge, Mass.: Harvard University Press, 1968], pp. 104–6, 206–8) discusses Dickinson's use of antithesis, arguing that Dickinson relies on schemes of opposites in theme or pattern. Lindberg-Seyersted does not notice the similarity between the synthetic parallelism of the Bible and Dickinson's poetry.

11. Other examples of synonymous parallelism, in either two- or four-line pairings, occur in #162, "My River runs to thee—"; #219, "She sweeps with many-colored Brooms—"; #311, "It sifts from Leaden Sieves—"; #598, "Three times—we parted—Breath—and I—"; #622, "To know just how He suffered—would be dear—"; #643, "I could suffice for Him, I knew—"; #820, "All Circumstances are the Frame"; #842, "Apology for Her"; #1090, "I am afraid to own a Body—"; #1338, "What tenements of clover."

12. Poems showing this kind of parallelism also include #1297, "Go slow, my soul, to feed thyself"; #1314, "When a Lover is a Beggar"; and #1381, "I suppose the time will come."

13. Lindberg-Seyersted, *Voice of the Poet*, p. 204 n. 4.

14. Roston, *Prophet and Poet*, p. 140.

15. For a discussion of the influence of Watts on Dickinson's poetry, see James

Davidson, "Emily Dickinson and Isaac Watts," *Boston Public Library Quarterly* 6 (1954): 141–49; Martha Winburn England, "Emily Dickinson and Isaac Watts: Puritan Hymnodists," *Bulletin of the New York Public Library* 69 (1965): 83–116; and William E. Stephenson, "Emily Dickinson and Watts's Songs for Children," *English Language Notes* 3 (1966): 278–81. Stephenson, while agreeing with Davidson and England on the similarities in meter and vocabulary between Watts's hymns and Dickinson's poetry, helpfully points out that the similarity stops there; he notes that Davidson actually brings out more differences than similarities in his attempt to show a more extensive influence. Stephenson goes on to argue that the technical resemblances of meter and vocabulary could have come as easily from Watts's *Divine Songs Attempted in Easy Language for . . . Children.*

16. Porter, *Dickinson*, p. 4. Karl Keller (*The Only Kangaroo among the Beauty: Emily Dickinson and America* [Baltimore: Johns Hopkins University Press, 1979], pp. 169–83) and Conrad Aiken ("Emily Dickinson," in *The Recognition of Emily Dickinson since 1890*, ed. Caesar R. Blake and Carlton F. Wells [Ann Arbor: University of Michigan Press, 1968], pp. 110–17) connect her aphorizing with Emerson, who may also have derived the technique from the biblical prophets. But Dickinson undoubtedly knew the Scriptures and their model of employing proverbs far better than she knew Emerson.

17. John Calvin discusses the prophetic office of Christ in the *Institutes* (see *Calvin: Institutes of the Christian Religion*, 2 vols., trans. Ford Lewis Battles, ed. John T. McNeill [Philadelphia: Westminster, 1960], 2:494–96); he notes Christ's preaching and prophetic function, citing Isa. 61:1–2, which Christ reiterated in Luke 4:18: "Jehovah has anointed me to preach" (2:496). And he associates Christ's prophetic office with Christ's "perfect wisdom," drawing on 1 Cor. 1:30: "He was given to us as our wisdom" (*Institutes*, 2:496), Calvin writes, and he calls Christ "the Wisdom of God . . . revealed in the flesh" (2:1154). Certainly, Christ was the master sage, as Dickinson would have known, fulfilling this Old Testament office alongside those of prophet, priest, and king. He reflected the wisdom school particularly in his proverbs and parables drawn from nature and in his ability to pose and solve puzzling questions. The connection between the biblical prophets, including Christ, and the wisdom techniques would have appealed to Dickinson, as both the prophet and the wisdom sayer stood as utterers of spiritual truth, given in the form of the Hebrew poetry. Of course, in Dickinson's day, students of the Bible did not draw the firm lines between the genres that scholars do today.

For other Calvinist treatments of Christ's prophetic role, see Charles Hodge, *Systematic Theology*, 3 vols. (London and Edinburgh: T. Nelson, 1872–1873), 2:459–609; and the Westminster Confession (larger catechism). For a discussion of Christ as wisdom sayer, see James M. Robinson, "Jesus as *Sophos* and *Sophia*: Wisdom Tradition and the Gospels," in *Aspects of Wisdom in Judaism and Early Christianity*, ed. Robert L. Wilken (Notre Dame, Ind.: University of Notre Dame Press, 1975).

18. Keller, *The Only Kangaroo*, p. 177; his entire list appears on pp. 172–78.

19. Charles Anderson, *Emily Dickinson's Poetry: Stairway of Surprise* (1960; reprint, Garden City, N.Y.: Doubleday, 1966), p. 5.

20. William H. Shurr, ed., *New Poems of Emily Dickinson* (Chapel Hill: University of North Carolina Press, 1993), pp. 14–37.

21. Lindberg-Seyersted, *Voice of the Poet*, p. 104. Given the close connection between the biblical prophets and the wisdom sayers, both models for Dickinson, it is of some interest to find in a book about proverbs, read by Dickinson, a passage on indirection pencil-marked, apparently by her: "Hints, shrewdly strown, might-

ily disturb the spirit / Where a barefaced accusation would be too ridiculous for calumny: / The sly suggestion toucheth nerves, and nerves contract the fronds" (in Martin F. Tupper, *Proverbial Philosophy: A Book of Thoughts and Arguments, Originally Treated* [New York: Wiley & Putnam, 1846], quoted in Lindberg-Seyersted, p. 104 n. 3).

22. Benjamin Franklin, *Poor Richard's Almanac*, in *The Papers of Benjamin Franklin*, 30 vols. to date, ed. Leonard W. Larabee (New Haven: Yale University Press, 1959–), 7:345.

23. Richard Sewall, *Life of Emily Dickinson*, 2 vols. (New York: Farrar, Straus & Giroux, 1974), 2:712.

7. FEMALE PROPHECY IN NEW ENGLAND

1. For explorations of female power in colonial America, see Lyle Koehler, *A Search for Power: The "Weaker Sex" in Seventeenth-Century New England* (Urbana: University of Illinois Press, 1980); Amy Schrager Lang, *Prophetic Woman: Anne Hutchinson and the Problem of Dissent in the Literature of New England* (Berkeley and Los Angeles: University of California Press, 1987); Ben Barker-Benfield, "Anne Hutchinson and the Puritan Attitude toward Women," *Feminist Studies* 1, 2 (Fall 1972): 65–96.

2. For a description of the proceedings of the trial, see "The Examination of Mrs. Anne Hutchinson at the Court at Newtown," in *The Antinomian Controversy, 1636–1638: A Documentary History*, ed. David D. Hall (Middletown, Conn.: Wesleyan University Press, 1968), pp. 311–48; the remark by Winthrop appears on p. 316.

3. Lang, *Prophetic Woman*, esp. pp. 41–77. Lang traces the retellings of Hutchinson's events throughout her study.

4. Michael J. Colacurcio, "Footsteps of Ann Hutchinson: The Context of *The Scarlet Letter*," *English Literary History* 39 (1972): 459–78.

5. Wendy Martin, *An American Triptych: Anne Bradstreet, Emily Dickinson, and Adrienne Rich* (Chapel Hill: University of North Carolina Press, 1984), pp. 79–80.

6. Koehler, *Search for Power*, pp. 219, 221.

7. Lang, *Prophetic Woman*, p. 42.

8. See, among others, Joanne A. Dobson, *Dickinson and the Strategies of Reticence: The Woman Writer in Nineteenth-Century America* (Bloomington: Indiana University Press, 1979); Lynn Keller and Cristanne Miller, "Emily Dickinson, Elizabeth Bishop, and the Rewards of Indirection," *New England Quarterly* 57 (1984): 533–53; and Vivian R. Pollack, *Dickinson: The Anxiety of Gender* (Ithaca, N.Y.: Cornell University Press, 1984).

9. Mary Maples Dunn, "Saints and Sinners: Congregational and Quaker Women in the Early Colonial Period," *American Quarterly* 30, 5 (1979): 582–601; Fox's quotation appears on p. 596.

10. Koehler, *Search for Power*, p. 258. As Koehler explains, Fox and other Quakers "saw Paul's injunction against women speaking in church assemblies as directed only at the 'ignorant women' of the Corinthians" (p. 257). Fox's argument, Koehler continues, "was that since it was specified, 'If they learn anything, that is, if they be farther instructed concerning some points of doctrine, Let them ask their husbands at home.' Obviously, a woman must be ignorant if she had to ask her husband for advice, whereas the women who experienced Christ's inner light could edify" (p. 257).

11. Ralph Waldo Emerson, "Woman: A Lecture Read before the Women's

Rights Convention, Boston, September 20, 1855," reprinted in *The Complete Writings of Ralph Waldo Emerson*, 12 vols., ed. Edward W. Emerson (Boston: Houghton Mifflin, 1903–1904), 1:405, 418, 426.

12. Lillian O'Connor, *Pioneer Women Orators: Rhetoric in the Ante-Bellum Reform Movement* (New York: Columbia University Press, 1954), p. 109.

13. Caroline May [Kirkland], preface to *The American Female Poets*, ed. Caroline May (Philadelphia: Lindsay and Blakiston, 1848), p. vi.

14. Doris Yoakum, "Women's Introduction to the American Platform," in *A History and Criticism of American Public Address*, ed. William Norwood Brigance (New York: Russell & Russell, 1960), pp. 185–87. As Yoakum points out (p. 185), the *New York Daily Tribune*'s lyceum list for 1859 contained names of 203 lecturers; 12 were women. Only two decades before, women were generally not allowed to speak before the general public.

15. Elizabeth Oakes Smith, "An Incident," in *American Women Poets of the Nineteenth Century: An Anthology*, ed. Cheryl Walker (New Brunswick, N.J.: Rutgers University Press, 1992), p. 71.

16. Paula Bennett, *Emily Dickinson: Woman Poet* (Iowa City: University of Iowa Press, 1991), p. 137.

17. O'Connor, *Pioneer Woman Orators*, pp. 186–87.

18. Richard Sewall, *Life of Emily Dickinson* (New York: Farrar, Straus & Giroux, 1974), 1:240.

19. Nathaniel Hawthorne, "Mrs. Hutchinson," in *Salem Gazette*, 7 Dec. 1830, reprinted in *Tales, Sketches, and Other Papers*, 13 vols. (1850; reprint, Boston and New York: Houghton Mifflin, 1891), 12:217–19; Lang, *Prophetic Woman*, pp. 2–3.

20. See Rosamond Rosenmeier, *Anne Bradstreet Revisited* (Schenectady, N.Y.: Twayne, 1991), who places Bradstreet in a tradition of biblical wisdom that she claims to be especially important to women's spirituality.

21. Cheryl Walker, *The Nightingale's Burden: Women Poets and American Culture before 1900* (Bloomington: Indiana University Press, 1982), p. 9.

22. Pattie Cowell, *Women Poets in Pre-Revolutionary America, 1650–1775* (Troy, N.Y.: Whitson, 1981), pp. 7–10. According to Cowell, many colonial women poets refused to allow publication of their work to avoid such censure; women who did seek publication frequently did so anonymously. Bradstreet herself did not decide to publish her poems but discovered that her brother-in-law John Woodbridge had published them (as *The Tenth Muse, Lately Sprung Up In America*) without her knowing. In 1650, Woodbridge carried a manuscript to England without her knowledge; "The Author to Her Book," published in the next (1678) edition, makes this abundantly clear, as Bradstreet pointed out that she had not given the "rambling brat" permission to leave the family circle. See *The Works of Anne Bradstreet*, ed. Jeannine Hensley (Cambridge, Mass.: Harvard University Press, 1967), p. 221. It was not until later, after she was published, that she was conscious of a broader audience, revising the poems for later editions. See Cowell, *Women Poets*, pp. 7–12, for a discussion of the social, psychological, and practical barriers facing colonial women poets in their writing and in their publishing.

23. Quoted in Koehler, *Search for Power*, p. 227; see pp. 227–28 for a brief discussion of other seventeenth-century women—contemporaries of Hutchinson and Bradstreet—who were prosecuted for their religious outspokenness, and pp. 246–59, as well as Dunn, "Saints and Sinners," for discussions of Quaker women as affecting many Puritan women after the Antinomian Controversy by their assertive example.

24. Anne Bradstreet, "The Prologue," in *Works*, p. 16.

25. Beth Maclay Doriani, "'Then Have I . . . Said with David': Anne Bradstreet's Andover Manuscript Poems and the Influence of the Psalm Tradition," *Early American Literature* 24 (Spring 1989): 52–69. Ann Stanford (*Anne Bradstreet: The Worldly Puritan* [New York: Burt Franklin, 1974], p. 81) and Charmenz S. Lenhart (*Musical Influence on American Poetry* [Athens: University of Georgia Press, 1967], p. 44), have commented on the musical influence of the metrical psalms, noting the similarity in metrics between the *Bay Psalm Book* and Bradstreet's Andover poems.

26. A sample of her verse is reprinted in Cowell, *Women Poets*, p. 213.

27. Quoted in Cowell, *Women Poets*, p. 125.

28. Rufus W. Griswold, *The Sacred Poets of England and America for Three Centuries* (New York: Appleton, 1848), p. 326.

29. See Sewall, *Life*, 2:742–50.

30. George Frisbie Whicher, *This Was a Poet: A Critical Biography of Emily Dickinson* (New York: Scribner's, 1938; reprint, Ann Arbor: University of Michigan Press, 1957), p. 170. Jack L. Capps (*Emily Dickinson's Reading: 1836–1886* [Cambridge, Mass.: Harvard University Press, 1966], pp. 128–43) discusses the newspapers and periodials that Dickinson read and their content, including women's verse. Sewall (*Life*, 2:671–74) points out Dickinson's reading of prose.

31. Sarah Edgarton Mayo, "The Supremacy of God," in *The Female Poets of America*, ed. Rufus Griswold (Philadelphia: Henry Baird, 1853), p. 299.

32. Lydia H. Sigourney, "Death of a Friend," in Griswold, *Sacred Poets*, p. 473.

33. Lydia H. Sigourney, "Lord, Remember Us," in Griswold, *Sacred Poets*, p. 474.

34. Emily Stipes Watts, *The Poetry of American Women Writers from 1632–1945* (Austin: University of Texas Press, 1977), p. 6.

35. Ann Douglas, *The Feminization of American Culture* (New York: Avon, 1977), pp. 10–11.

36. Jane Tompkins, *Sensational Designs: The Cultural Work of American Fiction, 1790–1860* (New York: Oxford University Press, 1985), p. 163.

37. Walker, *Nightingale's Burden*, p. 19.

38. Tompkins, *Sensational Designs*, pp. 122–46.

39. Dobson (*Dickinson and the Strategies of Reticence*, esp. pp. 48–55) discusses acceptable motives for publication available to women. Karen Dandurand offers evidence that Dickinson could have published her poems but chose not to, in "Why Dickinson Did Not Publish" (Ph.D. diss., University of Massachusetts, 1985). For a brief survey of extant contemporary comments about Dickinson and publication wherein several people unsuccessfully encouraged her to publish, see Dobson, *Dickinson and the Strategies of Reticence*, Appendix 1, pp. 128–30.

40. Dobson, *Dickinson and the Strategies of Reticence*, p. xii. David S. Reynolds (*Beneath the American Renaissance: The Subversive Imagination in the Age of Emerson and Melville* [New York: Knopf, 1988]), too, notices the ways in which Dickinson adapted the stereotypes and stylistic strategies of her female contemporaries, emphasizing her affinities with writers he identifies as "subversives." Dobson, meanwhile, focuses on the conventional—the cultural emphasis on feminine privacy and domesticity, conventions of the female self in writing, conventions of female literary style, etc. The conventional is at least as influential as the subversive, Dobson demonstrates, and it showed Dickinson a broad range of feminine expression associated with her own Christian tradition, in which she continued to retain some interest. See Reynolds, *Beneath the American Renaissance*, chap. 14, pp. 387–437.

8. "AND I SNEERED—SOFTLY—'SMALL'!"

1. Richard Wilbur, "Sumptuous Destitution," in *Emily Dickinson: Three Views* (Amherst, Mass.: Amherst College Press, 1960), pp. 39, 38.

2. Some scholars have suggested that Dickinson's unwillingness to "give up the world" (as she termed it in a letter) may have been a large part of why she did not want to profess Christianity when she was twelve. But her retreat into her father's house and her life as a poet can also be seen as a form of "giving up the world." Viewing her renunciation as a positive gesture (not a defensive one) that characterizes Dickinson as a wisdom giver solves some of the problems of these inconsistencies.

3. Karl Keller, *The Only Kangaroo among the Beauty: Emily Dickinson and America* (Baltimore: Johns Hopkins University Press, 1979), p. 65.

4. Henry David Thoreau, *Walden* (1854), ed. F. B. Sanborn, vol. 2 of *The Writings of Henry David Thoreau*, ed. F. B. Sanborn and Bradford Torrey (Boston: Houghton Mifflin, 1906), 101, 100.

5. Keller, *The Only Kangaroo*, p. 94.

6. See Charles Anderson, *Emily Dickinson's Poetry: Stairway of Surprise* (1960; reprint, Garden City, N.Y.: Doubleday, 1966), pp. 165–222, for an exploration of the "ecstasy" and "despair" clusters.

7. Barbara J. Williams, "A Room of Her Own: Emily Dickinson as Woman Artist," in *Feminist Criticism: Essays on Theory, Poetry, and Prose*, ed. Cheryl L. Brown and Karen Olson (Metuchen, N.J.: Scarecrow, 1978), p. 79. Inder Nath Kher (*The Landscape of Absence: Emily Dickinson's Poetry* [New Haven: Yale University Press, 1974], pp. 229–69) also connects reward with renunciation in Dickinson's poetry, this time in terms of her "quest for identity" entailing "infinite venture and infinite suffering" (p. 231).

8. Focusing on the contradictions between the poet's gender and her chosen vocation, critics have discussed the poems that seem to express rage, rebellion, madness, and creative anguish. Vivian Pollack (*Dickinson: The Anxiety of Gender* [Ithaca, N.Y.: Cornell University Press, 1984]) identifies gender as Dickinson's "generative obsession," maintaining that "most of Emily Dickinson's poetry, and all of it that matters, originates in frustration," the frustration of sexual identity (p. 9). Sandra M. Gilbert and Susan Gubar (*Madwoman in the Attic: The Woman Writer and the Nineteenth-Century Literary Imagination* [New Haven: Yale University Press, 1979]) similarly view Dickinson as a frustrated woman, arguing that she enacted (but eventually resolved) "both her anxieties about her art and her anger at female subordination" (p. 583). Barbara A. C. Mossberg (*Emily Dickinson: When a Writer Is a Daughter* [Bloomington: Indiana University Press, 1982]) focuses on Dickinson's identity as a daughter, arguing that the poet's feeling of entrapment in this pose of self-denying daughter fueled her art, while Suzanne Juhasz (*The Undiscovered Continent: Emily Dickinson and the Space of the Mind* [Bloomington: Indiana University Press, 1983]) has argued that Dickinson's patriarchal world demanded a renunciatory or subordinate position of her. See Suzanne Juhasz, ed., *Feminist Critics Read Emily Dickinson* (Bloomington: Indiana University Press, 1983), for a collection of essays, most of which explore Dickinson's struggle to overcome societal strictures including the cultural expectation of female renunciation. See also Sharon Cameron, "'A Loaded Gun': Dickinson and the Dialectic of Rage," *PMLA* 93 (1978): 423–37, for an exploration of the conflict between the forces of sexuality and death, a dialectic based on sacrifice and protest.

9. John Cody, *After Great Pain: The Inner Life of Emily Dickinson* (Cambridge, Mass.: Harvard University Press, Belknap Press, 1971).

10. Cheryl Walker, *The Nightingale's Burden: Women Poets and American Culture before 1900* (Bloomington: Indiana University Press, 1982), p. 93.

11. Lawrence Buell, "Calvinism Romanticized: Harriet Beecher Stowe, Samuel Hopkins, and *The Minister's Wooing*," in *Critical Essays on Harriet Beecher Stowe* (Boston: G. K. Hall, 1980), p. 271.

12. Nathanael Emmons (1745–1840) carried Hopkins's thinking to the generation of ministers that Dickinson heard, widely influencing antebellum religious life, according to Williston Walker, *History of the Congregational Churches in the United States* (New York: Christian Literature, 1894), p. 300. The more moderate theologian Timothy Dwight (1752–1817) also perpetuated Edwards's ideas, including an emphasis on self-denial.

13. Walker, *Nightingale's Burden*, pp. 92–93.

14. Joanne A. Dobson, *Dickinson and the Strategies of Reticence: The Woman Writer in Nineteenth-Century America* (Bloomington: Indiana University Press, 1979), p. 123.

15. Cameron ("'A Loaded Gun'") sees as its subject anger; Adrienne Rich "'Vesuvius at Home': The Power of Emily Dickinson," *Parnassus* 5, 1 [1976]: 449–74) ambition; Cody (*After Great Pain*), sexuality; to name a few of the possible readings.

16. Dobson, *Dickinson and the Strategies of Reticence*, p. 123.

17. Buell, "Calvinism Romanticized," p. 271.

18. Keller, *The Only Kangaroo*, p. 83.

19. Jane Tompkins, *Sensational Designs: The Cultural Work of American Fiction, 1790–1860* (New York: Oxford University Press, 1985), p. 163.

20. Charlotte Louise Nekola, "Emily Dickinson and the Poetry of Silence" (Ph.D. diss., University of Michigan, 1984), p. 42.

21. David T. Porter (*Dickinson: The Modern Idiom* [Cambridge, Mass.: Harvard University Press, 1981], p. 2) views her art as "feeding" on her deprivation; Sharon Cameron (*Lyric Time: Dickinson and the Limits of Genre* [Baltimore: Johns Hopkins University Press, 1979], p. 2) calls her a "hoarder of loss"; Albert J. Gelpi (*Emily Dickinson: The Mind of the Poet* [New York: Norton, 1971], p. 168) decides that she projected "a calculated mask." These approaches feed the notion that her behavior and poetic strategies were aberrant, even neurotic—that her art was provoked by her neurosis. Cody's psychological study *After Great Pain* especially reads like a catalogue of psychoses, neuroses, and repressions. This pathological model fails to consider the wider context of her life and times, encouraging us to view the content of her work as purely personal. It seems more accurate to view her work as commenting on the value of loss.

22. Wendy Martin, *An American Triptych: Anne Bradstreet, Emily Dickinson, Adrienne Rich* (Chapel Hill: University of North Carolina Press, 1984), p. 80.

23. For a discussion of Dickinson's strategy as continued by a twentieth-century poet, see Suzanne Juhasz, "Renunciation Transformed, the Dickinson Heritage: Emily Dickinson and Margaret Atwood," *Women's Studies* 12 (1986): 251–70.

24. In Luke 9:57–62, Christ explains to a would-be prophetic follower the principle of renouncing one's family and home: "Let the dead bury their dead [meaning, tend to family matters]: but go thou and preach the kingdom of God" (v. 60), pointing out that he—and, by inference, prophetic followers—"hath not where to lay his head" (v. 58). See Jean McClure Mudge, *Emily Dickinson and the Image of Home* (Amherst: University of Massachusetts Press, 1973), for a demon-

stration, through an analysis of the letters and poems, of how Dickinson's physical home played a significant part in her artistry throughout her lifetime. Mudge also discusses Dickinson's emotional responses to home and her ambivalence about it.

25. See Jay Leyda, *The Years and Hours of Emily Dickinson* (New Haven: Yale University Press, 1960; reprint, New York: Archon, 1970), 1:255.

26. Amanda Porterfield, *Feminine Spirituality in America: From Sarah Edwards to Martha Graham* (Philadelphia: Temple University Press, 1980), p. 144.

27. Ann Douglas (*The Feminization of American Culture* [New York: Avon, 1977]) argues that, in their sharing of cultural values such as the importance of self-denial, nineteenth-century women and ministers triumphed in "feminizing" (or "sentimentalizing") American culture, as both groups turned to the popular press to find an audience; the minister even began courting a "feminized" image (p. 93). While Douglas's work underscores the availability of the preacherly model to Dickinson, she neglects to emphasize the empowering effects of the model of the (male) minister, who, as a man, represented an important version of the American self.

28. Jonathan Edwards, "Christ the Example of Ministers," in *The Works of President Edwards*, 10 vols. (Edinburgh, 1847; reprint, New York: Burt Franklin, 1968), 10:515, 520–21.

29. Ibid., 518.

30. Ibid., 521, 523. Edwards also uses the figure of "crown" in association with self-abasement in *Images or Shadows of Divine Things*, ed. Perry Miller (New Haven: Yale University Press, 1948), p. 43: like the rose that grows upon briars, the "crown of glory is to be come at in no other way than by bearing Christ's cross, by a life of mortification, self-denial, and labour."

31. Aaron Kramer, *The Prophetic Tradition in American Poetry, 1839–1900* (Rutherford, N.J.: Fairleigh Dickinson University Press, 1968).

32. Jonathan Edwards, "Treatise on Religious Affections," in *Works*, 4:983.

33. F. D. Huntington, *Christian Believing and Living: Sermons* (Boston: Crosby, 1860), p. 276.

34. Shira Wolosky ("Emily Dickinson's War Poetry: The Problems of Theodicy," *Massachusetts Review* 25 [1984]: 22–41) shows Dickinson's uneasiness with the war as a "problem of theodicy," but Wolosky gives the impression that all suffering disturbed Dickinson. It was only senseless, random suffering or suffering for the wrong cause that disturbed her—such as the war, which, as Wolosky shows, was romanticized by Dickinson's contemporaries. Spiritual suffering—suffering for one's faith or calling—as Christ and the other biblical prophets underwent was of another order and was justified (as Dickinson explained in #527).

35. Paula Bennett, *Emily Dickinson: Woman Poet* (Iowa City: University of Iowa Press, 1991), p. 124.

36. Ibid.

37. Eliza New, "Difficult Writing, Difficult God: Emily Dickinson's Poems beyond Circumference," *Religion and Literature* 18, 3 (Fall 1986): 5. New calls Dickinson's position "Kierkegaardian" in the sense that the poet maintains a theological doubt.

38. With its references to sight and blindness, the poem carries special weight when we consider the impact of Dickinson's own vision problems on her poetry. Cynthia Griffin Wolff (*Emily Dickinson* [New York: Knopf, 1986]), among others, understands Dickinson's "crisis since September" as that of her sudden loss of sight, important for a poet and, I would add, a "seer," a prophet.

39. Porter, *Dickinson*, p. 46.

40. Edwards, "Treatise on Religious Affections," 4:983.

41. Some examples of biblical prophets who underwent deprivation because of their prophetic calling include Jeremiah, who was put in stocks, threatened for prophesying, imprisoned, and later thrown into a cistern (Jer. 20:1–3; 11:18–26; 37; 38); Daniel, who was thrown into a lion's den (Daniel 6); and John the Baptist, who was arrested and beheaded (Matt. 4:12; 14:1–12).

42. Keller, *The Only Kangaroo*, p. 87.

43. Porterfield, *Feminine Spirituality*, p. 145.

44. Examples of "sea" imagery include #284, "The Drop, that wrestles in the Sea"; #1217, "Fortitude incarnate"; #1428, "Water makes many Beds"; possibly #520, "I started Early—Took my Dog"; and #1599, "Though the great Waters sleep."

45. Porterfield, *Feminine Spirituality*, p. 135.

46. Gary Lee Stonum, *The Dickinson Sublime* (Madison: University of Wisconsin Press, 1990), pp. 15–16.

47. I adopt the word choices Dickinson apparently preferred, as indicated in her packet copy (lines 5, 6, 7, 15).

48. Porterfield, *Feminine Spirituality*, pp. 16–17.

9. "'TIS SO APPALLING—IT EXHILARATES"

1. See, for example, Lyman Beecher's famous 1823 sermon, *The Faith Once Delivered to the Saints* (Boston: Crocker and Brewster, 1824). The key disputed issue within the orthodox Congregationalism of Dickinson's contemporaries, between the "conservative" (i.e., strictly Calvinist) and Arminian (or Taylorite) camps, became the relative emphasis on the human role in the regeneration of the soul. Yet, if we accept Beecher's definition of orthodoxy, the two camps bore more in common than the opposing "liberalism," which, according to Joseph Haroutunian, was "Calvinism in reverse," that is, centered on humans instead of God, identifying human happiness with the glory of God. See Joseph Haroutunian, *Piety versus Moralism: The Passing of the New England Theology* (New York: H. Holt, 1932), p. 145, for a discussion of this change in religious outlook; also William G. McLoughlin, introduction to *The American Evangelicals, 1800–1900: An Anthology*, ed. William G. McLoughlin (New York: Harper & Row, 1968), pp. 5–10, and "The Second Great Awakening, 1800–1830," in *American Evangelicals*, pp. 109–15.

2. McLoughlin, introduction to *American Evangelicals*, p. 14.

3. Quoted in Richard Wilbur, "Sumptuous Destitution," in *Emily Dickinson: Three Views* (Amherst, Mass.: Amherst College Press, 1960), p. 35.

4. Lawrence Buell, *New England Literary Culture from Revolution through Renaissance* (New York: Cambridge University Press, 1986), pp. 68–69.

5. Margaret Homans (*Women Writers and Poetic Identity: Dorothy Wordsworth, Emily Bronte, and Emily Dickinson* [Princeton: Princeton University Press, 1980], pp. 31–32), for example, is one critic who sees the conception of poet-prophet as patriarchal and therefore unacceptable to Dickinson. At its finest, however, the feminist approach usually does not dismiss totally the idea that Emerson influenced Dickinson but objects to the oversimplification of the influence. Still, feminist critics have tended to prefer exploring Dickinson's relationship to communities of women.

6. Buell, *New England Literary Culture*, pp. 69, 70.

7. Louise Bogan, "A Mystical Poet," in *Emily Dickinson: Three Views*, p. 34.

Index to Dickinson's Poems

Poems that are mentioned or quoted are listed in roman type. Entries in italics indicate longer discussions.

226

General Index

afterworld, 195–97, 199
Amherst, 14, 24, 44, 45, 53, 81, 207n. 15
Anna (New Testament prophet), 22
apocalypse, 8, 157, 197

Barnes, Albert, 19, 108, 187
Beecher, Lyman, 187–88, 224n. 1
Bible, 8, 9, 10, 18, 21–22, 25–26, 32, 59,
    92, 114–15, 122–23, 129, 137, 138, 140,
    141, 145, 147, 153, 179–80, 198; as liter-
    ature, 17–20, 107–13, 145, 208n. 26,
    216n. 9; travel literature of, 92–94;
    wisdom literature of, 3–4, 25, 107,
    114–15, 141
Blair, Hugh, 19, 211n. 22; *Lectures on
    Rhetoric and Belles Lettres,* 20, 108,
    131
Blake, William, 36, 37
Bowles, Samuel, 103
Bradstreet, Anne, 25, 28, 122, 123, 124,
    142–45, 146, 147, 149, 172, 219nn.
    20, 22; "Meditations Divine and
    Morall," 4
Browne, Antoinette, 129
Browning, Elizabeth Barrett, 42

Calvin, John, 15, 18, 21, 31, 114, 217n. 17
Calvinism, 44, 185, 186–88, 189, 205n.
    2, 224n. 1
Canticles, 3
Channing, Edward T., 13; *Lectures
    Read to the Juniors in Harvard Col-
    lege,* 14
Channing, William Ellery, 74, 211n. 22
Child, Lydia Maria, 21; *History of the
    Condition of Women,* 10
circumference, 120, 172
Civil War, 7–8, 223n. 34
Colton, Aaron, 49, 71, 210n. 7

dancing, 18, 21, 177–78, 184, 200–201
David (Old Testament poet), 17, 18,
    145, 147
Deborah, 3, 10, 21, 111, 122, 124, 201
Dickinson, Austin, 45, 46, 101–2
Dickinson, Edward, 46

Dickinson, Emily: and doctrine of
    election, 28, 200; and oratory, 48–
    49, 133, 136–37, 138; and publication,
    121, 144, 150–51, 163, 206n. 4, 207n. 3,
    209n. 6, 220n. 39; and white
    clothing, 88, 182
Dickinson, Emily, poetry of: and au-
    dience, 36–41, 49, 90–91, 199; and
    biblical texts, vivifying, 66–69, 213n.
    41; as consolation literature, 101–4;
    dashes, 29, 48–49, 61, 91, 210n. 14;
    diction, 16, 49, 50, 52, 54, 68, 110, 153;
    fascicles, 36, 38, 90, 133, 144, 163; and
    God, 29, 61, 63, 74–76, 80–81, 84–
    85, 89, 100, 171–72, 180–81, 197–98;
    imagery, 30, 32, 57–58, 74, 88, 96, 114,
    167, 193, 211n. 23, 224n. 44; and Jesus,
    69, 78, 80, 85, 87, 100, 154, 172–73,
    175, 180, 194–95, 198; and paradox,
    116–19; parallelism, 65, 109, 111–13,
    114, 115, 116, 119, 212n. 39, 216nn. 10,
    11, 12; as proverbs, 114–16, 119, 120,
    217n. 16; spoken quality, 16, 30, 48,
    50; voice, 17, 29–30, 33, 35, 36, 37,
    70–71, 75, 76, 92, 119, 127–28, 134–36,
    147, 201, 215n. 2
domesticity, 46–47, 125, 165, 194, 222n.
    24; Dickinson and, 158, 162–65,
    221n. 2, 222n. 24
Donald, E. Winchester, 24
dream. *See* vision
Dwight, Edward S., 23, 46, 49, 210nn.
    7, 8
Dwight, Timothy, 19, 187, 208n. 26;
    *On the History, Eloquence, and Po-
    etry of the Bible,* 19

Edwards, Jonathan, 15, 32, 43–44, 51,
    55, 56, 70, 72, 152, 153, 166, 167, 175,
    186, 187, 212n. 35, 223n. 30
Emerson, Ralph Waldo, 3, 4, 7, 8, 14–
    15, 20, 26, 38, 74, 75, 85, 88, 89, 107,
    110, 184, 189–90, 191, 206–7n. 3,
    207n. 15, 224n. 5; "Divinity School
    Address," 8, 14, 26, 104; "The Poet,"
    14, 88, 159; "Woman," 130, 207n. 5

228

proverb, 3–4, 114–15, 116, 119–20, 206n.
4. *See also* Bible, wisdom literature
of
Psalms, Book of, 18, 20, 114, 142, 145,
176
Puritanism, 6, 11, 15, 16, 44, 47, 50, 52,
53, 55, 69, 104, 125, 127–28, 143–44,
145, 171, 187, 190, 206n. 2, 212n. 28;
and women, 122–23, 125, 219n. 23

Quakers, 123, 125, 128–29, 143

Read, Thomas Buchanan, *The Female
Poets of America*, 2, 14, 146, 148
Revelation (Book of), 20, 29, 36, 52,
73–74, 82, 88, 93, 94, 95, 107, 176, 177,
214–15n. 11
rhetoric textbooks, 20, 48, 50, 108, 131
romanticism, 8–9, 18–20, 190, 191, 196
Rossetti, Christina, 37

"separate sphere" ideology, 47, 125, 156,
221n. 8
singing, 3, 9, 17, 18, 22, 43, 92, 111, 133,
145, 147, 184, 200–201
Smith, Elizabeth Oakes, 134–36, 147
Smith, Henry Boynton, 45
song. *See* singing

Song of Solomon, 3
spirituality, women's, 9–11, 177, 184
Stone, Lucy, 129, 137
Stowe, Harriet Beecher, 149, 150, 154,
185; *The Minister's Wooing*, 159; *Uncle
Tom's Cabin*, 150
submission, 127, 149, 151, 154, 159, 165,
166, 170, 176, 178–81

Taylor, Nathaniel W., 187
Thoreau, Henry David, 7, 25, 40, 75,
155, 156, 162, 184, 189, 191; *Walden*, 7,
139–40, 155
transcendentalism, 8–9, 17, 74, 130, 185;
poetics, 8
Tyler, William S., 49–50, 53–54, 55–56,
58

Unitarianism, 51, 54–55, 67, 69, 74, 104,
185, 187, 211n. 17

vision, 72, 81–85, 87, 92–98

Wadsworth, Charles, 23, 46, 56, 210n.
9, 211n. 23, 212n. 37
Watts, Isaac, 92, 113–14, 145, 184, 216–
17n. 15
Whitman, Walt, 7, 8, 25, 40, 75, 184